I0810696

IMAGES
of America

HISTORIC FALLS CHURCH

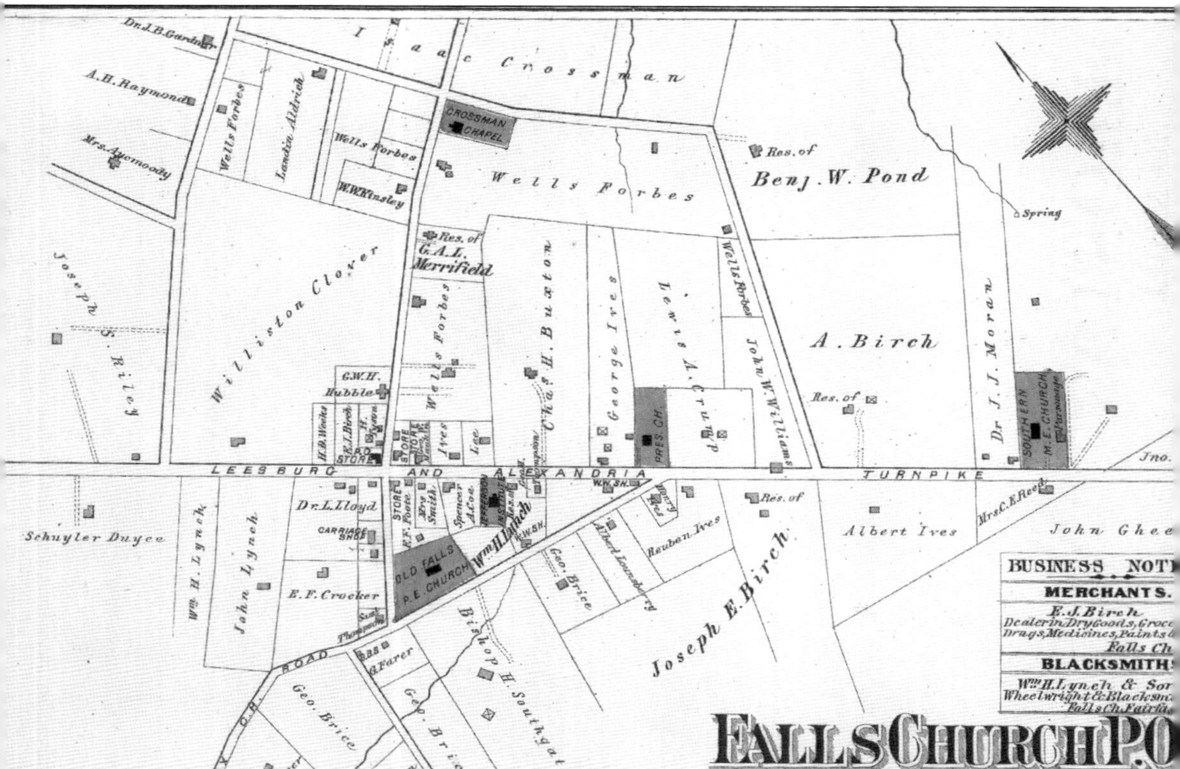

The Hopkins Atlas of Fifteen Miles Around Washington in 1879 identifies some of the families living in Falls Church in the post–Civil War era. During this time, large plantations and farms began being subdivided, and more people moved to Falls Church, including many government workers, who believed the air was more refreshing. Broad Street was then called the Leesburg-Alexandria Turnpike. The map also listed local businesses, such as Wm. H. Lynch, Blacksmith. Falls Church incorporated in 1875 but was still a part of Fairfax County until 1948. (Courtesy of the Library of Congress, Maps Division.)

ON THE COVER: A welcome wagon in front of DeSoto Motors (now the taxi company), at the convergence of Lee Highway and Hillwood Avenue, greets a new citizen of Falls Church. The Koons family, which still runs car dealerships, originally hailed from Falls Church. Maintaining a small-town feel, new city residents are greeted with welcome packages upon moving in. (Courtesy of the Mary Riley Styles Public Library.)

IMAGES
of America

HISTORIC FALLS CHURCH

Cathy Taylor

ARCADIA
PUBLISHING

ISBN 978-0-7385-9262-6

Published by Arcadia Publishing
Charleston, South Carolina

Printed in the United States of America

Library of Congress Control Number: 2011946071

For all general information, please contact Arcadia Publishing:
Telephone 843-853-2070
Fax 843-853-0044
E-mail sales@arcadiapublishing.com
For customer service and orders:
Toll-Free 1-888-313-2665

Visit us on the Internet at www.arcadiapublishing.com

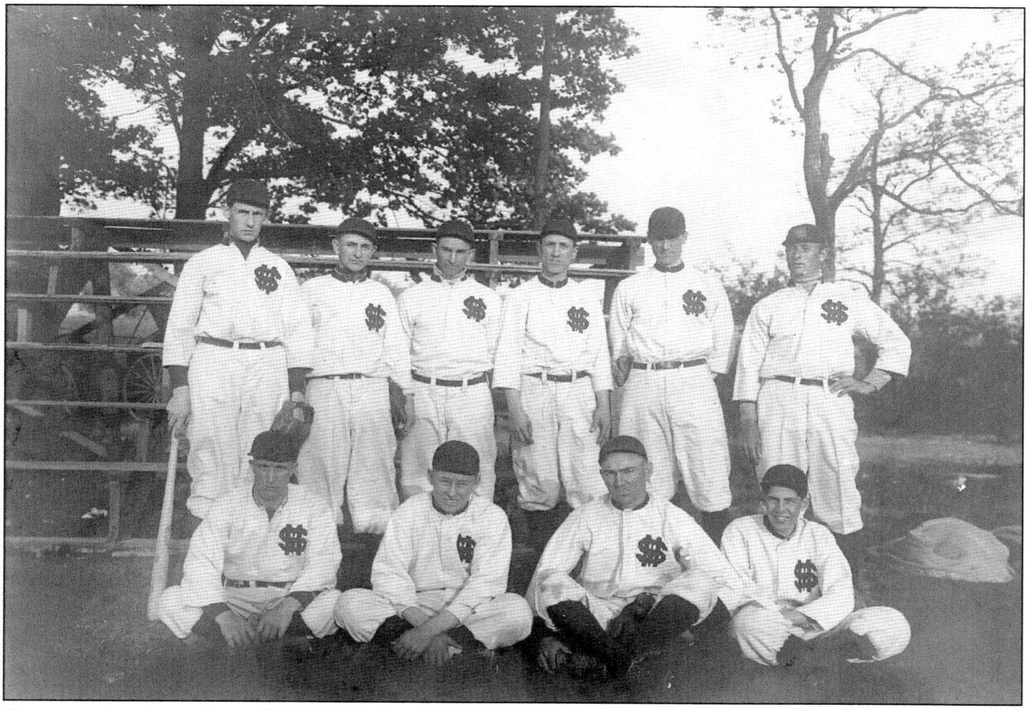

Community has always been a defining factor in Falls Church. (Courtesy of the Mary Riley Styles Public Library.)

Contents

ACKNOWLEDGMENTS

I would like to sincerely thank the following people for their help in providing historic information or images: Ron Anzalone from the Falls Church Historical Commission; Barb Cram, who is involved in too many programs to name; Linda Lau from the Victorian Society of Falls Church; Marshall, Janet, Brenda, and Shirley at Mary Riley Styles Public Library; Nikki Graves Henderson and Ed Henderson from Tinner Hill Heritage Foundation; Tracy Gillespie from the Northern Virginia Regional Park Authority; Catherine Speakman of the DePutron family; and Bonnie Darden and Donna Jean Bonner.

History is often open to interpretation and not an exact science, containing many conflicting stories. I tried to be as accurate as possible, but please forgive if any mistakes were made. This is not a complete historic architectural inventory of the city, as there was not enough space and other such books exist. I tried to touch upon all the important people and places that greatly influenced the development and maturation of the town. I sincerely appreciate everyone who cherishes, preserves, and shares both the physical history of Falls Church and the stories that carry on for generations.

Unless otherwise noted, images can be credited to the Mary Riley Styles Public Library. Images from the Virginia Room Collection with a second credit are denoted with (MRSPL) and the second credit. Images from the Library of Congress (LOC) and Northern Virginia Regional Park Authority (NVRPA) are noted as well.

INTRODUCTION

Native Americans traversed two main trails that crossed at a point where one led to Alexandria and the other to a favored fishing spot at the Potomac falls, where the shallow water served as the easiest crossing point into Maryland. One of these trails followed a natural ridge in the geography, providing easier terrain to traverse between the hills and abundant creeks feeding the fields of the countryside. Where the heavily trafficked trails crossed—now roughly the intersection of Broad Street and Little Falls Street—an ivy-encased log cabin sealed with oyster shell mortar and containing enormous towering chimneys on either end staked its claim. A wooden church soon followed nearby. The legacy of that first church near the falls of the Potomac River ultimately gave the evolving village its name.

The community around the church grew with the birth of the US government, even before its seat was relocated from Philadelphia to the opposite shores of the Potomac, a mere six miles away. As vestrymen of Truro Parish—the parish The Falls Church belonged to—George Washington, George Mason, and Charles Broadwater were actively involved in Falls Church activities before the Revolution. Due to its close proximity to what became the nation's capital, the history of the country and this small town were—and still are—inseparably intertwined. Despite living in the shadow of big government and being a passenger on its coattails through time, the town managed to maintain a unique identity with a story of its own to tell containing surprising twists.

Wars have profoundly impacted the town and its evolution, as every war fought has swept citizens of Falls Church along not as mere spectators but often as awkward participants. The town's popular ordinary, Wren's Tavern, was the site of much of this history, from getting visits and a recommendation from Ben Franklin to harboring War of 1812 refugees from Washington and even a visit from passing Pres. James Madison while in search of his wife. One of the founding families associated with one of the most recognizable historic sites and community spaces in the city, Cherry Hill, may not have met had it not been for the arrest of an accused female spy during the Civil War.

Military history was also made in the skies above the village during the Civil War as the war marked a key turning point for the village. Falls Church had been devastated by battles fought on its edges and soldiers tromping through local farms, stealing anything in sight. However, many soldiers who fought in and around Falls Church decided to settle there after the war, causing the first boom in population. Leading up to the Civil War and beyond, several key African American families successfully championed equality in education and stature, with the positive impact of their unending efforts felt nationwide.

Influences of war aside, the founders of the developing town laid a foundation of core beliefs in education and community involvement, which have persisted in modern times. Several early families donated the land and financial resources for early churches and schools. Nature and preservation programs to beautify the village and involve citizens began more than a century ago, resulting in several noteworthy historic trees, which are still alive throughout town.

As the country matured and technology advanced, the little village grew up and the population continued to boom—at one point it was the most populous municipality in Fairfax County. Rutted dirt paths gave way to railroads and trolley tracks, which in turn gave way to a paved network of roads and highways. Residents along the tracks enjoyed home-side service by the electric trolley line in its heyday, building shelters on their property. The railroad suffered greatly during the Civil War and never met its aggressive goal of reaching the coal industry in Ohio like its competitor to the north in Baltimore. After the trains died out, the track bed was transformed into a popular recreation trail, with Falls Church on the leading edge of the transformation.

The ability to get in and out of the town easily improved access to Washington and made Falls Church a desirable place to live, not just to own a summer country home. Thus a commuter town was born. The down side of demand for such roads was the loss of the shade trees lining the main thoroughfares of yesteryear. Despite that, Falls Church has striven to maintain a vast tree canopy and has been named a Tree City, USA, for 33 consecutive years.

With the influx of new residents came the necessity for a public infrastructure with electricity, phones, and a water and sewer system. Outdoor privies gave way to indoor plumbing as the town secured its own water source. Telephones and electricity can largely be attributed to one enterprising resident who also founded the city's first bank.

Of course, improved transportation meant people could travel to all Northern Virginia communities easily, and Falls Church found its business district competing to retain customers amid the growing sprawl. Major shopping centers cropped up on the east and west sides of the little city, attracting shoppers from the region despite steps taken by early visionaries to route major roads through the heart of town.

Villains and heroes, successes and disappointments, occupy the city's history. Above all, it has strived to be an All-American City, an honor it won in 1962, for which Pres. John F. Kennedy congratulated the town personally. The spirit of community involvement and pride in the school system keeps Falls Church remaining the "Little City" its founders envisioned.

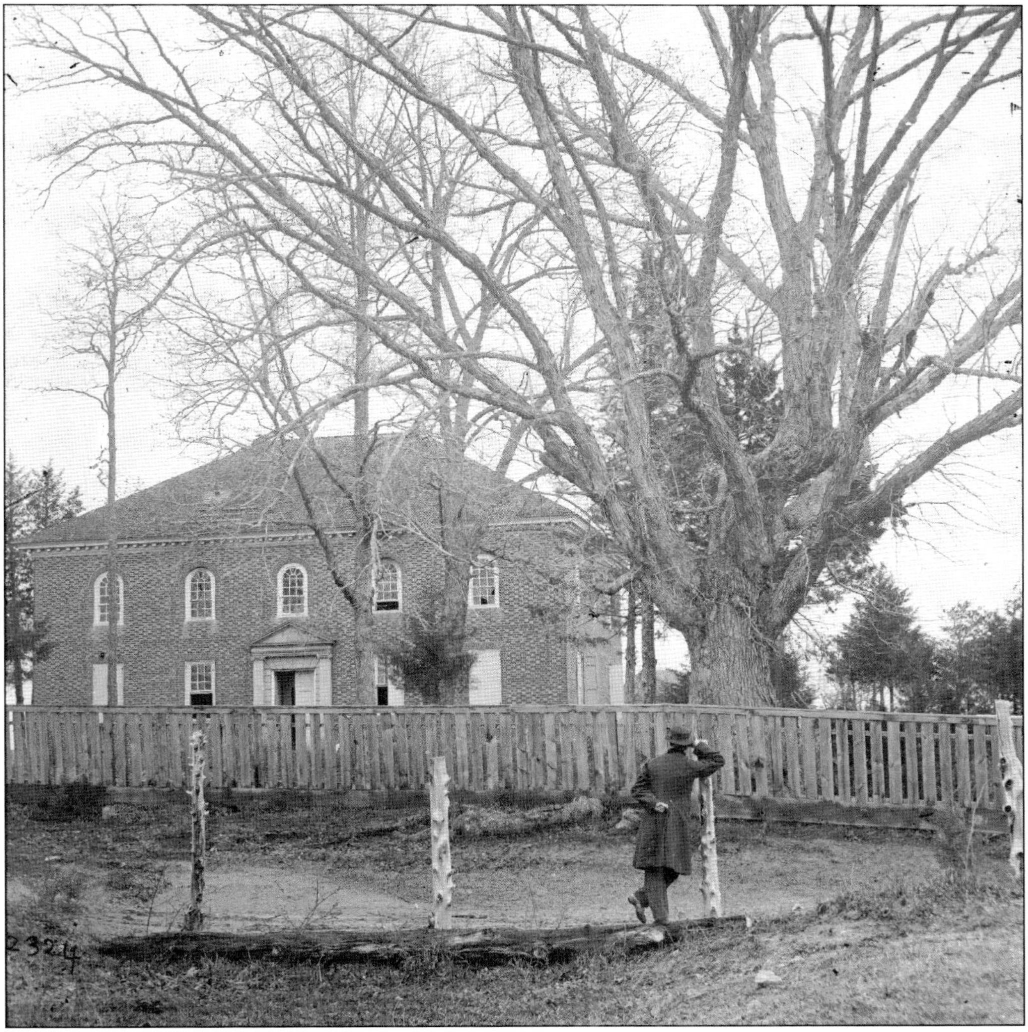

"At a Vestry held at the Falls Church March 28th, 1763—Present, Henry Gunnell, William Payne jun. Church Wardens, John West, William Payne (sen.) Chas. Broadwater. Thos. Wren, Abra. Barnes, Danl. McCarty, Robt. Boggess, and Geo. Washington, Vestrymen, Who being there met to examine into the state of the said Church, greatly in decay and want of repairs, and likewise whether the same should be repaired or a new one built, and whether at the same place or removed to a more convenient one; Resolved it is the opinion of this Vestry that the old Church is rotten and unfit for repair, but that a new Church be built at the same place. Ordered that the Clerk of the Vestry advertise in the Virginia and Maryland Gazettes for workmen to meet at the said Church on the 29th day of August next, if fair, if not the first fair day, to undertake the building a Brick, Church to contain 1600 feet on the floor, with a suitable gallery," read the Truro Parish Vestrybook. (LOC.)

One

The Falls Churches

There is no better place to start than with the churches of Falls Church, given that the town was named after the Colonial–era church, The Falls Church. Churches oversaw moral codes in the Colonial community, mustered the military, saw to the poor, ill, and feeble, and taxed the landowners in their parishes. Taverns, also known as ordinaries, served as local community gathering places to share news and events and also welcomed travelers with food and a place to sleep.

The vestry for Truro Parish was responsible for collecting tithes from the parishioners and establishing land boundaries. The men elected to the vestry were of the utmost trustworthy and discreet character. Most landowners at that time owned grants from the British crown on their plantation acreage. Tobacco served as the main form of currency of the time, with church builders and pastors being paid in such. Little Falls Street was known as the "rolling road," as merchants wheeled casks filled with tobacco to the warehouses and ports in Alexandria, where it was checked for quality. With the change from Anglican to Episcopalian after the Revolution and the separation of church and state, more churches from other denominations sprang up in Falls Church, most of which are still in existence today.

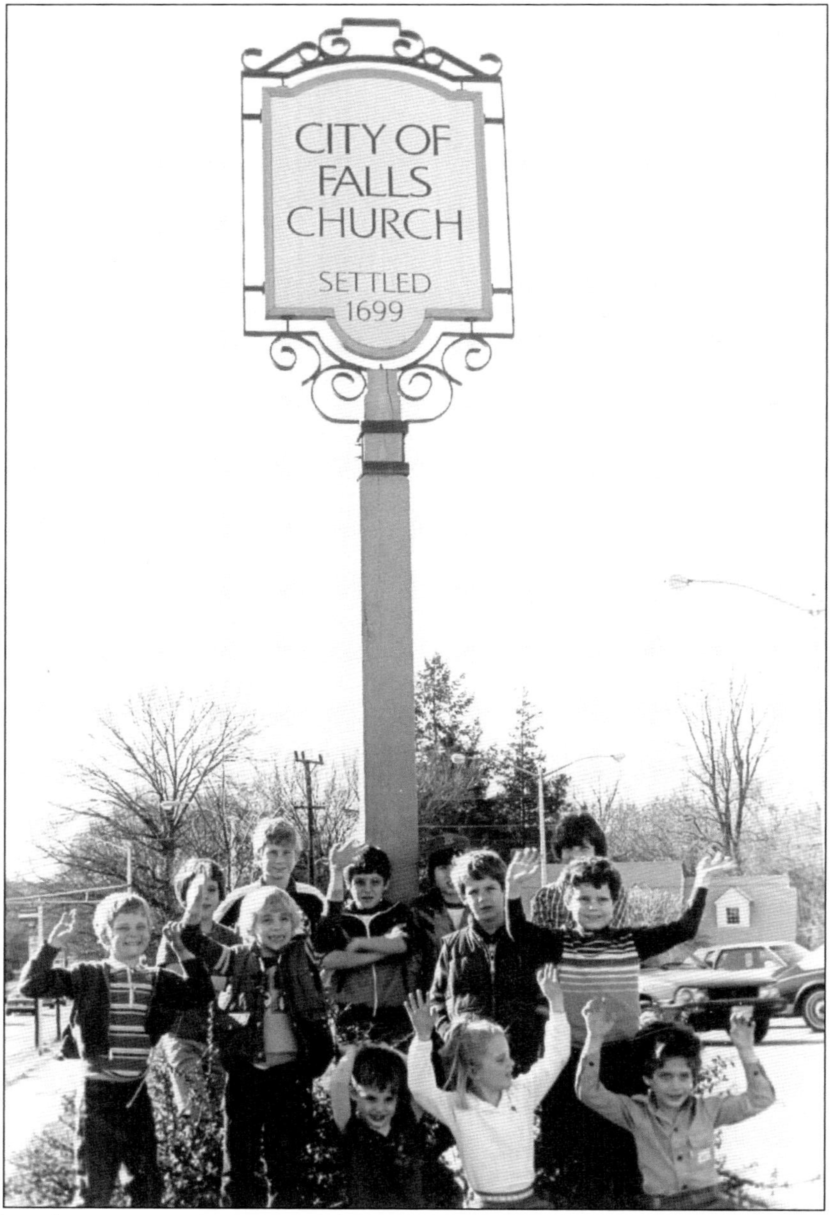

Long before the young government of the United States of America situated itself across the riverbanks of the Potomac, Colonial settlers claimed the fertile fishing and hunting land previously occupied by Native Americans. Acquiring vast acreage for farming, a handful of settlers laid claim to the lands now containing the city of Falls Church. The climate, never hitting the extremes of freezing or heat, appeared ideal for harvesting abundant crops. Often, owners of land grants leased their land to other farmers in order to get the tobacco crops out of the ground and pay back the English crown. Trails to the Little Falls of the Potomac already existed, because it was a favorite fishing spot for the Native Americans and the easiest crossing point to the shores of Maryland. Where the trail to the falls met another trail to Alexandria sat the oldest known residence in Falls Church, a log cabin nicknamed "Big Chimneys."

Big Chimneys, a log cabin so named because of its large bookending chimneys, one containing a date stone marked 1699, was the first known dwelling in the city, and 1699 was marked as the year the town was settled. Situated at the crossroads to the Potomac River and Alexandria, the cabin served as an ordinary, welcoming travelers for the night with food and drink and a place to sleep. A nearby spring provided fresh water, and the dwelling was described as ivy-covered, resembling an English cottage.

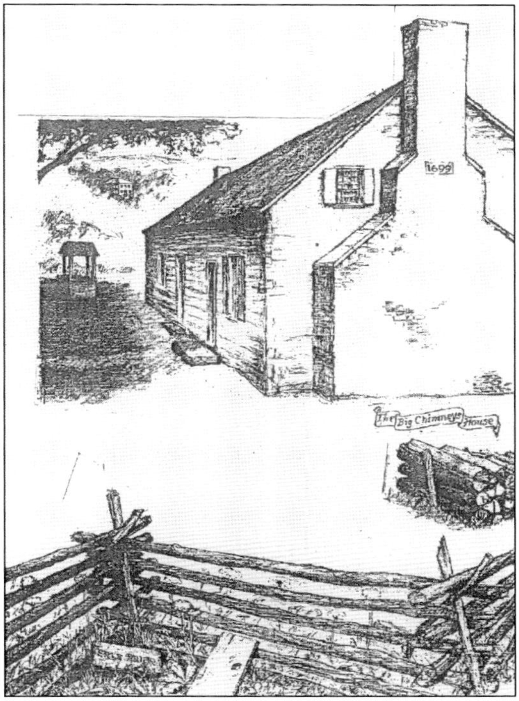

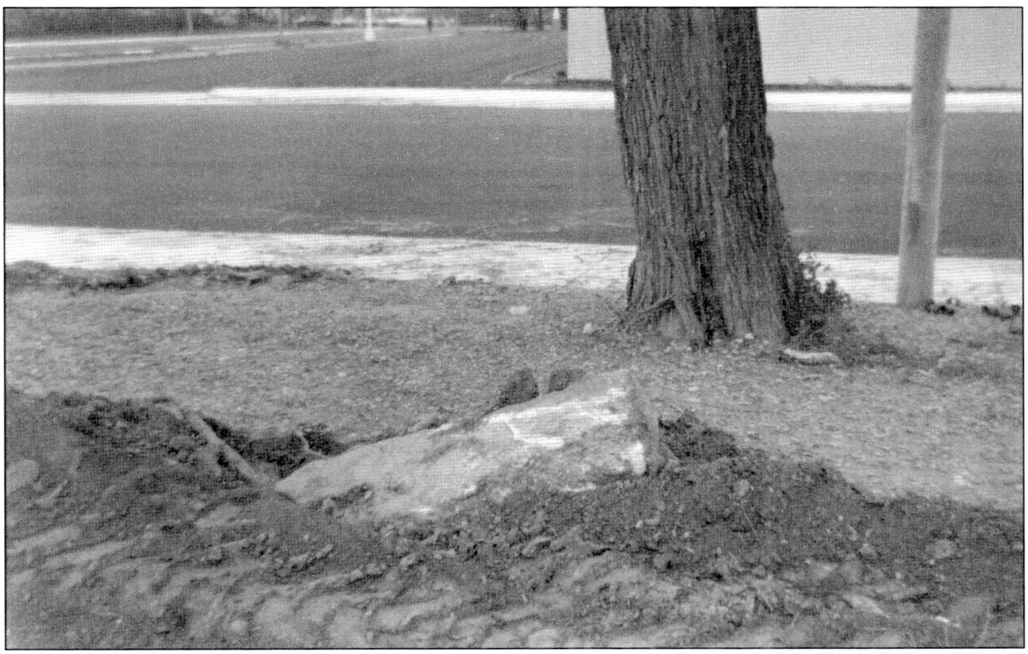

James Wren, one of the earliest known residents of Falls Church and the builder of the original brick Falls Church, owned Winter Hill, a nearby plantation, and also ran another popular ordinary, Wren's Tavern. Despite hints to the location of Wren's Tavern and archeolcgical excavation, the exact location has never been pinpointed. However, the site chosen for the Truro Parish church near the falls sat very near Big Chimneys.

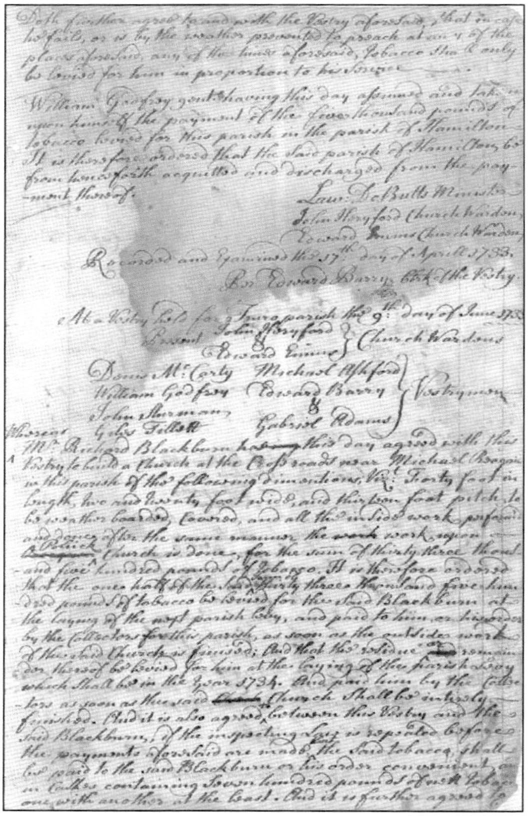

Doth further agree to and with the Vestry aforesaid, that in case he fails, or is by the weather prevented to preach at any of the places aforesaid, any of the times aforesaid, Tobacco shall only be levied for him in proportion to his service.

William Godfrey gent having this day assumed and taken upon himself the payment of the five thousand pounds of tobacco levied for this parish in the parish of Hamilton. It is therefore ordered that the said parish of Hamilton be from henceforth acquitted and discharged from the payment thereof.

Law: DeButts Minister
John Heryford Church Warden
Edward Emms Church Warden

Recorded and Examined the 17th day of April 1733.
Per Edward Barry Clerk of the Vestry.

At a Vestry held for Truro parish the 9th day of June 1733
Present John Heryford & Edward Emms } Church Wardens
Dennis McCarty, William Godfrey, John Sturman, Giles Tillett, Michael Ashford, Edward Barry & Gabriel Adams } Vestrymen

Whereas Mr. Richard Blackburn hath this day agreed with this Vestry to build a Church at the Cross roads near Michael Reagan's in this parish of the following dimensions, Viz: Forty feet in length, two and twenty feet wide, and thirteen feet pitch, to be weather boarded, covered, and all the inside work perform'd and done after the same manner the work upon Pohick Church is done, for the sum of thirty three thousand and five hundred pounds of Tobacco. It is therefore ordered that the one half of the said thirty three thousand five hundred pounds of tobacco be levied for the said Blackburn at the laying of the next parish levy, and paid to him, or his order by the Collectors for this parish, as soon as the outside work of the said Church is finished; And that the residue or remainder thereof be levied for him at the laying of the parish levy which shall be in the year 1734. And paid him by the Collectors as soon as the said Church shall be intirely finished. And it is also agreed between this Vestry and the said Blackburn, if the inspecting Law is repealed before the payments aforesaid are made, the said tobacco shall be paid to the said Blackburn or his order convenient in Casks containing seven hundred pounds of nett tobacco one with another at the least. And it is further agreed to

At the meeting of the Truro Parish Vestry held on March 26, 1733, it was "Ordered, that the Churchwardens give publick notice to workmen to appear at the next Vestry to be held for this parish to agree for the building of a Church at the cross roads near Michael Reagans in this parish." Michael Reagan was one of the original land patent holders in Falls Church. Richard Blackburn, credited with building Washington's Mount Vernon, agreed with the vestry to build a church at the crossroads near Michael Reagan's, "Forty feet in length, two and twenty feet wide, and thirteen feet pitch, to be weather boarded, covered, and all the inside work perform'd and done after the same manner the work upon Pohick Church is done, for the sum of thirty-three thousand five hundred pounds of tobacco." The wood-frame church born of that meeting was the predecessor to the permanent brick church built only three decades later due to the rapid deterioration of the church, which may have replaced an even earlier one built in 1709. (Both, LOC.)

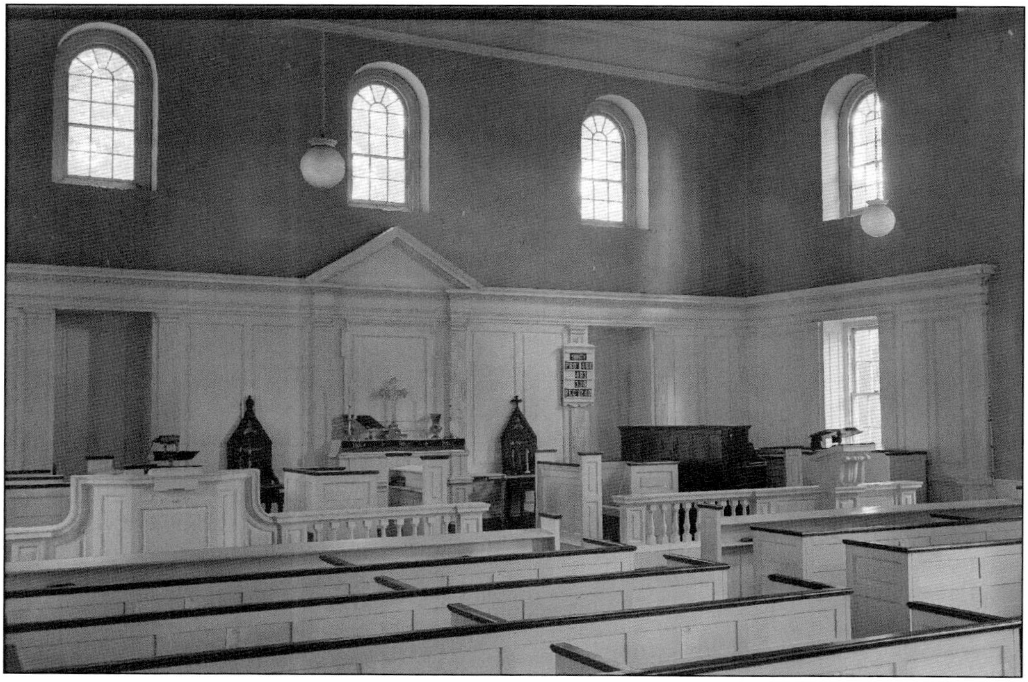

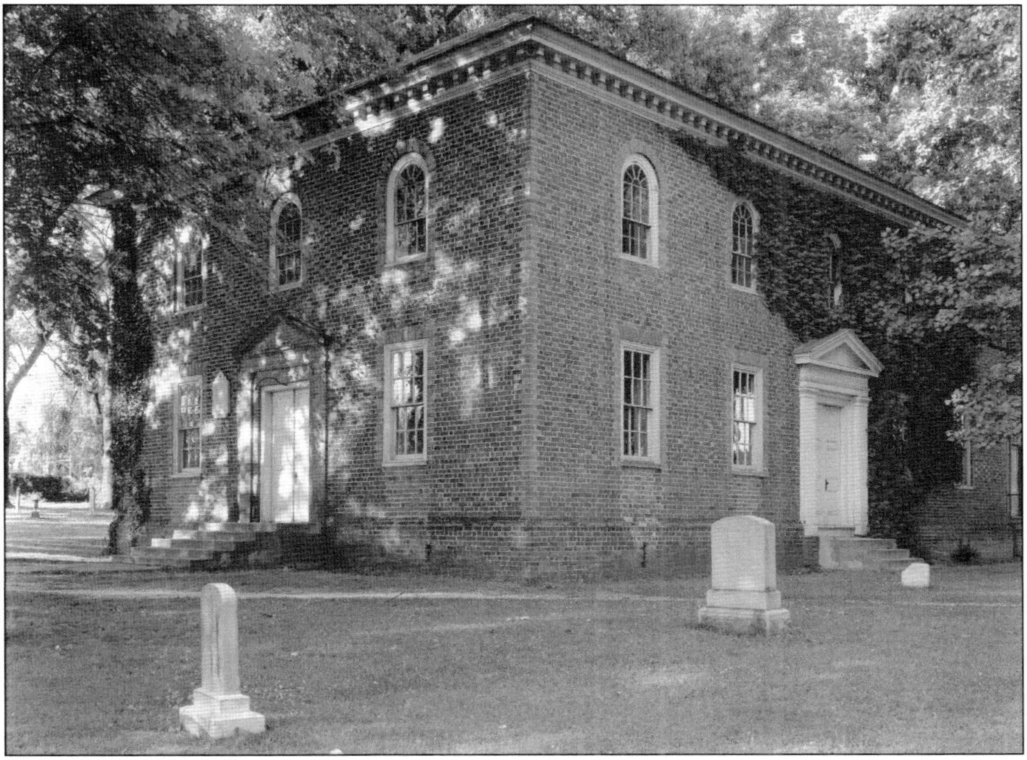

Notable vestrymen of the church included Augustine Washington; his son, future president George Washington; and George Mason, who wrote the Virginia Resolutions later used in the Bill of Rights. George Washington was elected to the vestry in 1762, the year before the resolution to build a more substantial church to replace the wooden church in disrepair. (LOC.)

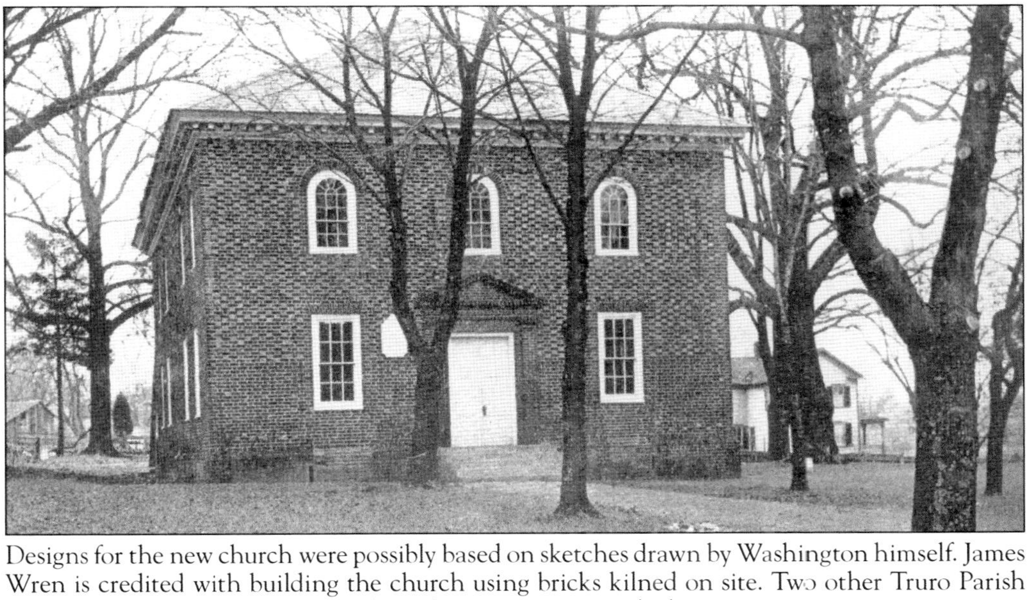

Designs for the new church were possibly based on sketches drawn by Washington himself. James Wren is credited with building the church using bricks kilned on site. Two other Truro Parish churches surviving today were built in the same era in much the same manner.

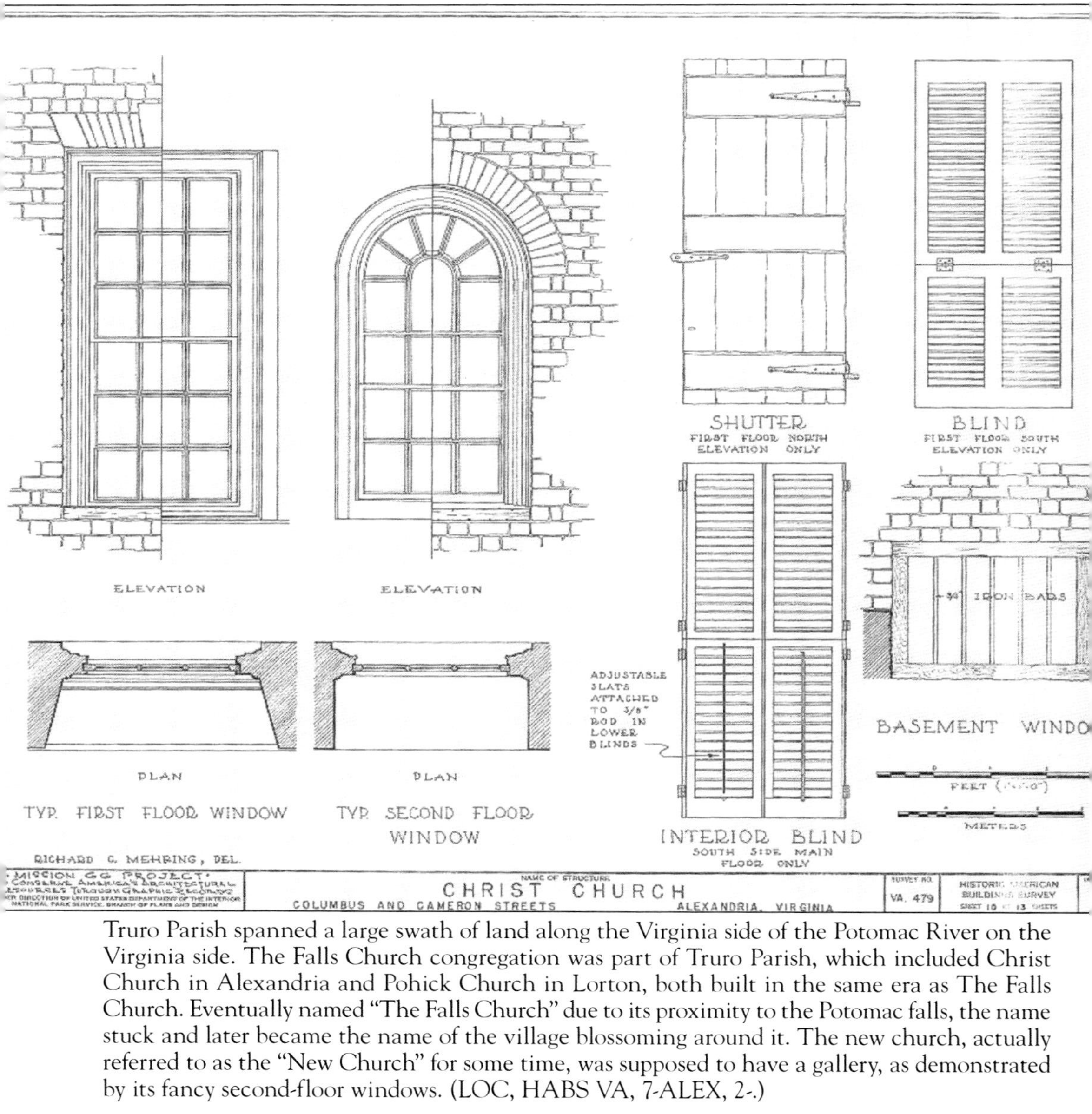

Truro Parish spanned a large swath of land along the Virginia side of the Potomac River on the Virginia side. The Falls Church congregation was part of Truro Parish, which included Christ Church in Alexandria and Pohick Church in Lorton, both built in the same era as The Falls Church. Eventually named "The Falls Church" due to its proximity to the Potomac falls, the name stuck and later became the name of the village blossoming around it. The new church, actually referred to as the "New Church" for some time, was supposed to have a gallery, as demonstrated by its fancy second-floor windows. (LOC, HABS VA, 7-ALEX, 2-.)

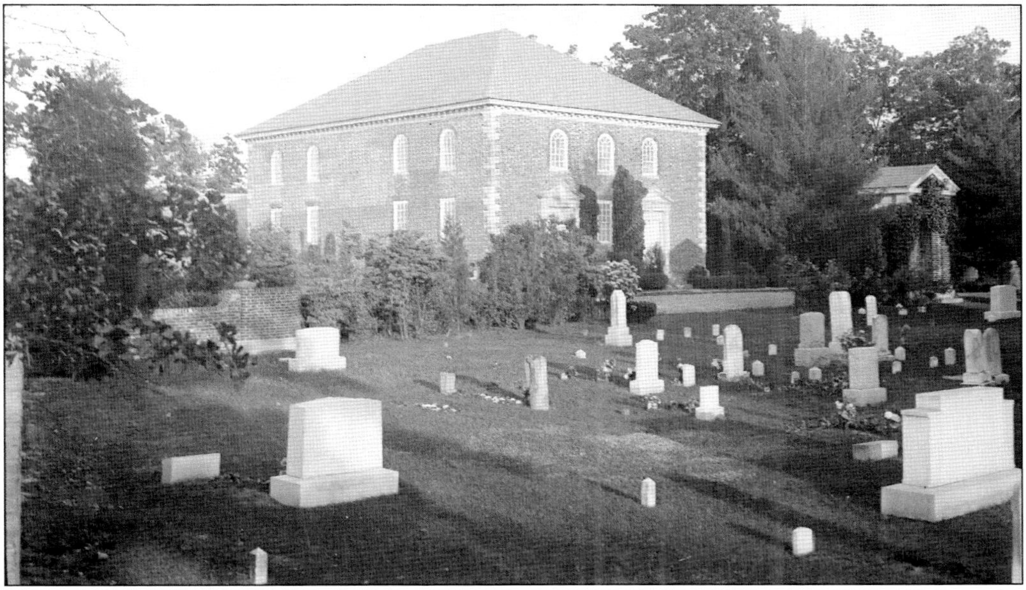

Pohick Church looks almost identical to The Falls Church and was built in 1774 apparently from the same basic plans. It contains the same two rows of windows and brick features. Pohick was devastated during the Civil War and has been restored twice since. (LOC, HABS VA, 30-POHI, 1–3.)

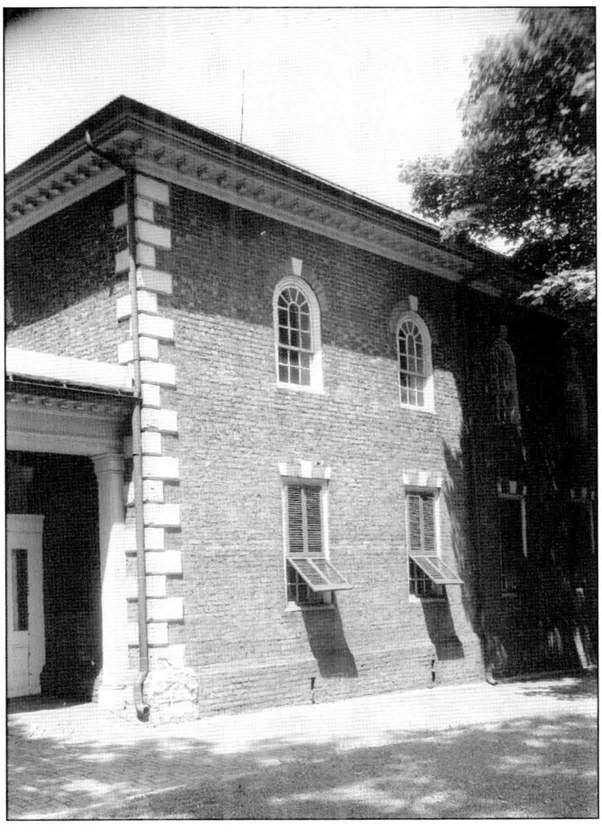

The windows and shutters of Christ Church in Alexandria also reflect the design of The Falls Church. Once all things England were shunned with the disestablishment of the Anglican Church, The Falls Church fell into a state of neglect after 1789, used only occasionally and left open for any traveler or animal to wander in until Capt. Henry Fairfax had it repaired at his expense. (LOC, HABS VA, 7-ALEX, 2-.)

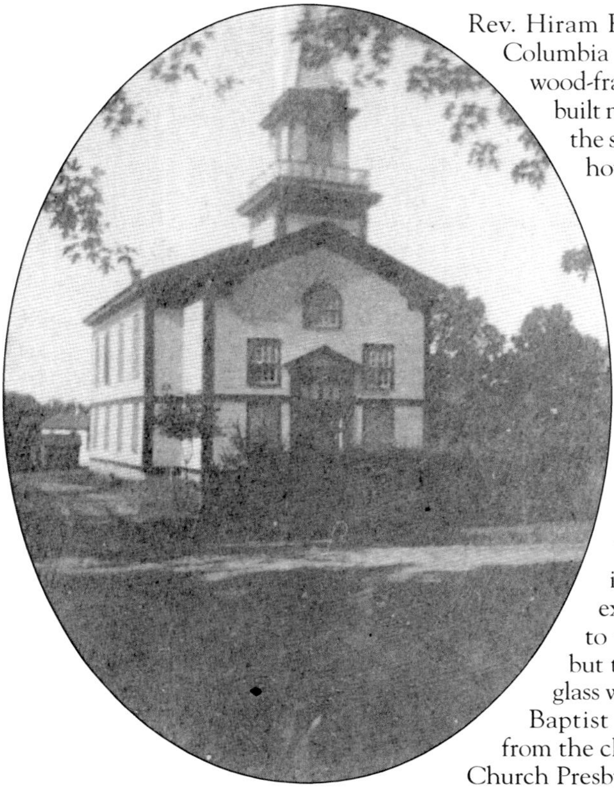

Rev. Hiram Reed organized the congregation for Columbia Baptist Church in 1856. The original wood-frame house of worship with a steeple was built near The Falls Church in 1857. The life of the structure was short-lived in this location, however, because of the Civil War.

Using rocks from the local quarry on South Washington Street at Tripps Run, construction of a new Columbia Baptist Church (below) on North Washington Street was begun in 1909. Every denomination in town except the Catholics sent a representative to the building committee and assisted, but the Catholics did contribute a stained-glass window from their old church. Columbia Baptist was demolished in 1968, but stone from the church was used in the addition to Falls Church Presbyterian.

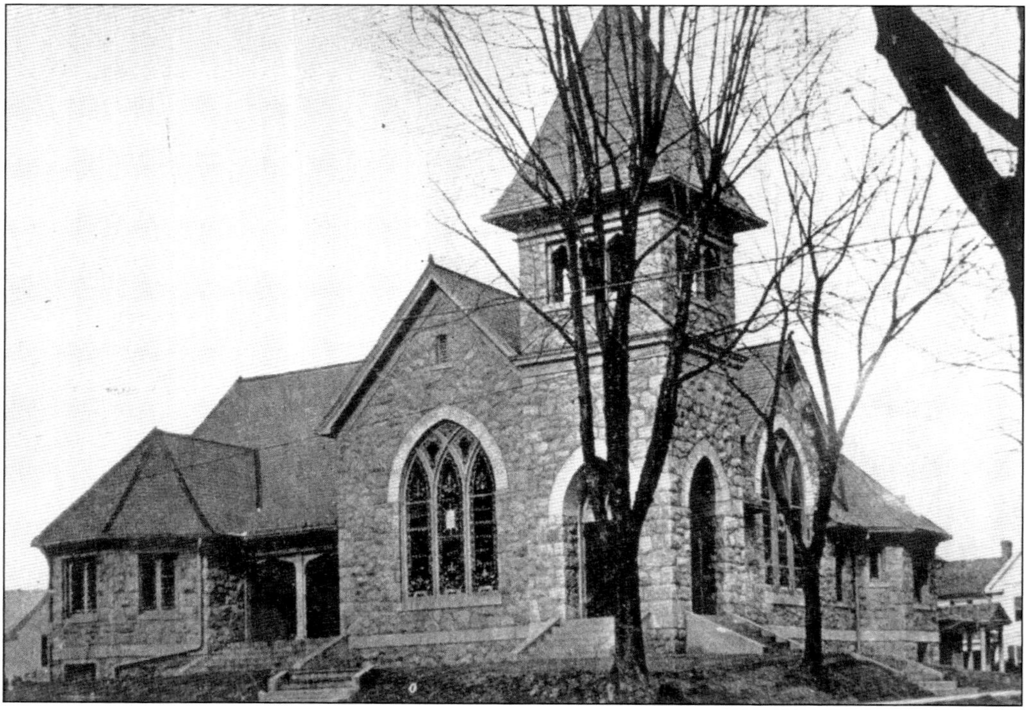

Catholicism entered Falls Church by way of the mission of St. James, which congregated at Sabilla Sewall's home, later called Walnut Hill, beginning in 1873. Sewall donated property from her land on South West Street at Fowler Street to build the original wood-frame St. James Church in 1892 on the property that is now the St. James Cemetery.

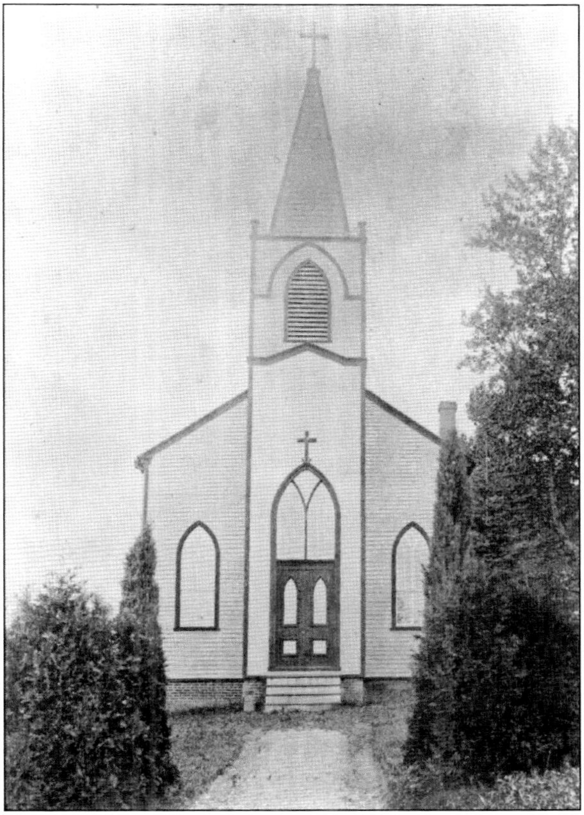

The original Sherwood family farmhouse (below) north of Broad Street at Spring Street stood on the land now occupied by St. James Catholic Church. The Sherwoods played a prominent role in the development of Falls Church. The Catholic congregation outgrew the small mission church on South West Street and had a new church erected on what was part of the Sherwood farm between Broad Street and Park Avenue in 1902. (Courtesy of Catherine Speakman.)

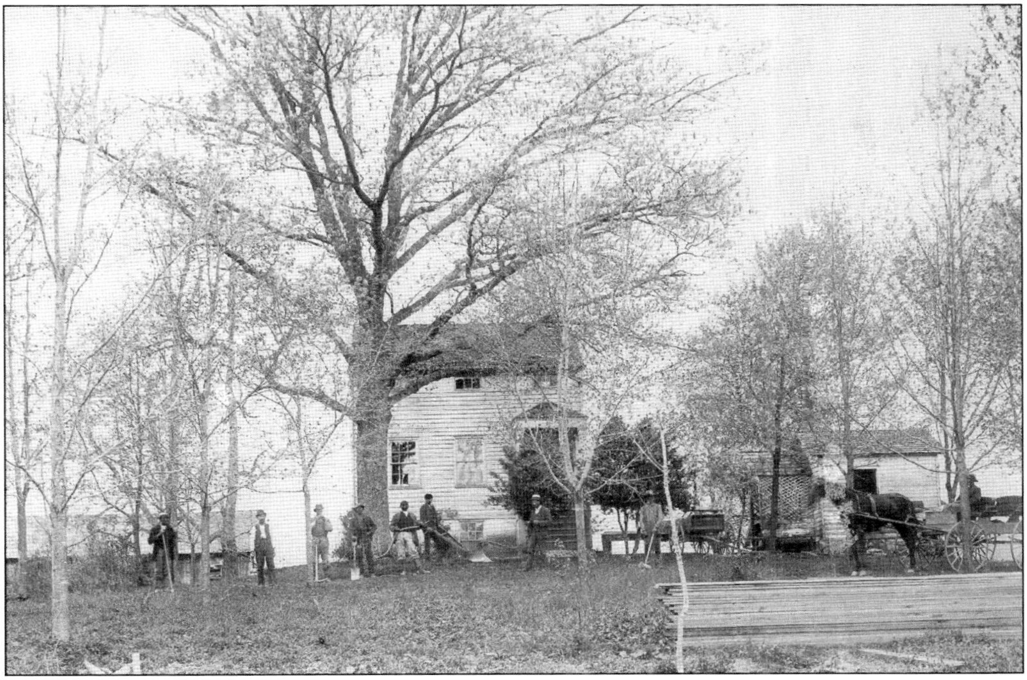

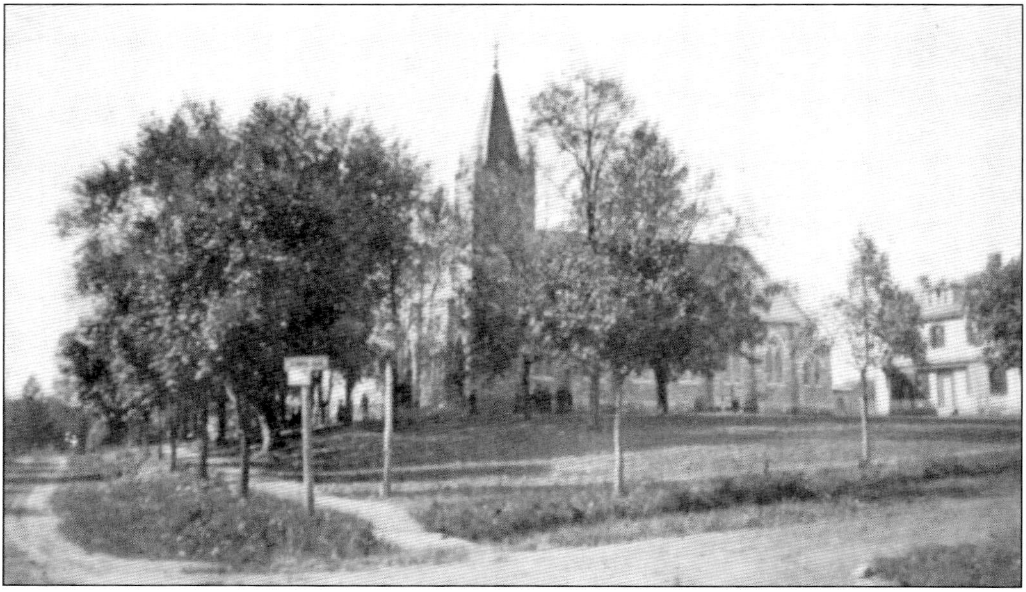

Through the generosity of Ida Mary (Barry) Ryan, the wife of Thomas Fortune Ryan, the new church was built near the center of town. Exhibiting some of the finest Gothic architecture in all of Northern Virginia, the larger St. James Catholic Church on Park Avenue and Spring Street is built of sandstone from the local quarry. Village resident A.O. Von Herbulis was the architect of the new church, and Thomas Hiller is credited with building the original center wing.

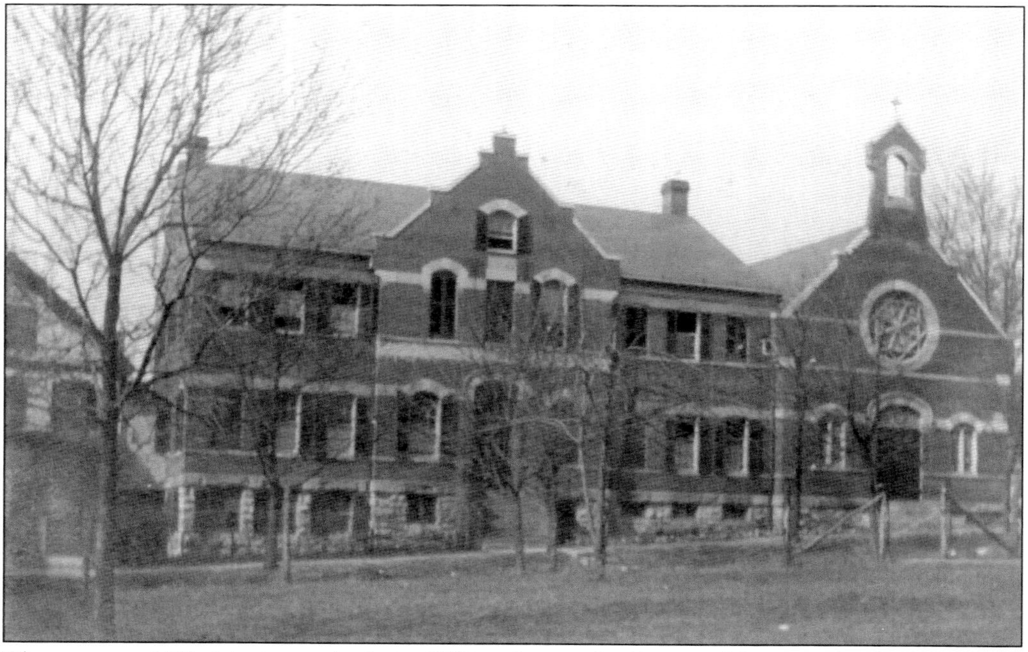

The convent Villa Maria was built in 1907 to house the Sisters of Perpetual Adoration, who arrived from New Orleans in 1905 to run the St. James School. Prior to the construction of the convent, the sisters had been living in the Sherwood home. A boarding school for girls was started in the cottage next door.

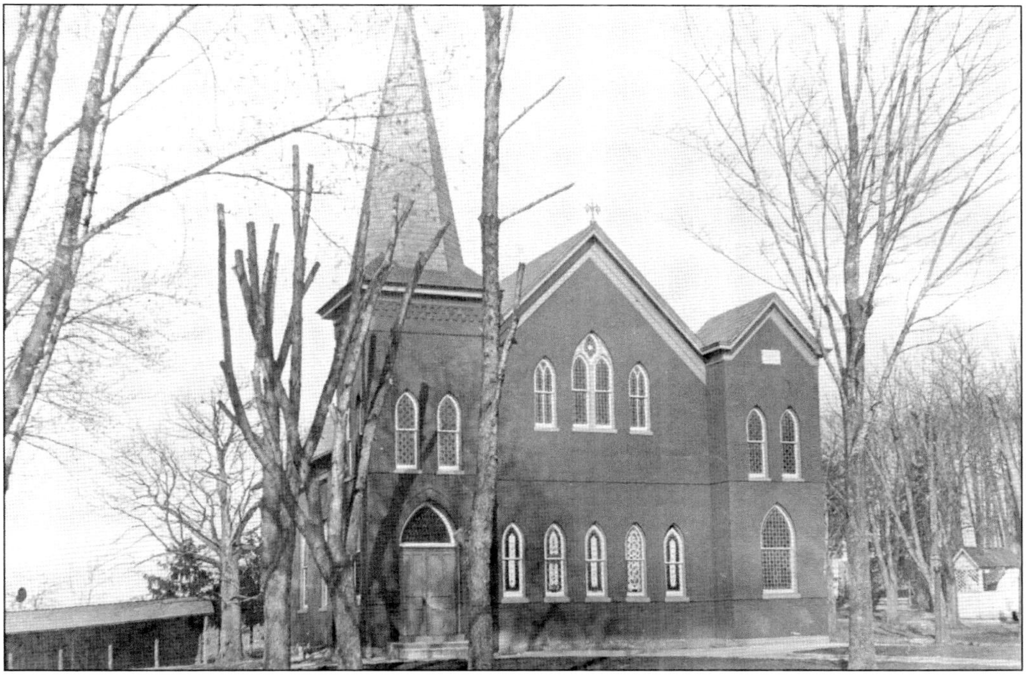

The first Methodist congregation in Falls Church worshipped at the log Fairfax Chapel, built in the 1770s on the Oakwood Cemetery hill. The first recorded sermon by a black Methodist preacher, Harry Hoosier, was held there. A larger church replaced the log structure around 1789, and a brick church was built in 1819 containing a gallery for the black congregants. The church closed prior to the Civil War and was ultimately destroyed during the war from soldiers removing bricks for their own chimneys, causing the church to collapse. The Methodist congregation split into north and south factions after the Civil War, and the southern faction built this church, Dulin Methodist, and parsonage (below) on land donated by William Dulin. Dulin stipulated that if the property was ever not used for church purposes, it would revert back to Dulin's heirs.

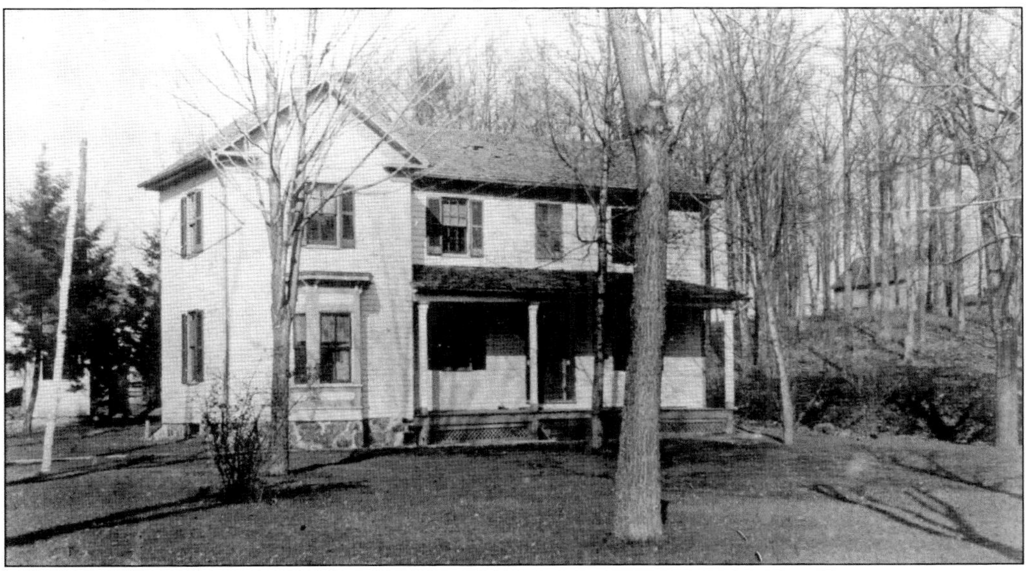

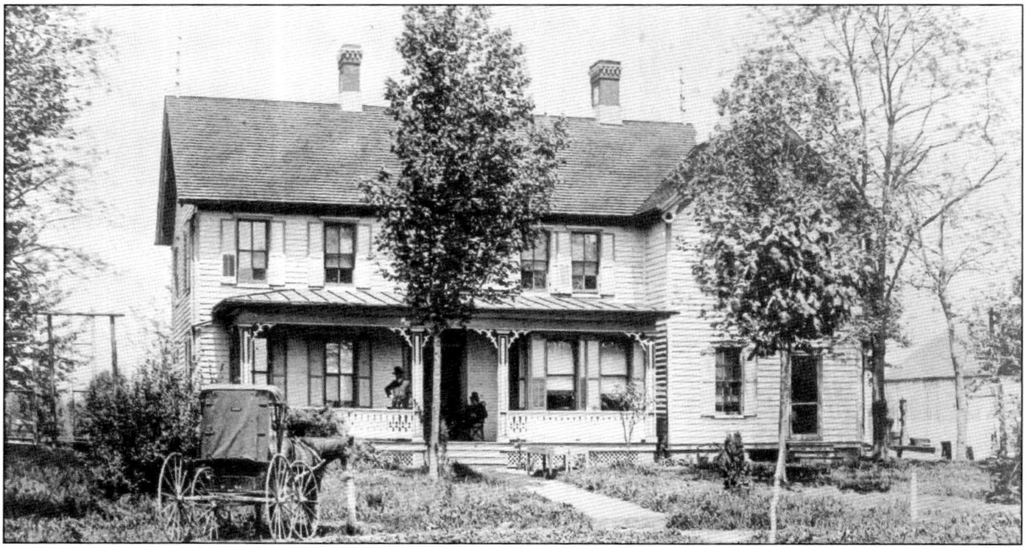

Isaac Crossman arrived in Falls Church from Pennsylvania shortly after the Civil War and began building his family farmhouse on North Washington Street in 1871 while living in a log cabin on the property. Crossman was among the first group of town councilmen appointed when Falls Church became an incorporated town in 1875.

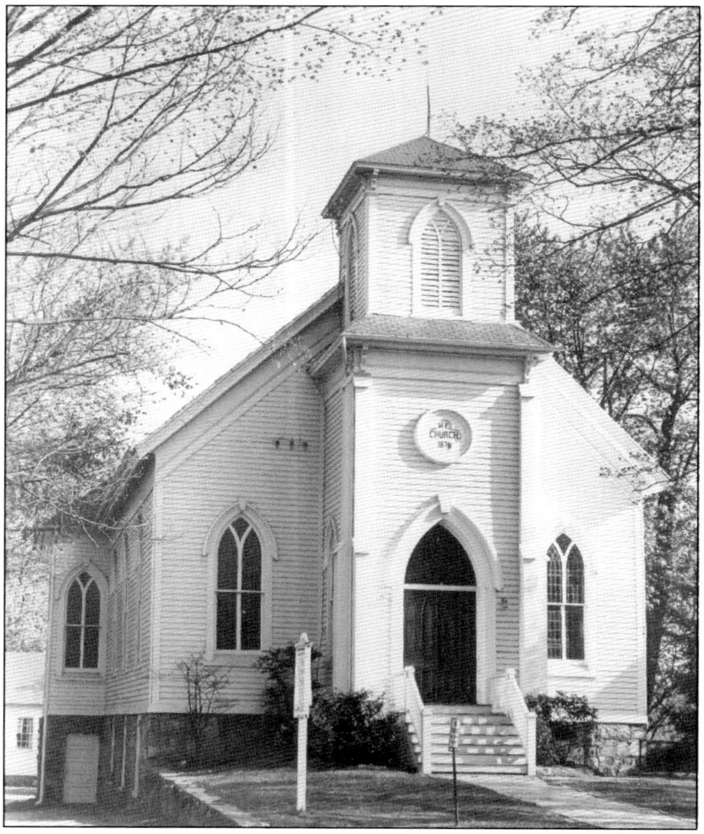

Crossman donated a slice of his vast farmland on North Washington Street and contributed financial support for the Crossman Methodist Church, serving the northern faction of the original Methodist congregation after the Civil War. This wood-frame Crossman Methodist was built in 1875 and demolished in 1963.

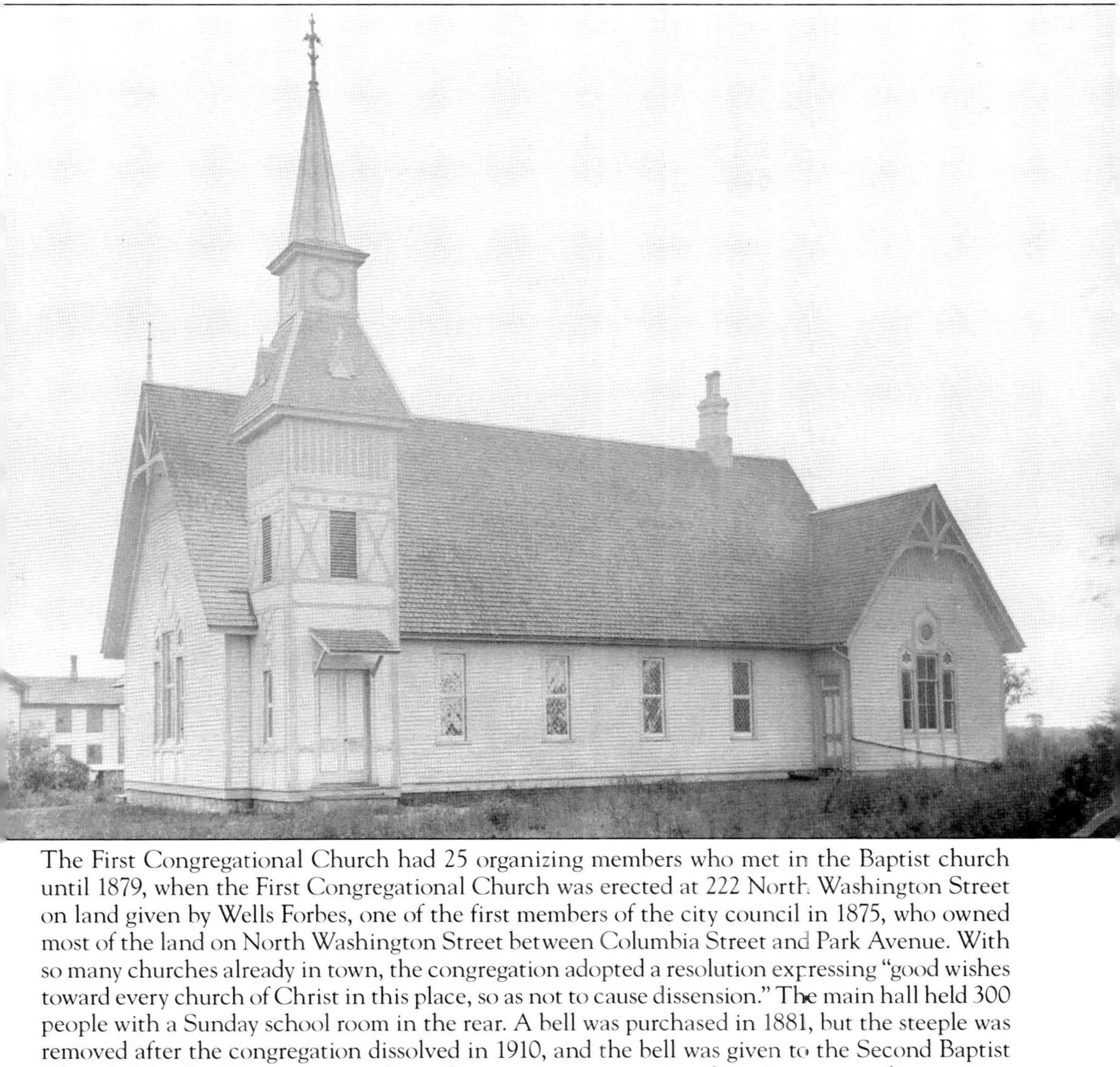

The First Congregational Church had 25 organizing members who met in the Baptist church until 1879, when the First Congregational Church was erected at 222 North Washington Street on land given by Wells Forbes, one of the first members of the city council in 1875, who owned most of the land on North Washington Street between Columbia Street and Park Avenue. With so many churches already in town, the congregation adopted a resolution expressing "good wishes toward every church of Christ in this place, so as not to cause dissension." The main hall held 300 people with a Sunday school room in the rear. A bell was purchased in 1881, but the steeple was removed after the congregation dissolved in 1910, and the bell was given to the Second Baptist Church. The building was transformed to serve many varying functions as a police station, town hall, school, recreation center, library, and general meeting place. Macon Ware's drugstore occupied the building in the late 1930s.

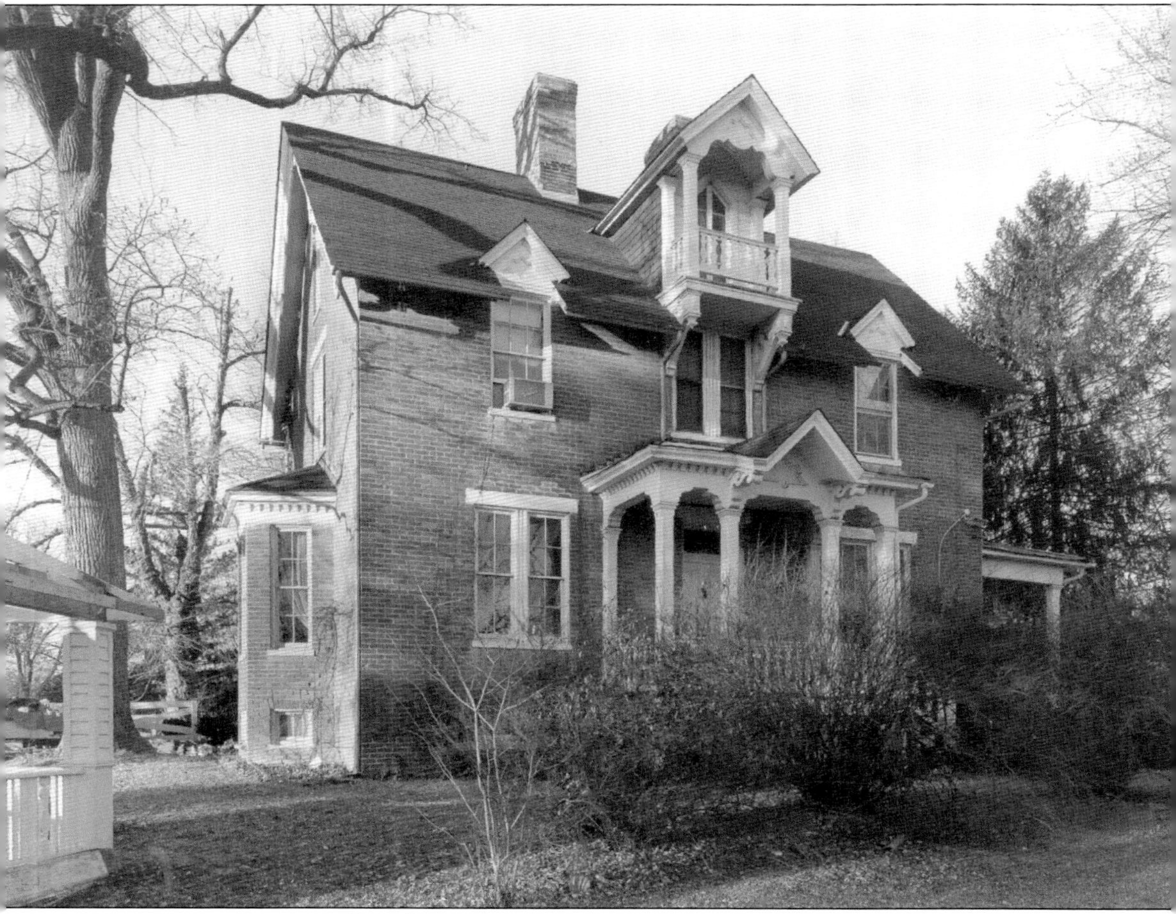

Mount Hope on South Oak Street served as the meeting place for local Presbyterians in the 1840s. At that time, the house only consisted of the frame saltbox-style portion, built between 1790 and 1815. The brick addition was not added until the 1870s. The house, at the top of a tree-lined drive, looked down toward Broad Street from the crest of the hill. Amzi Coe owned the property from 1842 until his death in 1866 and was likely the one who hosted the early meetings of the Presbyterians until Groot Hall was constructed in 1856.

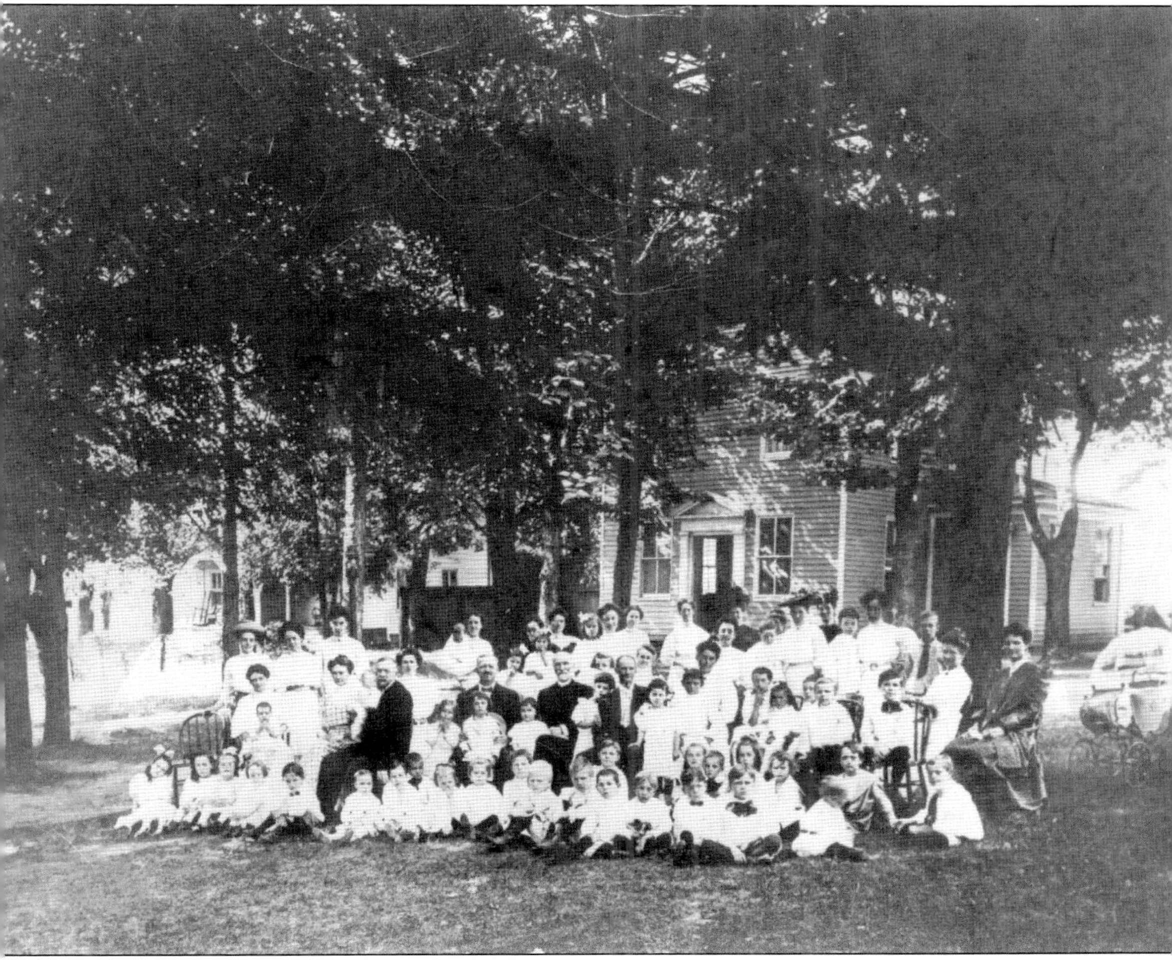

Groot Hall (above), built by Dr. Simon J. Groot, was formally dedicated as a church in November 1866. Initially, it hosted Presbyterian meetings until the Gothic-style Falls Church Presbyterian Church was erected in 1884 on East Broad Street, built of stone quarried on South Washington Street at Tripps Run. The Columbia Baptist building was demolished in 1968 and stone from it was used to construct the addition to Falls Church Presbyterian.

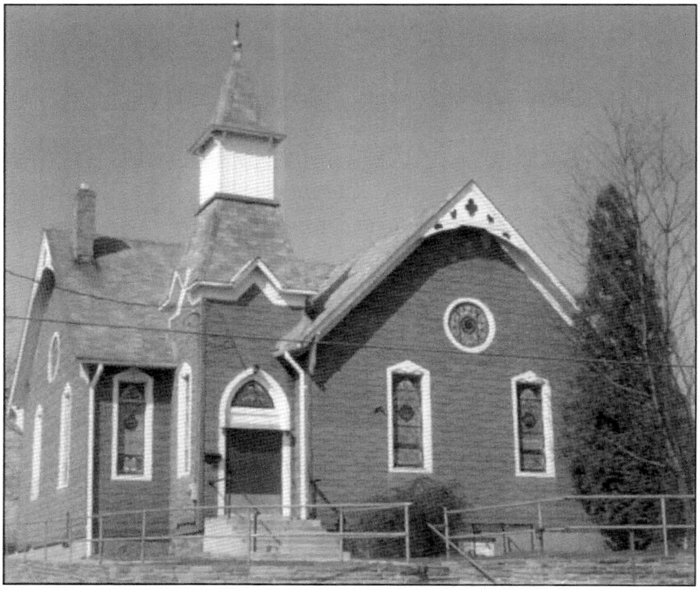

Shortly after hostilities of the Civil War ceased, the "colored settlement" built Galloway Methodist Church in a grove of trees on a hill where enslaved people had secretly worshipped before the war on part of the Dulany Plantation. George and Harriet Brice were church founders after Hiram Reed, minister of the First Baptist Church, now known as Columbia Baptist, encouraged them to begin their own church. (Courtesy of the Tinner Hill Heritage Foundation.)

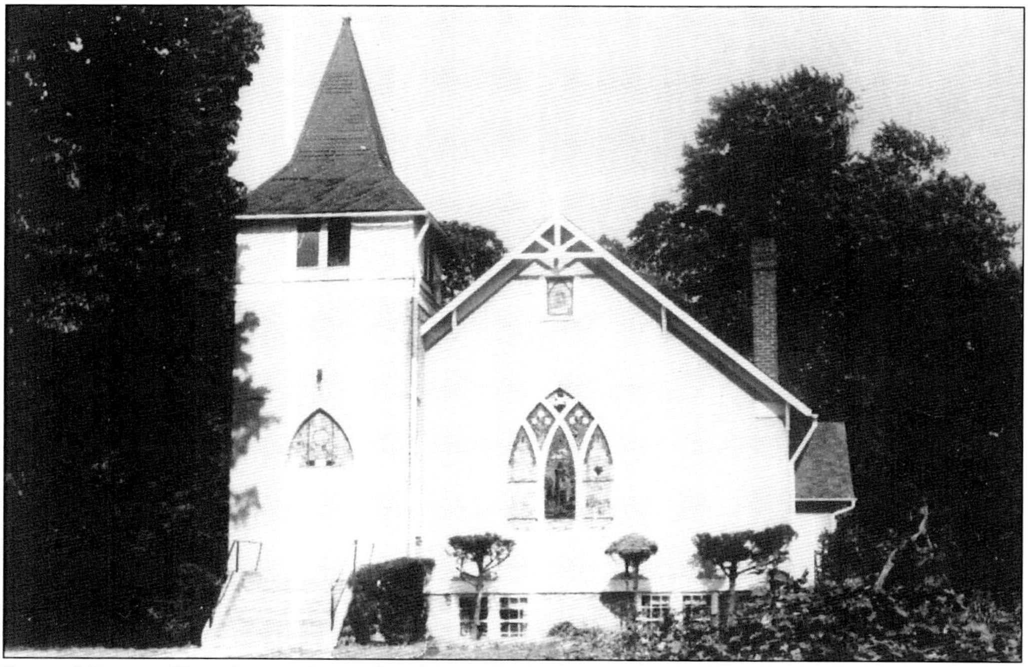

Second Baptist Church was planned and organized in a two-room log cabin on South Washington Street owned by Elder Hiram Reed of Columbia Baptist. After the Civil War, veteran Robert Johnson was persuaded and trained by Rev. Hiram Reed to qualify for the ministry. Reverend Johnson was ordained and became the first minister of Second Baptist in 1870. (Courtesy of the Tinner Hill Heritage Foundation, Barbara Williams Collection.)

Two

Parallel National History

Nothing has impacted the evolving village as much as the turbulence of war. From housing Navy Yard gunpowder during the final stages of the Revolution, to having a local pastor killed by John Mosby and "Mosby's Raiders" for his role in educating the local black community, to being a haven for Gen. Dwight D. Eisenhower as he strategized during World War II, Falls Church's history is intrinsically connected to that of the country as a whole.

Residents fought in every war, and some were lost to the cause of their country. Sides split drastically during the Civil War after Virginia voted itself out of the Union. The historic churches were ravaged and abused, becoming mere stables for animals during the Civil War. Local plantations were also not immune to the relentless hunger and need for warmth of soldiers fighting on both sides. Generals set up command posts within the village. Yet a romance sprang from the tragedy that forever impacted the future of the town and remains its legacy to this day.

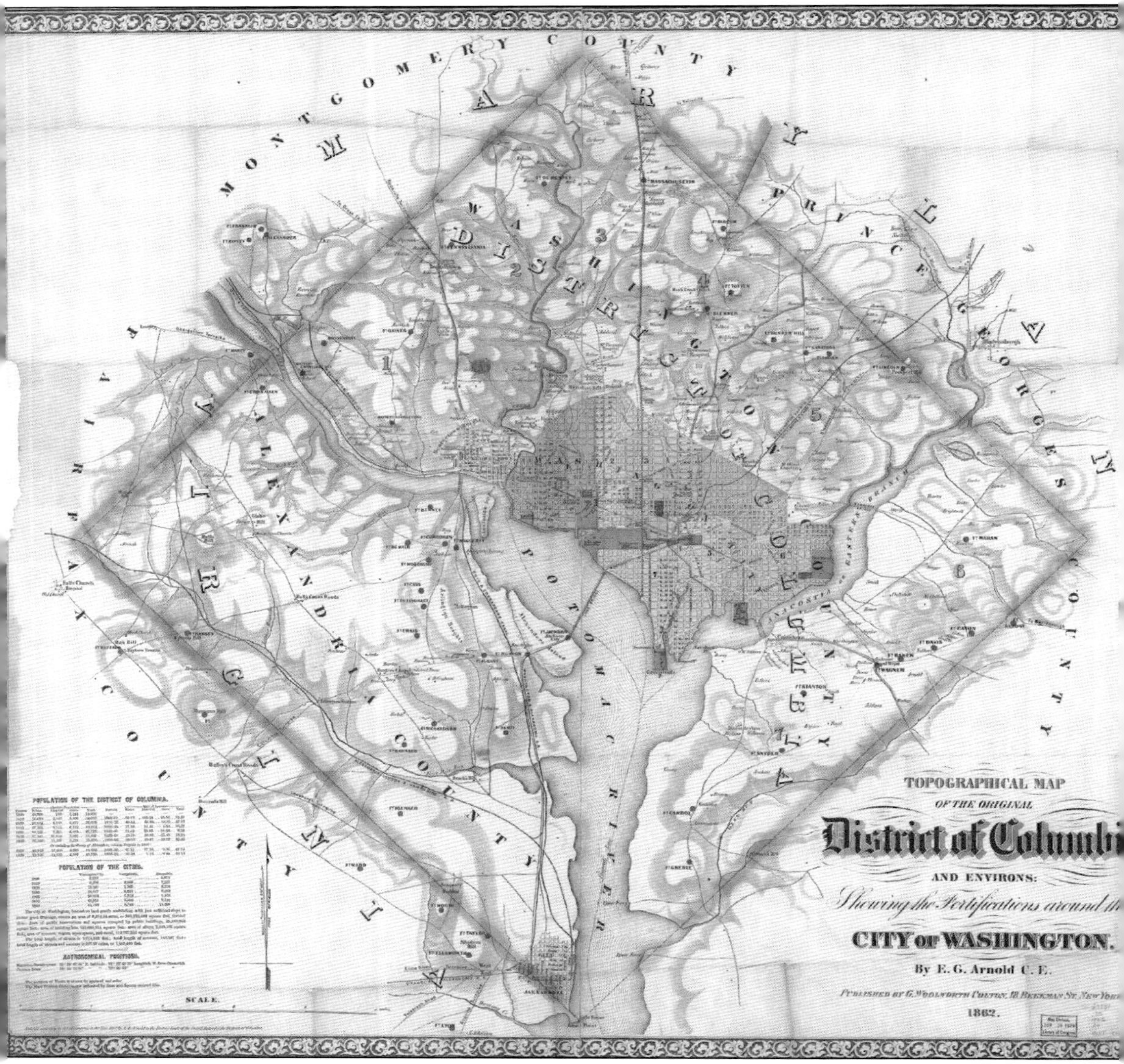

The federal District of Columbia was established in 1791 and formed a perfect diamond, taking some land from Arlington and Falls Church. Forty boundary stones were set at approximately one-mile intervals in 1791 and 1792. The work was done under the supervision of Maj. Andrew Ellicott, who was assisted by gifted astronomer Benjamin Banneker, a free black man. As the British invaded Washington in 1814, federal employees and families began to flee across the river. (LOC, Maps Division.)

The west cornerstone at the 400 block of Meridian Street, known as the "Ellicott Stone," marks the western tip of the original 10-mile-square federal district. That stone is also mentioned in the city charter as well as the DePutron farm as a boundary for the city limits.

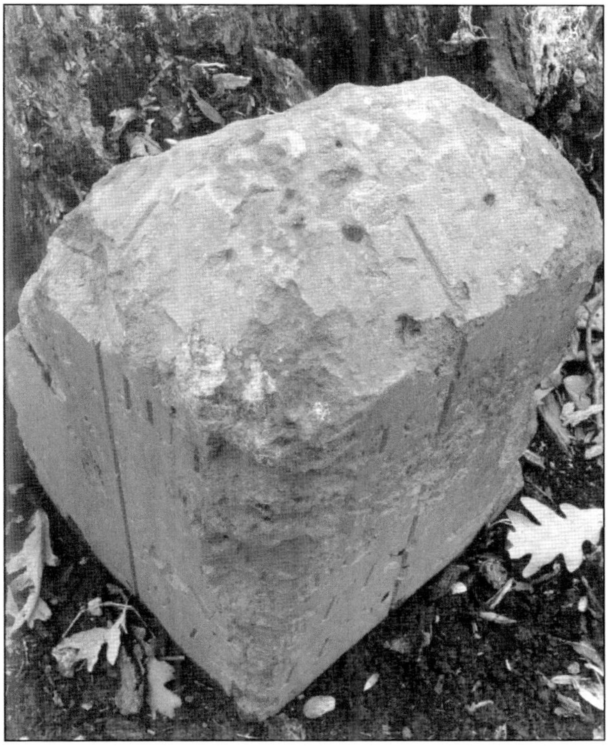

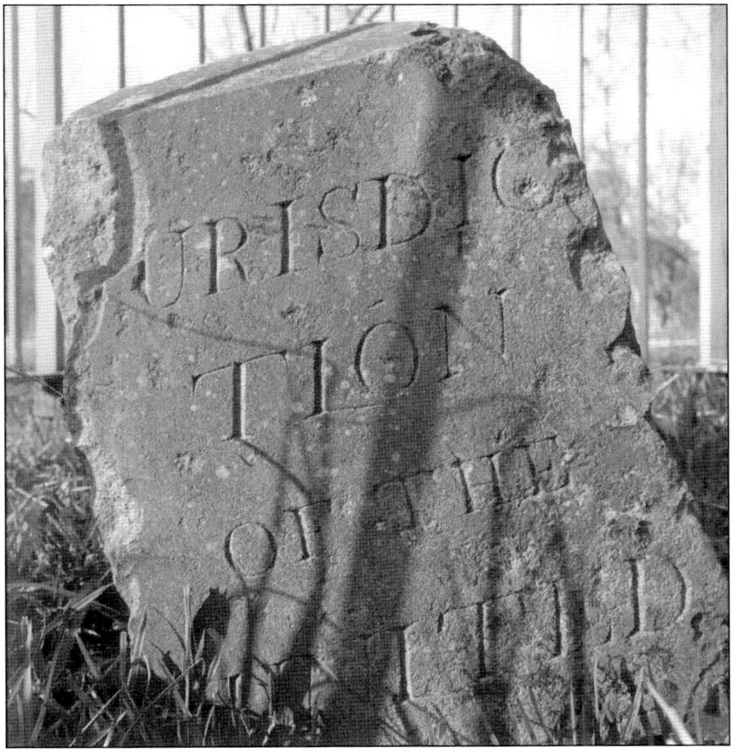

The 1791 boundary stone on Van Buren Street also marked the District of Columbia, Falls Church, and Arlington boundary in the northwest corner of DC. Once the new federal district was completed, congress and the president moved into Washington from Philadelphia in 1800.

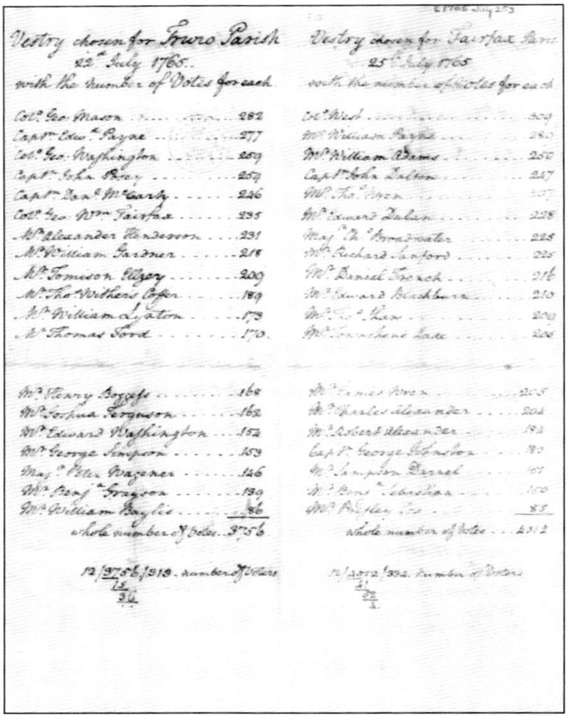

Vestry chosen for Truro Parish 22d July 1765. with the number of Votes for each		Vestry chosen for Fairfax Paris[h] 25th July 1765 with the number of Votes for each	
Colo. Geo. Mason	282	Colo. West	309
Captn. Edwd. Payne	277	Mr. William Payne	280
Colo. Geo. Washington	259	Mr. William Adams	250
Captn. John Posey	259	Captn. John Dalton	247
Captn. Danl. McCarty	246	Mr. Thos. Wren	237
Colo. Geo. Wm. Fairfax	235	Mr. Edward Dulan	228
Mr. Alexander Henderson	231	Majr. Chs. Broadwater	225
Mr. William Gardner	218	Mr. Richard Sanford	225
Mr. Tomison Ellzey	209	Mr. Daniel French	216
Mr. Thos. Withers Coffer	189	Mr. Edward Blackburn	210
Mr. William Lynton	173	Mr. Thos. Shaw	209
Mr. Thomas Ford	170	Mr. Townshend Dade	206
Mr. Henry Boggess	168	Mr. James Wren	205
Mr. Joshua Ferguson	162	Mr. Charles Alexander	204
Mr. Edward Washington	152	Mr. Robert Alexander	192
Mr. George Simpson	153	Captn. George Johnston	183
Majr. Peter Wagener	146	Mr. Sampson Darrel	167
Mr. Benja. Grayson	139	Mr. Benja. Sebastian	150
Mr. William Baylis	86	Mr. Presley Cox	85
whole number of Votes	3756	whole number of Votes	4012
12/3756/313 number of Voters		12/4012/334 number of Voters	

Falls Church vestrymen George Mason and George Washington, elected due to their most discreet and trustworthy character, were instrumental in the birth of the new United States of America. Col. George Mason was elected to the Truro vestry in 1748 and authored the Fairfax Resolves in 1774, presenting them to George Washington and Col. Charles Broadwater of Falls Church. Mason then drafted the Virginia Declaration of Rights, guaranteeing rights later used in the US Bill of Rights. George Washington fulfilled his Truro Parish vestry duties until military responsibilities during the Revolution demanded his full attention, but he did not resign from the vestry until 1784, after the Revolution. Colonel Broadwater, also a member of the vestry, drafted soldiers for the local militia in The Falls Church. It is believed that the Declaration of Independence was read to townspeople from the steps of The Falls Church. (Both, LOC.)

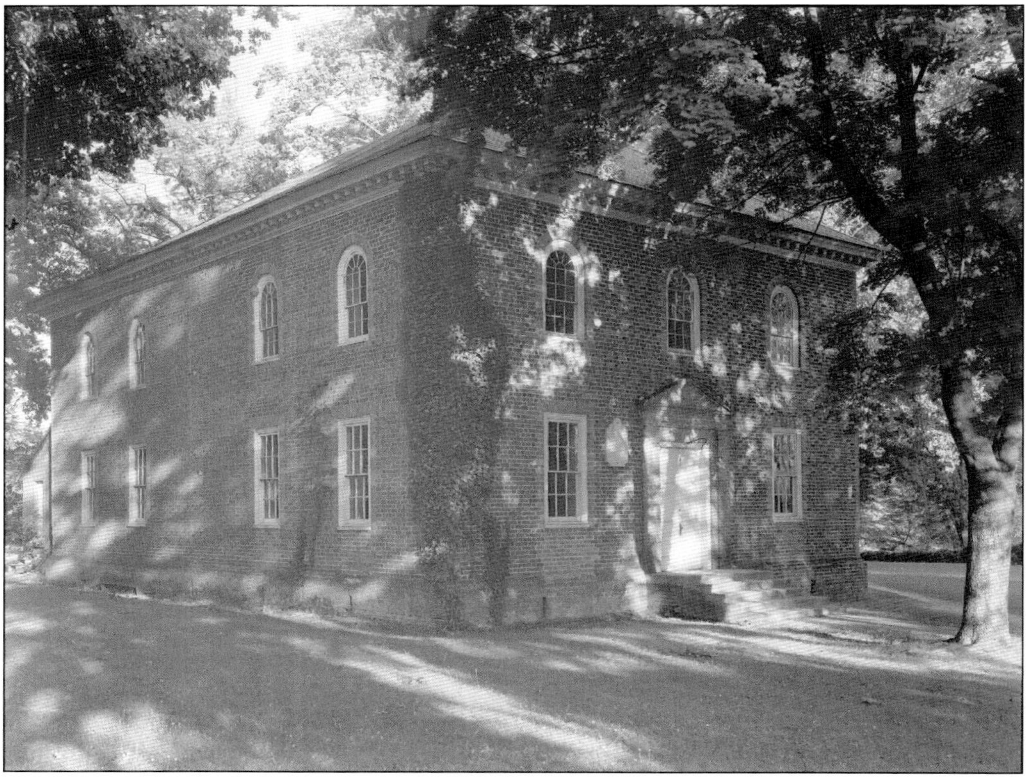

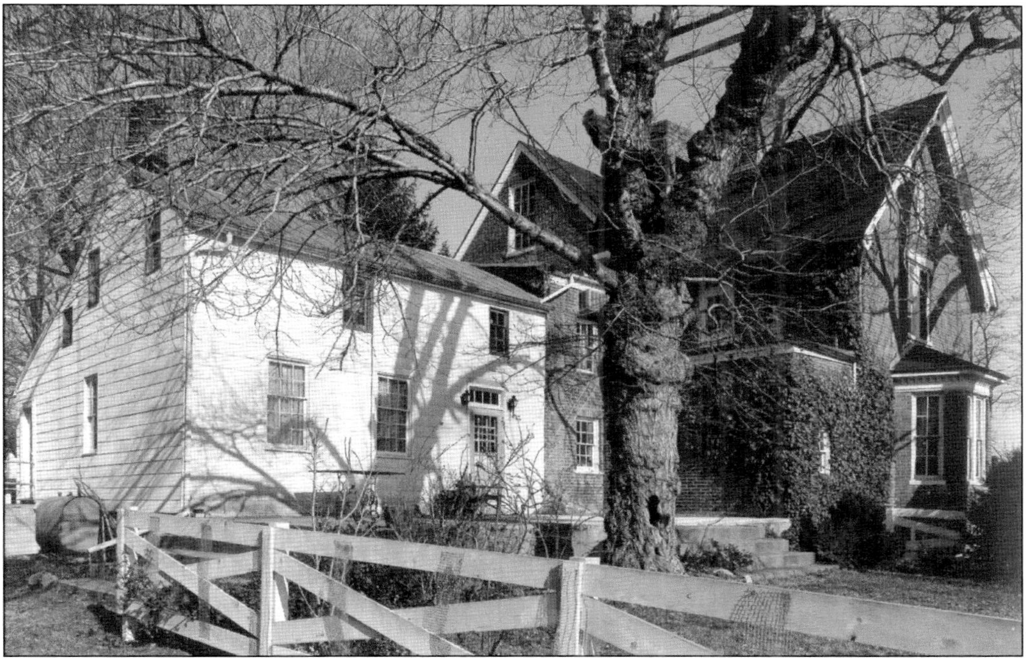

Falls Church was mostly a farming village, with only a smattering of families living within its borders as war with Britain loomed and drew nearer to the District in August 1814. The original frame portion of Mount Hope (above) had already been built. The Cloverdale farmhouse (below) was built in 1797 on a West Broad Street farm extending east past the current Lee Highway. Cloverdale is said to be identical to James Wren's Winter Hill, farther east on Broad Street. Documents including the Declaration of Independence were bustled out of DC through Falls Church. Dolley Madison fled the White House with a few artifacts and belongings, including a painting of George Washington, and sought refuge at a friend's house. Pres. James Madison came through Wren's Tavern in Falls Church while looking for his wife. The countryside, only sparsely mottled with plantation homes and farms, made the horrific burning of DC clearly visible from the village hillsides.

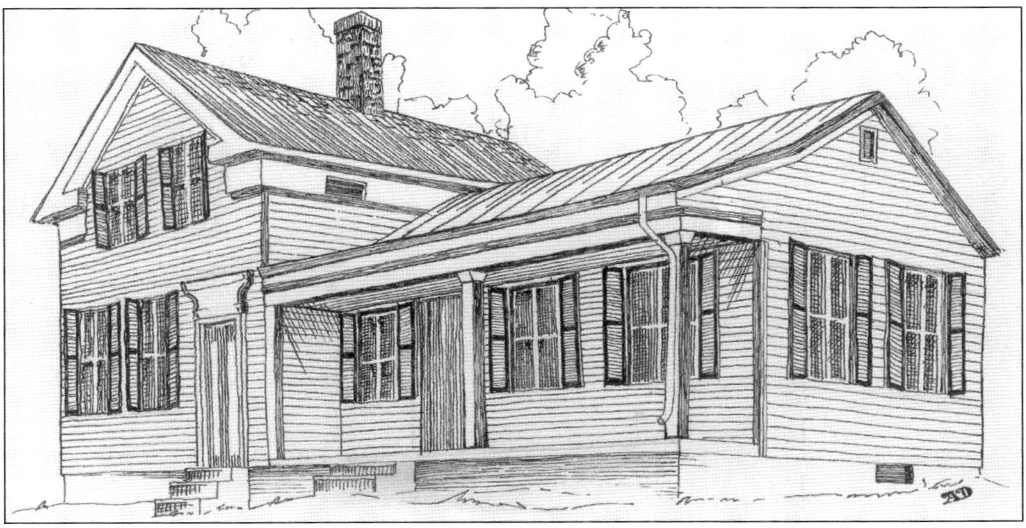

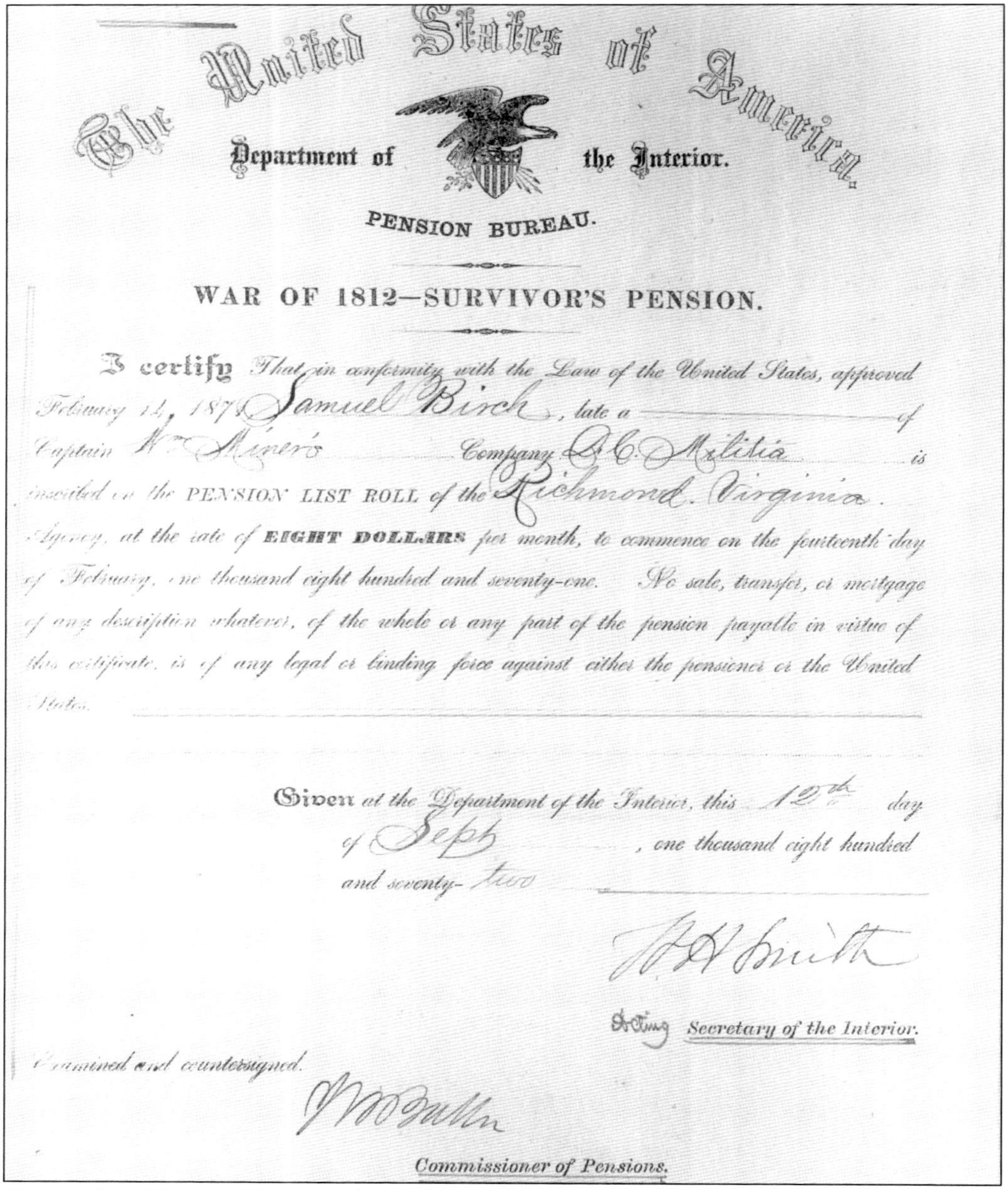

The United States of America

Department of the Interior.

PENSION BUREAU.

WAR OF 1812—SURVIVOR'S PENSION.

I certify That in conformity with the Law of the United States, approved February 14, 1871 Samuel Birch, late a ______ of Captain Wm Miner's Company D.C. Militia is inscribed on the PENSION LIST ROLL of the Richmond Virginia Agency, at the rate of EIGHT DOLLARS per month, to commence on the fourteenth day of February, one thousand eight hundred and seventy-one. No sale, transfer, or mortgage of any description whatever, of the whole or any part of the pension payable in virtue of this certificate, is of any legal or binding force against either the pensioner or the United States.

Given at the Department of the Interior, this 12th day of Sept, one thousand eight hundred and seventy-two

Acting Secretary of the Interior.

Examined and countersigned.

Commissioner of Pensions.

Commodore Thomas Tingey ordered the Washington Navy Yard gunpowder supply hastily evacuated from the city, and in the melee, wagons were difficult to acquire. Tingey's senior clerk, with a six-man guard assigned by Col. George Minor, spent the night at Wren's Tavern before supervising the storage of the 124 barrels of explosives in what the clerk felt was a woefully insecure Falls Church family barn. The barn belonged to the Dulanys, the daughter and son-in-law of the commodore. Upon returning to Wren's, the clerk learned he had just missed President Madison searching for his wife. Many Falls Church residents were actively involved in state duties and the militia. One of the earliest and longest-tenured families in the city were the Birches. Samuel Birch fought in the War of 1812, and this document shows his survivor's pension from the young government. Samuel Birch was about 22 when the War of 1812 began and ranked as a colonel.

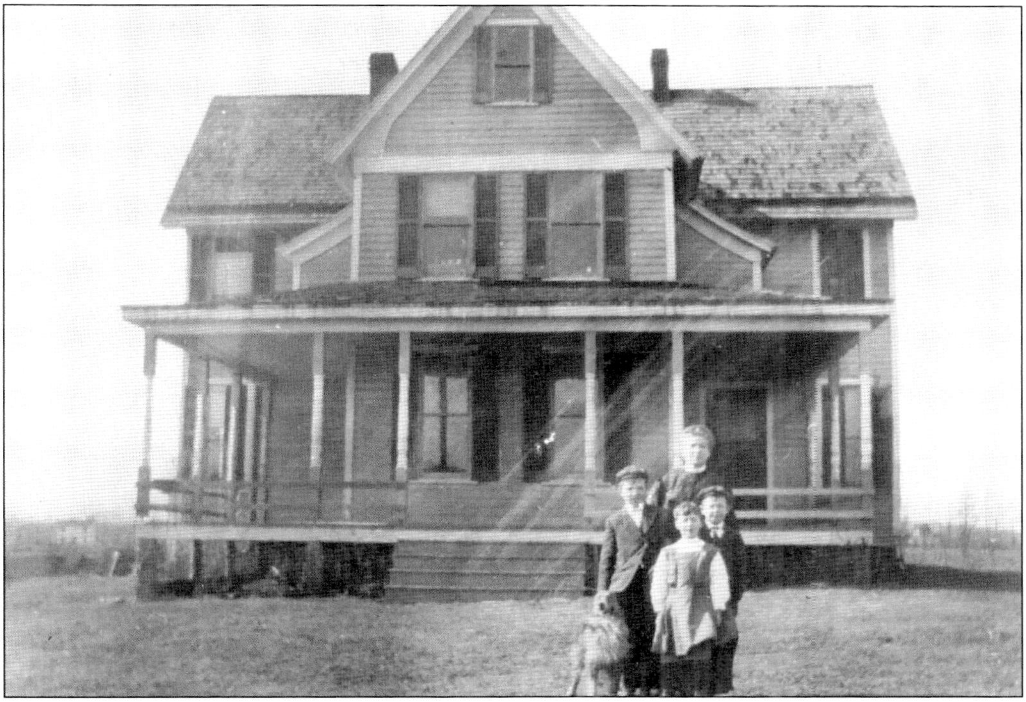

The Birches lived in a farmhouse on South Cherry Street and East Broad Street that was built about 1840 and owned it until 1976. Joseph Edward Birch was born in 1818, a son of Samuel Birch and Carrie Ann Richards of Alexandria. He first rented the house before purchasing it from his father-in-law, Orrin Orton, in 1852. The farm included a big-beam barn similar to Cherry Hill's and a pump house and privy. Joseph Birch's son, Frank Birch, married Flora Belle Crossman, a daughter of Isaac Crossman. Joseph Birch's daughter-in-law Margaret is seen above with her children, Tyler, Marian, and George. The house was originally one story and was later expanded. As one of the oldest founding families in the village, the Birches were instrumental in the development of the school system. Below, a story is read to the children in the Birch house on Valentine's Day.

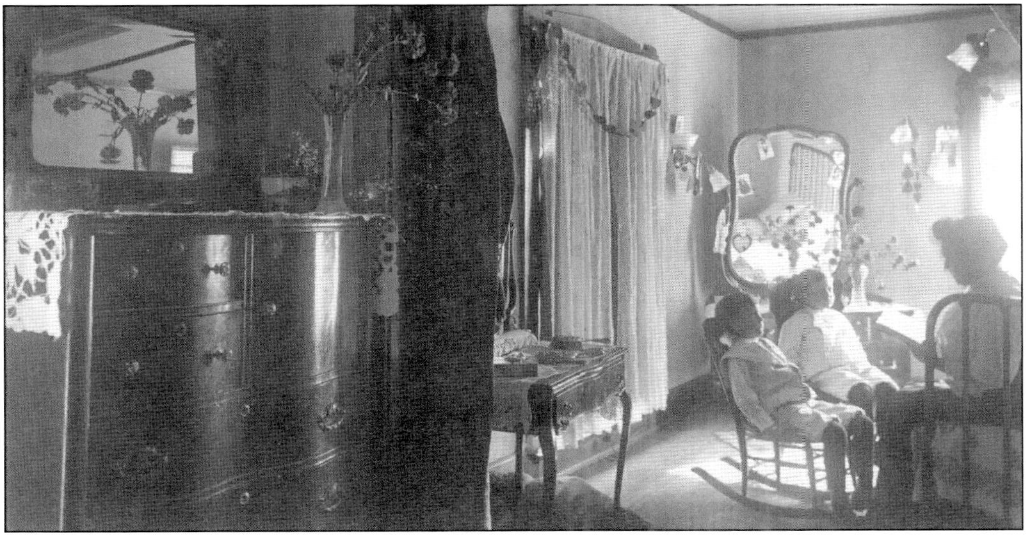

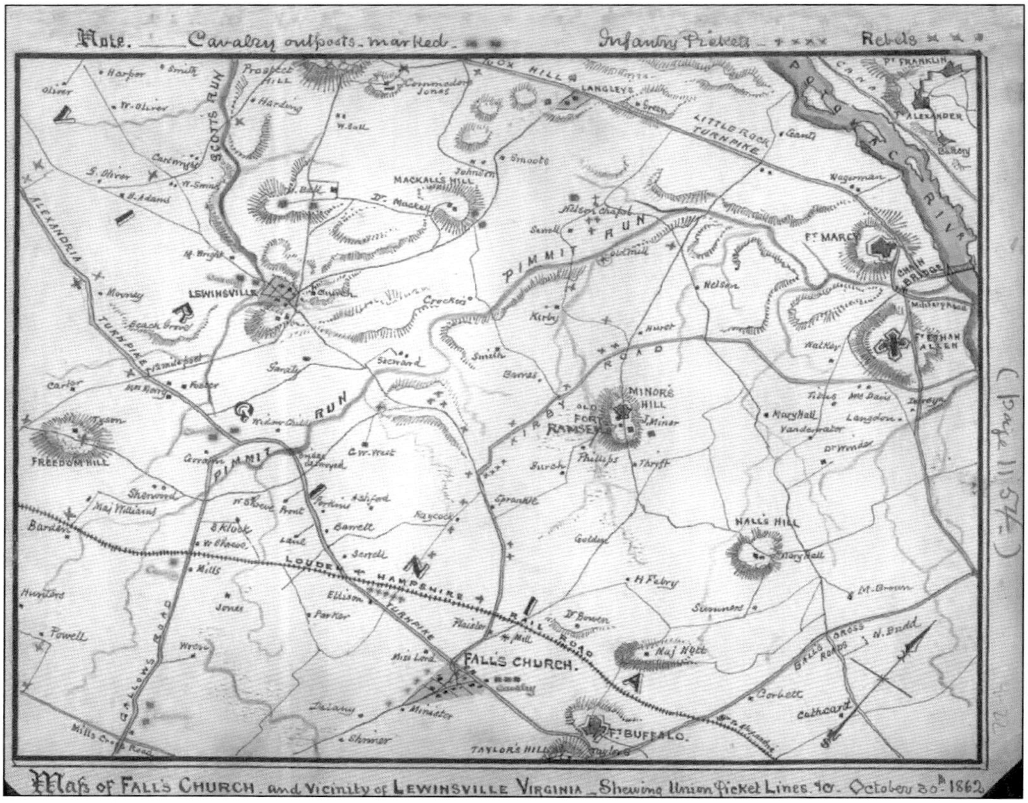

Life in Falls Church was only peaceful for a few decades before civil strife broke out again. Rumors flew about slaves rising up and attacking whites, and nerves were frazzled. Not everyone was fearful, however, and sentiments were widely split in Falls Church as it sat on a divide between Union and Confederate sides. (LOC, Maps Division.)

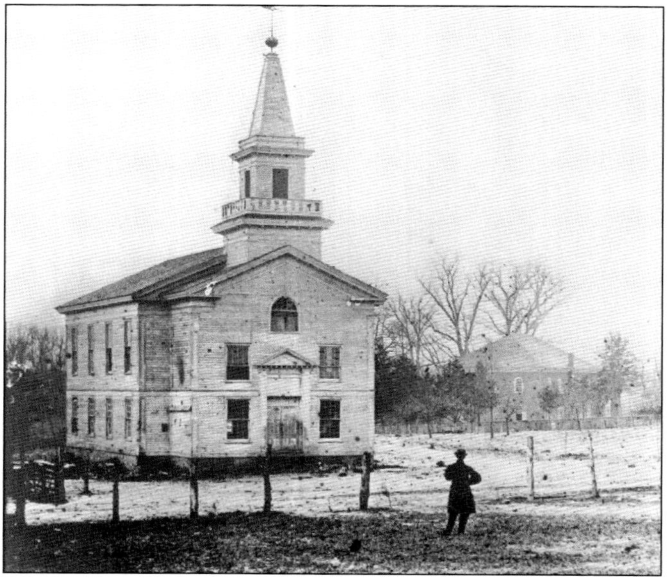

Rev. John Reed, a pastor at Columbia Baptist, the church his brother Hiram founded, taught Sunday school in his home to local free and enslaved blacks. One of his daughters, Lotta, also taught reading and writing during home visits. Reed, a Union-supporting member of the Falls Church Virginia Home Guard, had been threatened by Mosby and warned to keep his dealings in the church. Reed disregarded the threat and continued classes in his home.

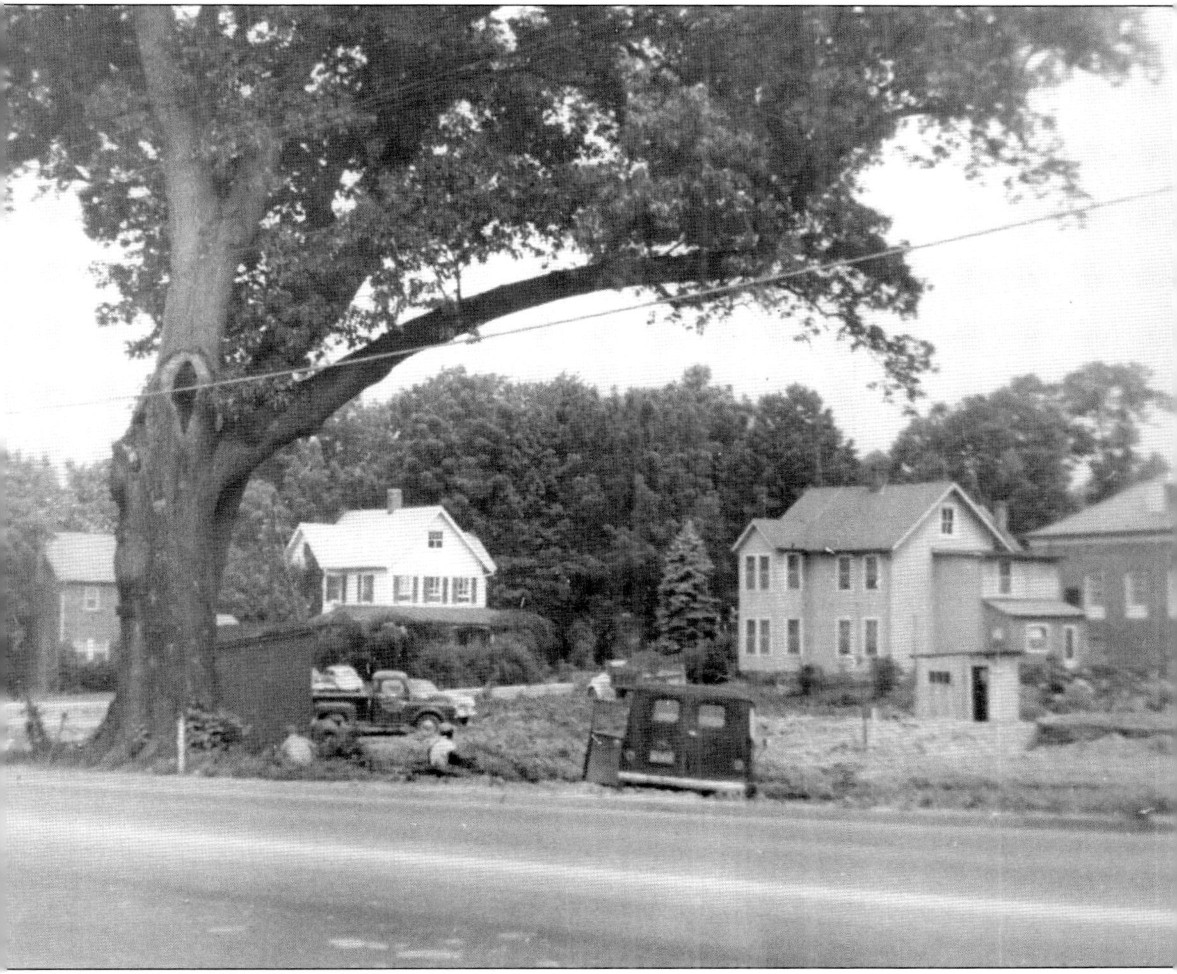

Reed and his daughter believed everyone should enrich their lives and be afforded the advantages allowed by a basic education. In the early morning hours of October 18, 1864, Mosby's men arrived at Reed's home posing as Union troops and took Reed and a black man, Jacob Jackson, 13 miles away to Vienna and shot both. Reed died, but Jackson survived, losing an ear and straggling back to Falls Church. Reed's family was assured safe passage to claim the body. John Singleton Mosby was a feared Confederate battalion commander familiar with Northern Virginia who led "Mosby's Raiders." A tree on East Broad Street at North Virginia Avenue was named Hangman's Tree based on the legend that Mosby hanged Union soldiers from it. The tree was cut down in 1968.

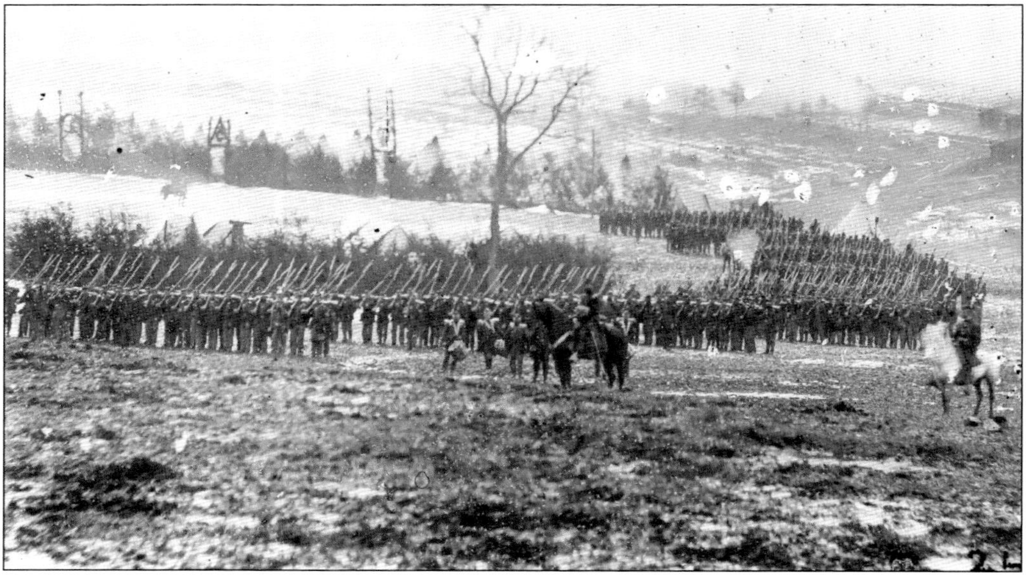

On May 23, 1861, Virginians voted themselves out of the Union, favoring secession. Local Union sympathizers were threatened, and Falls Church voted pro-secession in a 44-26 split. The village occupied a precarious position as soldiers from both sides traveled through and set up inside or around its borders. Taylor's Tavern and east to Alexandria was firmly controlled by Union troops, but everything west of Falls Church was under Confederate control. Over 85 regiments are known to have camped in or passed through Falls Church, all leaving havoc in their wake. Hunger-stricken soldiers snatched all the food, tools, and wood they could attain from local farms. (Both, LOC.)

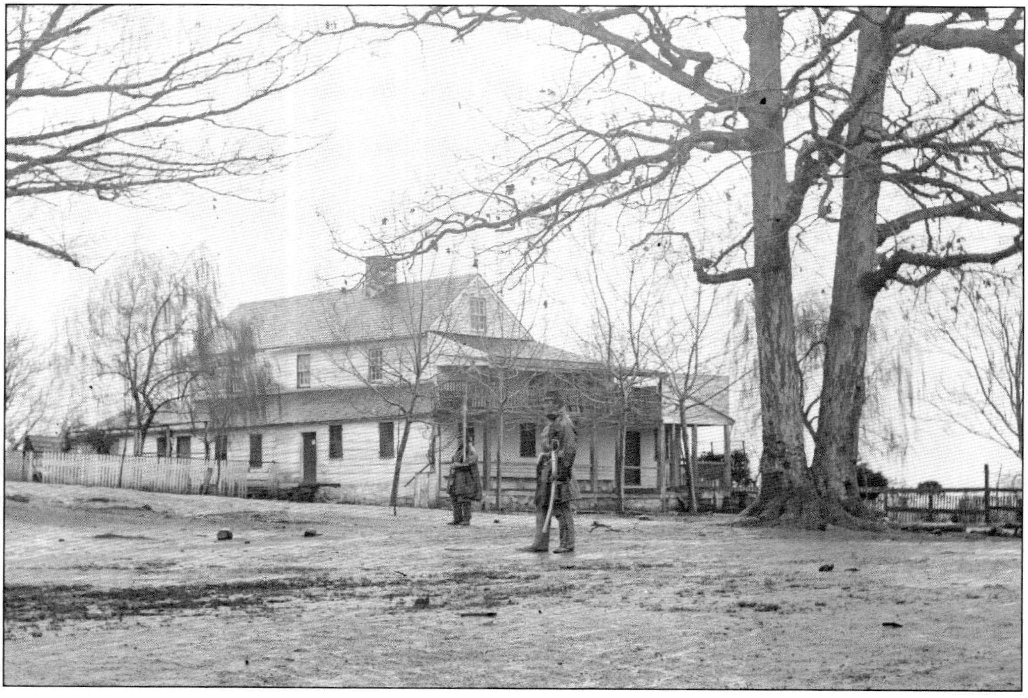

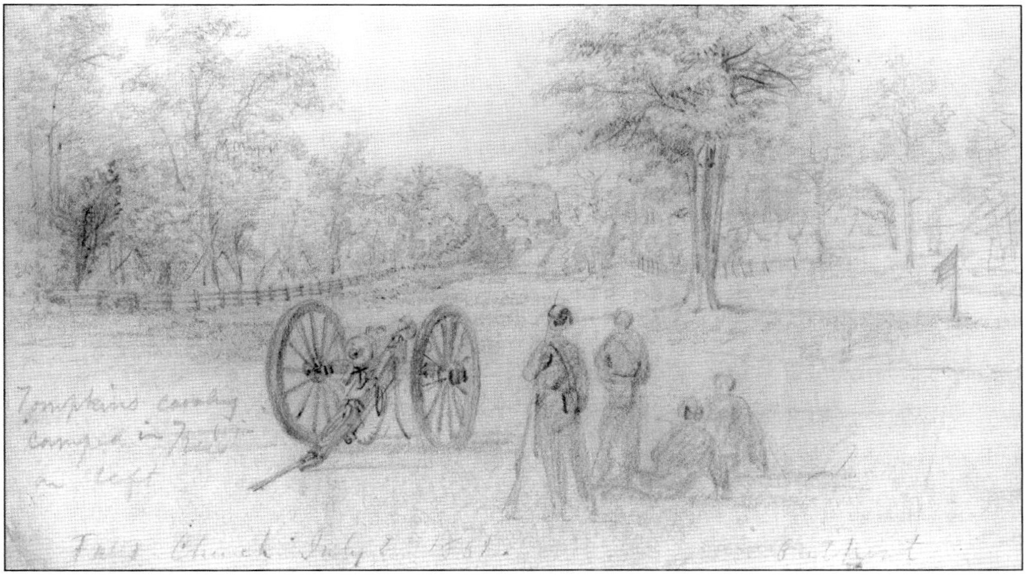

As fighting intensified and troops were in firing range of the village, many residents fled. Cannonading at the Battle of Bull Run near Manassas on July 21, 1861, could be heard in Falls Church. Union soldiers retreated in panic, streaming through Falls Church, leaving pro-Union citizens unnerved. This sketch of a cavalry outpost camped in Falls Church was drawn by Alfred Rudolph Waud in July 1961. (LOC.)

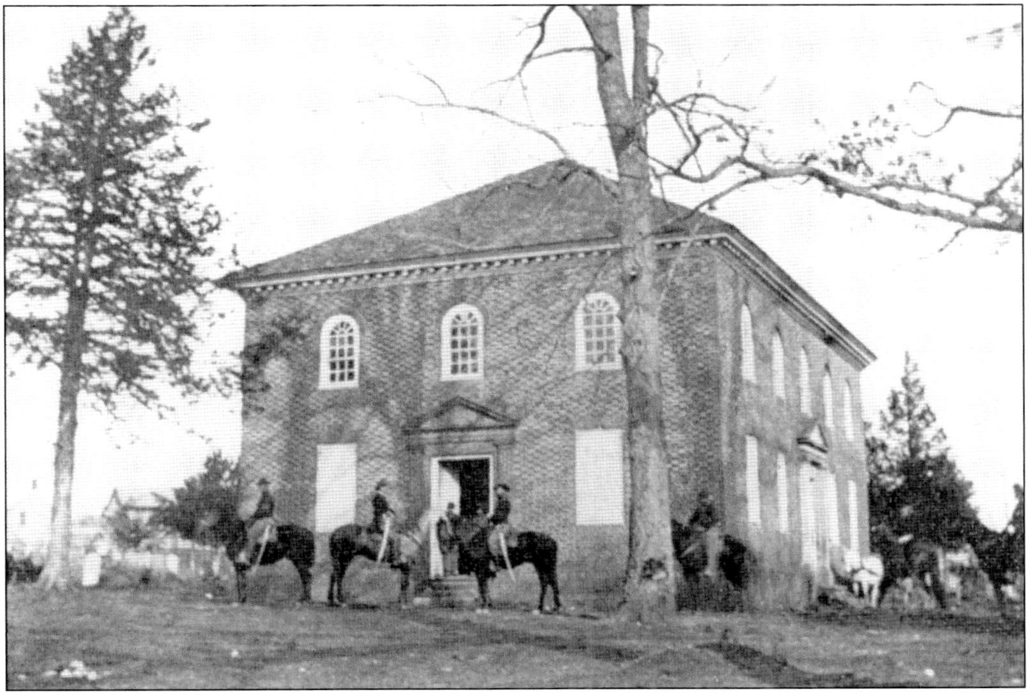

The Falls Church and other churches in the area also fell victim to war. The Falls Church served as a hospital and animal stable at various stages of the war. Services were suspended at nearly all of the Falls Church churches, although they were occasionally held for soldiers.

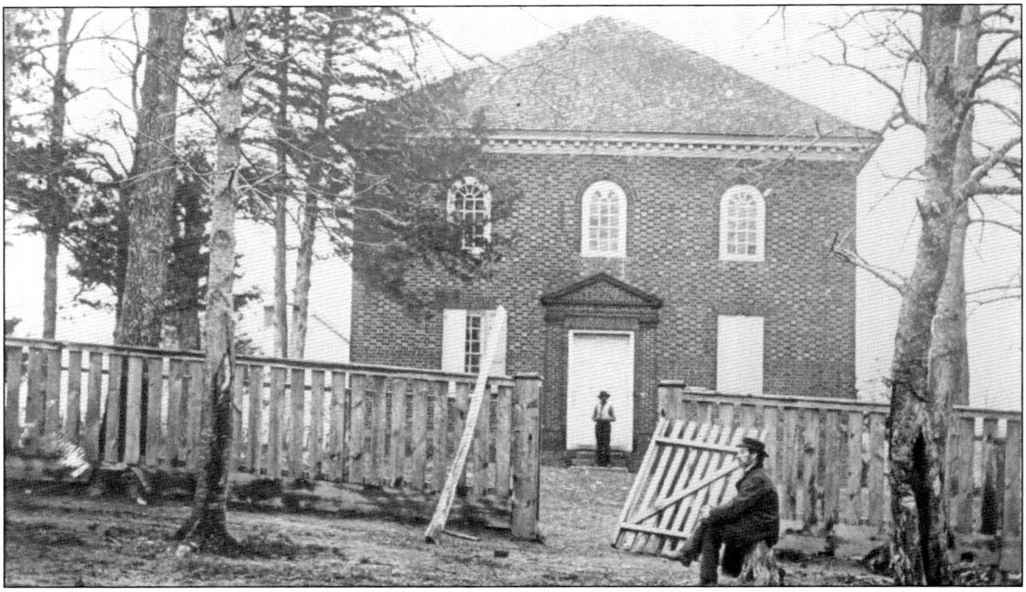

At the time of the Civil War, Falls Church contained about 25 houses and four churches. Some of the unmarked graves are the final resting place of Union soldiers. The bricks below the windows were removed to allow horses to enter and exit easily.

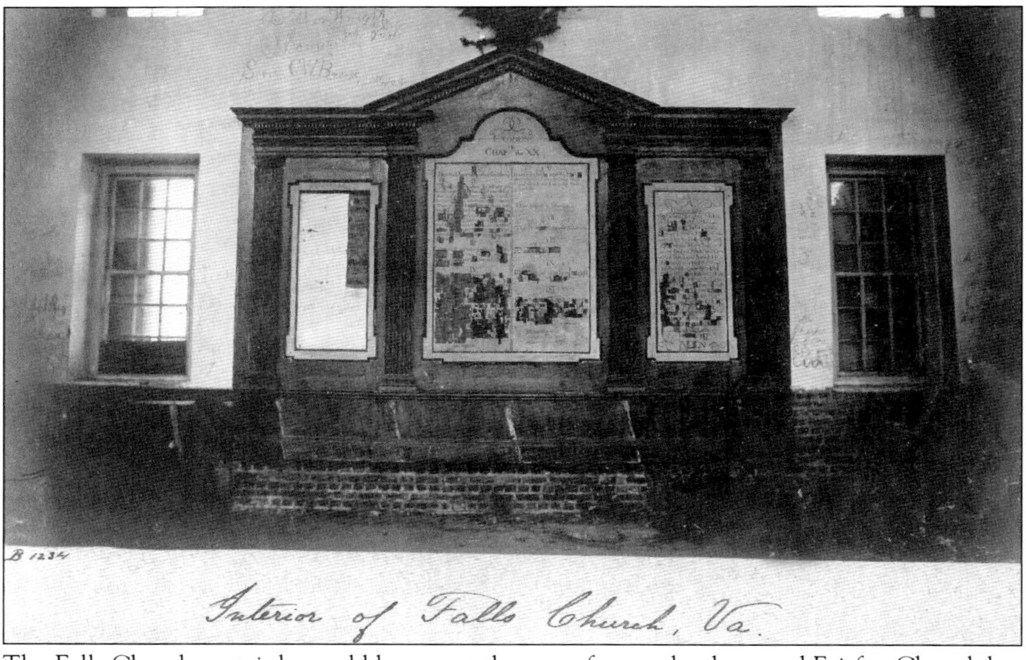

The Falls Church certainly would have met the same fate as the destroyed Fairfax Chapel, but its distinguished history and associations saved it. After Union cavalry damaged the church, residents George B. Ives and John Bartlett reported the damage to the military, and the US government paid for repairs to the church after the war. Pohick Church believes the graffiti in this popular image by Mathew Brady, wrongly attributed to The Falls Church, was discovered during renovations of Pohick Church. (LOC.)

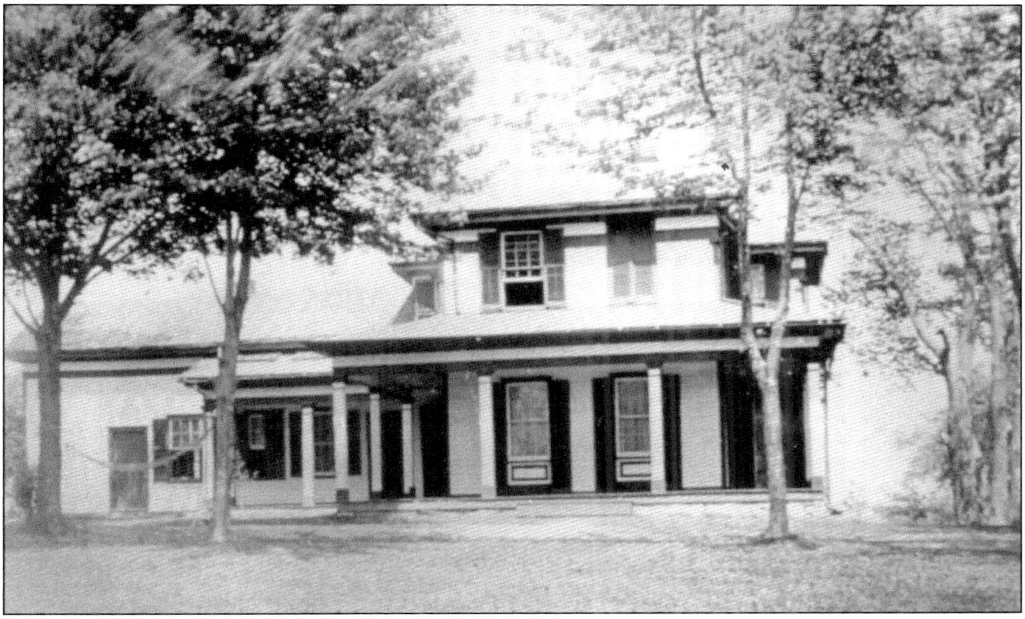

Home Hill, now known as Lawton House, on Lawton Drive, was the home of Union sympathizer John Bartlett and his family during the Civil War. The home was believed to be the headquarters for Confederate general James Longstreet early in the war. A piece of wood in the rafters bearing the names of companies of Union troops was discovered during repairs.

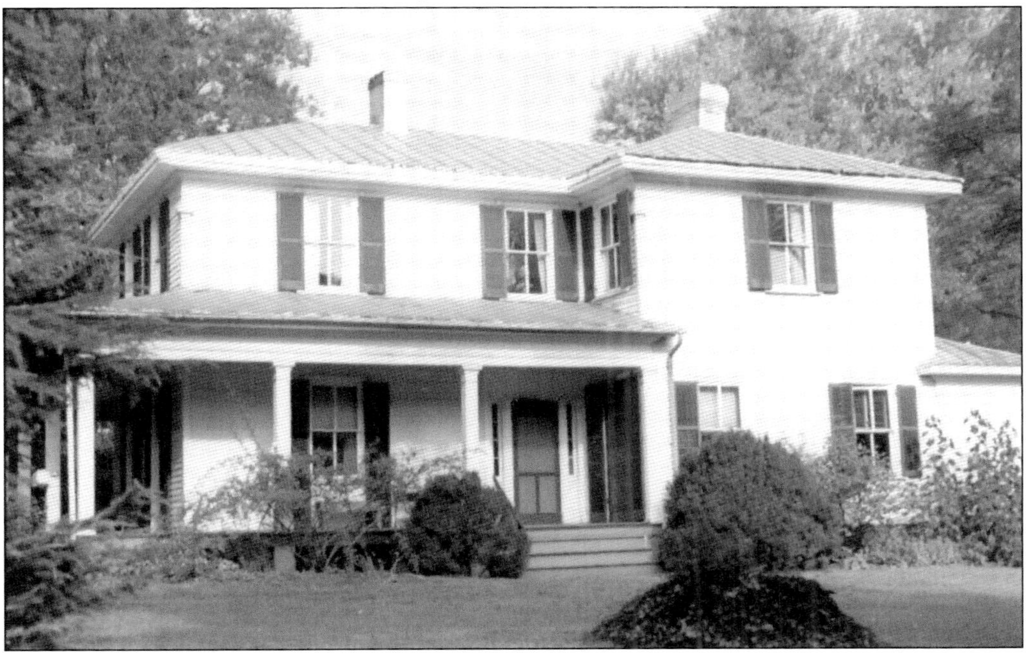

The home's military history continued beyond the Civil War, as Gen. Henry Ware Lawton bought the home in 1889 but was killed in the Philippines during the Spanish-American War. Merton E. Church, who figured prominently in the development of Falls Church, owned it and a large parcel of land in 1930.

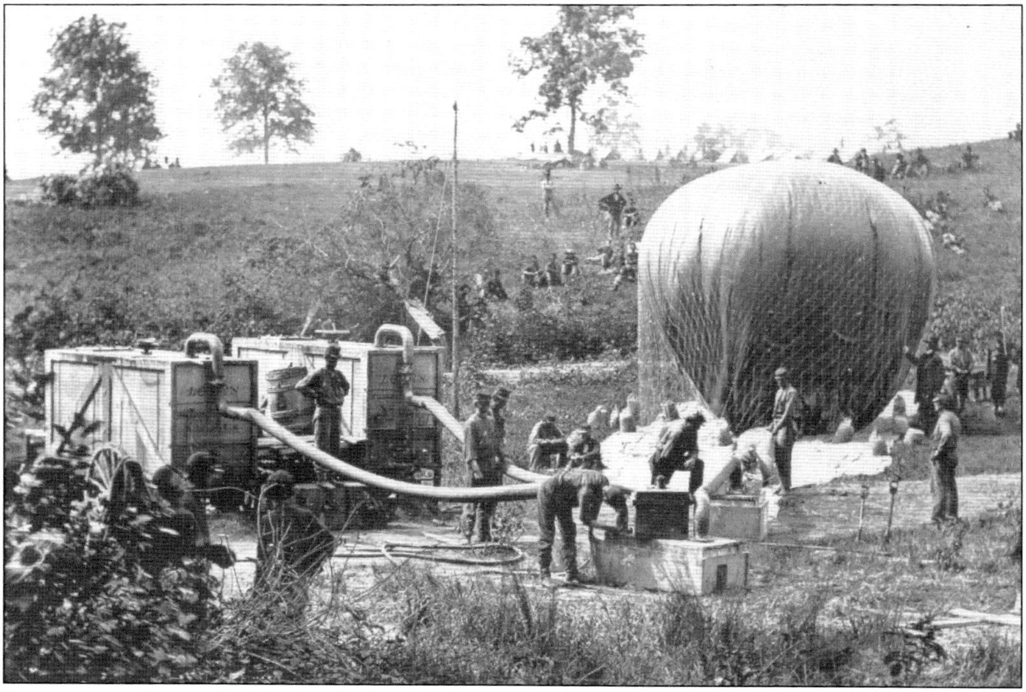

Every year at Cherry Hill Park, a balloon is flown over the historic site to commemorate the military history made in Falls Church during the Civil War. The first air-guided artillery was shot thanks to Prof. Thaddeus Lowe and one of his fleet of balloons. Lowe built his first balloon in 1858. In 1861, he set off on a flight that landing him smack-dab in Confederate South Carolina. Lowe realized the value of what he had seen from above troop positions and demonstrated the value to President Lincoln, including sending telegraph messages from the air. Lowe was then appointed by Lincoln as chief of the US Army Aeronautic Corps, the newly created balloon corps. Over the course of his career, Lowe made over 3,000 ascents in his hydrogen balloons, using portable hydrogen generators in the field and furthering the mobility of his balloons. (Both, LOC.)

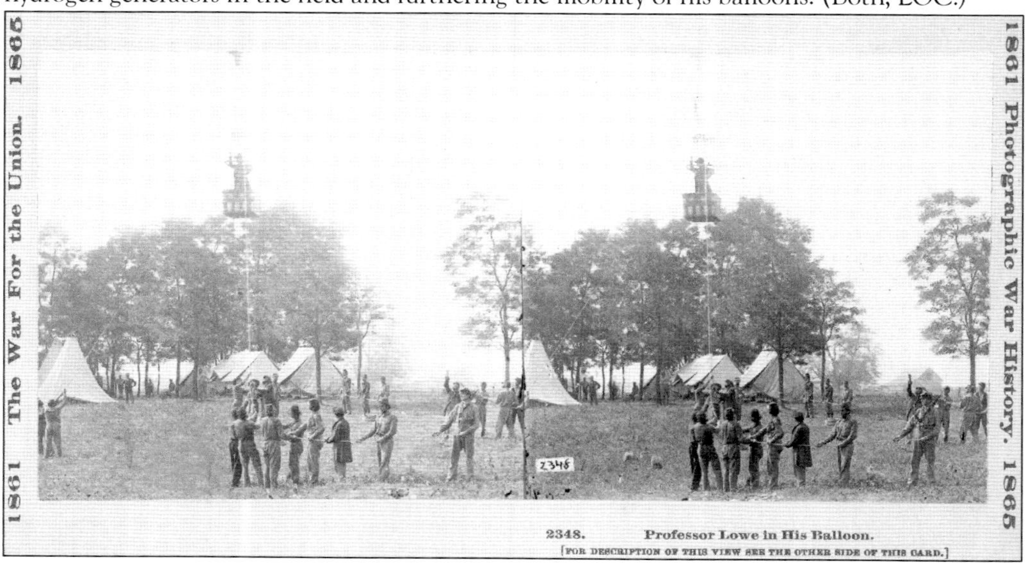

Lowe launched his balloon, the *Enterprise*, and traveled over Bailey's Crossroads and on past Taylor's Tavern in Falls Church. He could gaze three miles distant from the heights his balloons reached and relay enemy position information back to the ground using a telegraph rigged in his balloon. (LOC.)

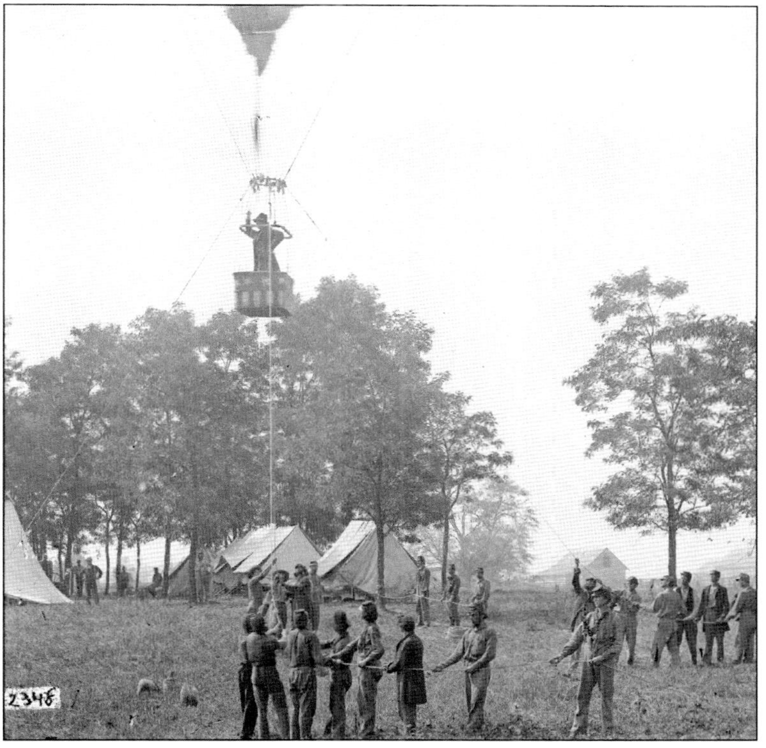

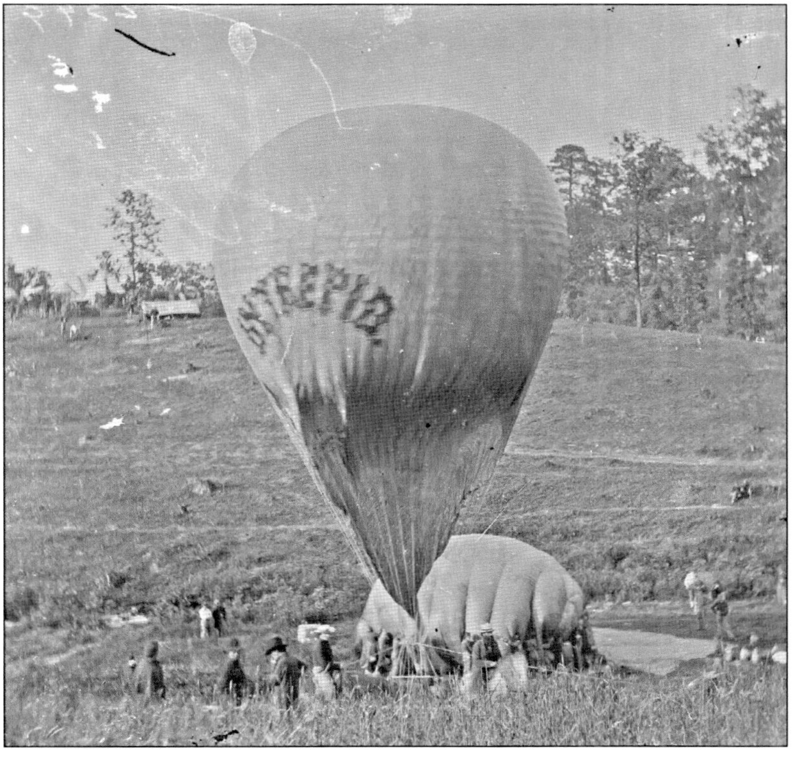

Using his telegraph method, Lowe was able to direct Union troops on the ground where to aim their artillery. If they were falling short or wide of the enemy, he telegraphed instructions for adjustments. The air-guided assault from Union troops was the first time in military history that accurately aimed artillery had been used against an invisible enemy. (LOC.)

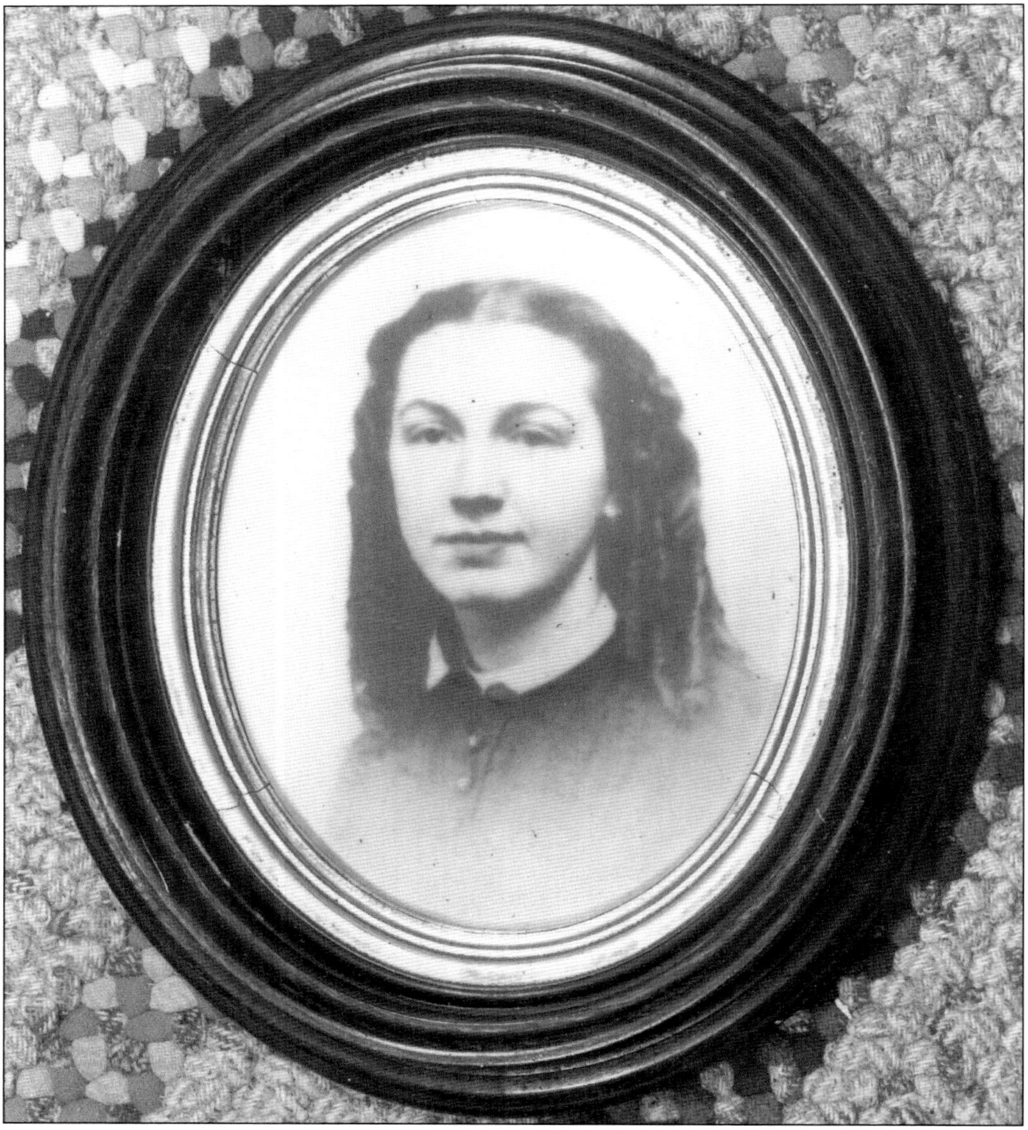

From the war, a surprising romance was born, impacting Falls Church forever. Mary "Mollie" Edwards Pultz grew up in what was Berkeley County, Virginia, at the time and was 17 when the war broke out. Stories vary, but one account says she was recruited to serve as a Confederate spy, a common practice in an area where most men were pro-Union while women were pro-Confederacy. Pultz passed innocent-seeming notes to friends in the Confederacy containing information gleaned from striking up conversations with Union soldiers. Another story says she was engaged to a Confederate soldier who was killed and wrote another recounting the devastation that had occurred in her valley. During a church service at Payne's Chapel with her mother, Pultz was arrested at 18 for spying and taken to a jail in Washington. In the old Capitol Prison, she met Belle Boyd, who she enjoyed exchanging lively notes with. A school friend of Pultz's, Ward Hill Lamon, had begun practicing law in an Illinois firm Lincoln was a member of and interceded on her behalf to get her paroled. She had to pledge allegiance to the Union and was released after a few days.

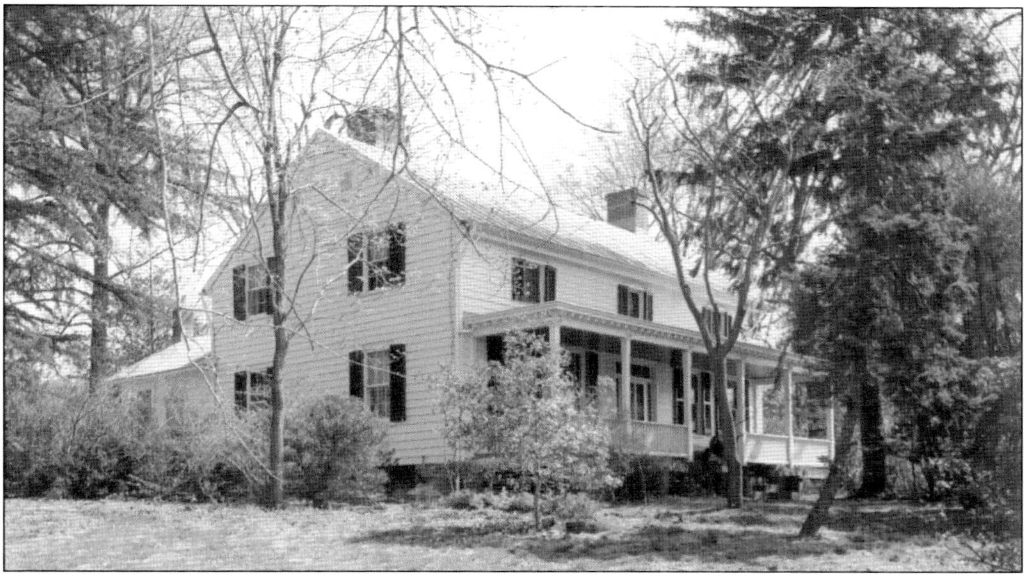

Cherry Hill Farm passed through several families before the Civil War. The farm extended to Leesburg Pike, with a lane of cherry trees leading from the house to the road. A dresser drawer was used as a horse trough, and the barn and corncrib are original from when the house was used as a farm. Soldiers ravaged the fields and crops during the war.

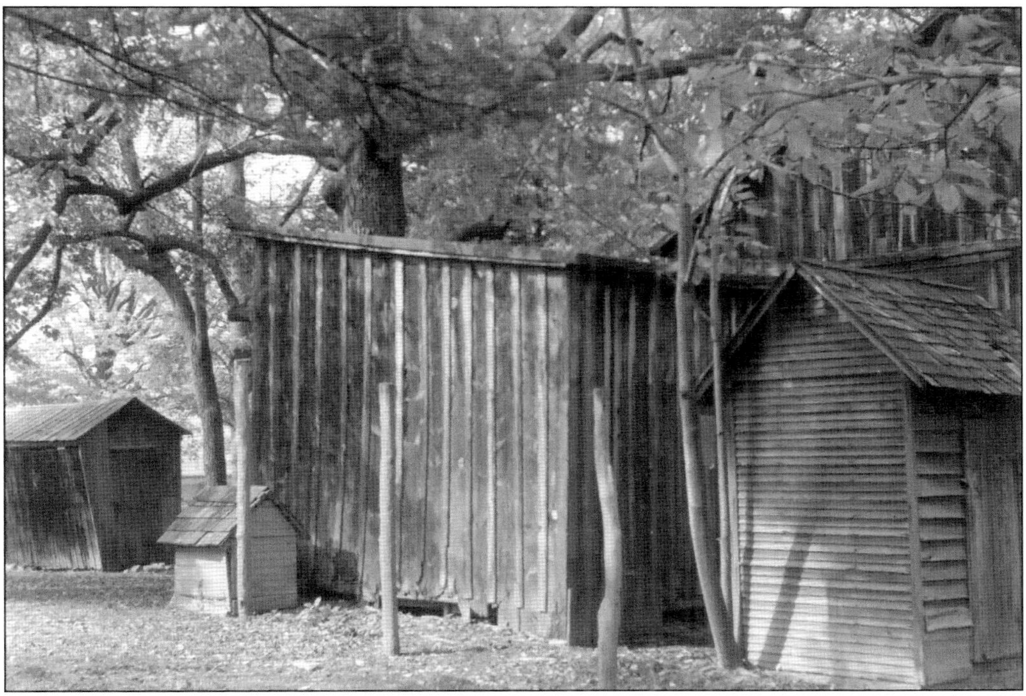

While her espionage trial never came about, Mollie Pultz frequently visited the Hughes family, who were responsible for her. There she met Joseph S. Riley, and the two fell in love. They married the following year and later moved to Cherry Hill Farm to start a family. The farmhouse was home to the Rileys, deeply ingrained in the development of the city, for 100 years.

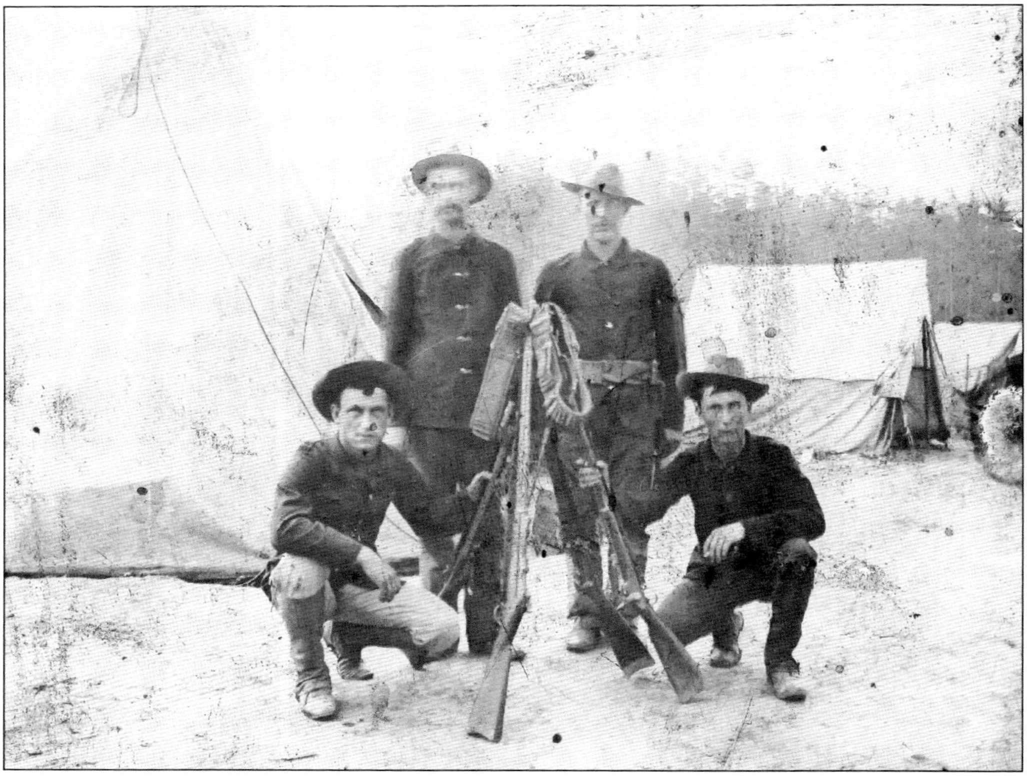

Falls Church bustled with growth after the Civil War but was again deeply affected when the warship *Maine* was sunk in early 1898, sparking the Spanish-American War. Two square miles of land in west Falls Church were designated Camp Russell A. Alger, and soldiers from many states were ordered to Falls Church. Life in the village was greatly disrupted with the military base on its borders, and residents going about their business were frequently stopped by army patrols. The ground beneath the tents and parades became wasted. When Pres. William McKinley visited to review troops, there was too much dust kicked up to see clearly. Clara Barton and Dr. Walter Reed also paid visits to the camp. Carl Sandburg was a soldier at the time, stationed at Camp Alger. (Both, NVRPA.)

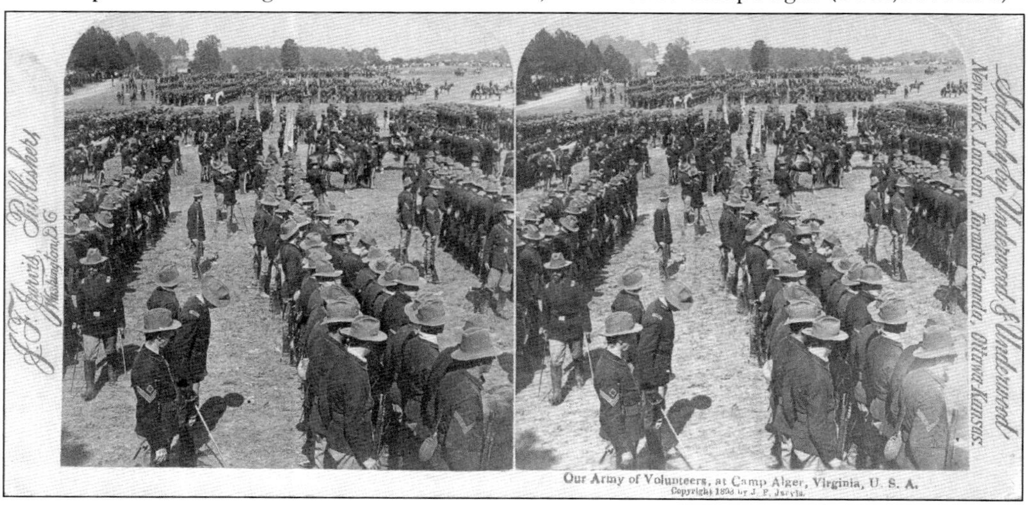

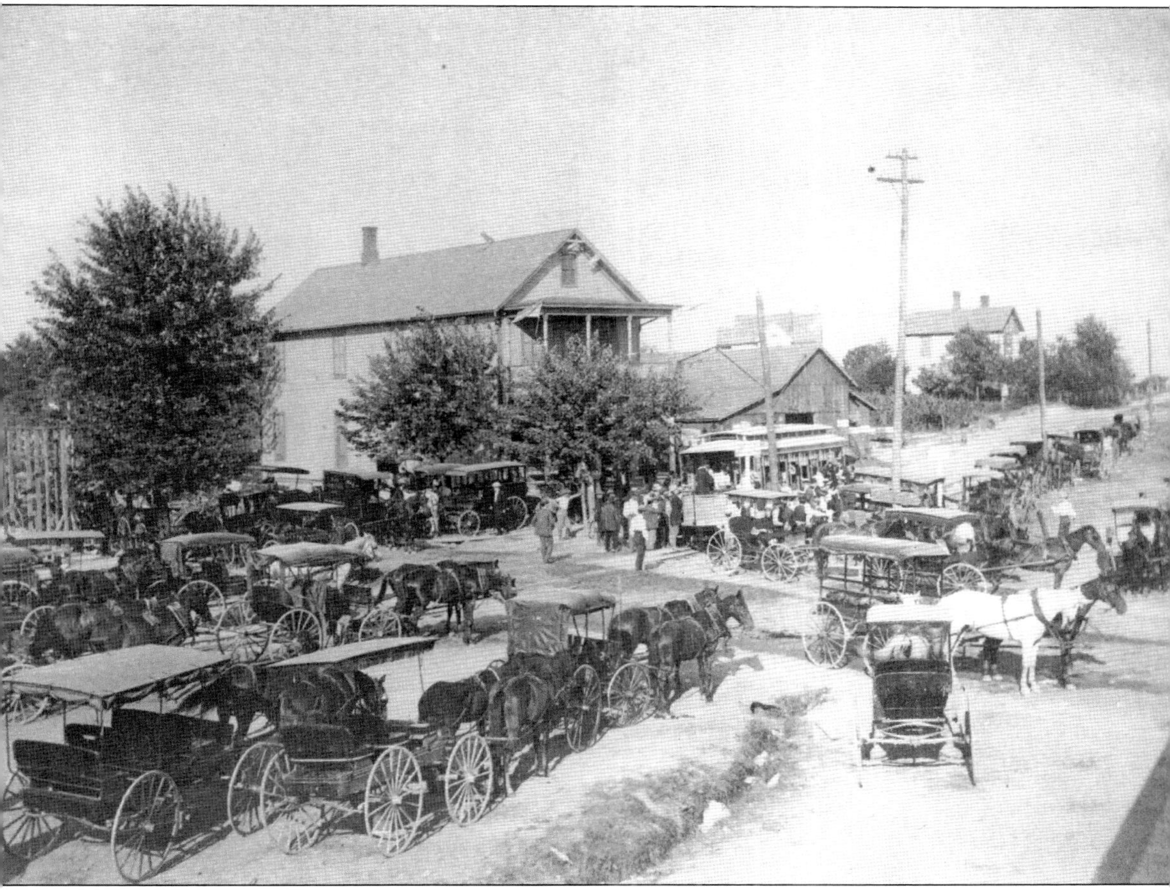

Disarray and disruption were common during the camp's existence. Troops enjoyed excursions into Washington, causing streets and train stations to become overwhelmed and chaotic. Provost guards from Camp Alger camped out at East Falls Church in order to direct traffic and attempt to maintain order. Buggies lined up outside the station to collect a fare for driving soldiers on clogged roads back to Camp Alger. The fare was "invariably 25 cents one way, no difference whether one rides in a farm wagon or a surrey," as Charles A. Hartley wrote in the July 27, 1898, *Tribune Telegraph*. Falls Church residents grew tired of the constant noise from the nearby encampment. When the war ended, the largest Independence Day fireworks display to date went off in the city to celebrate. The land the camp had occupied was laid completely barren by the encampment and was unusable for many years. Local resident Charles Parker Galpin was a sailor aboard the USS *Maine*, surviving the explosion that sparked the Spanish-American War.

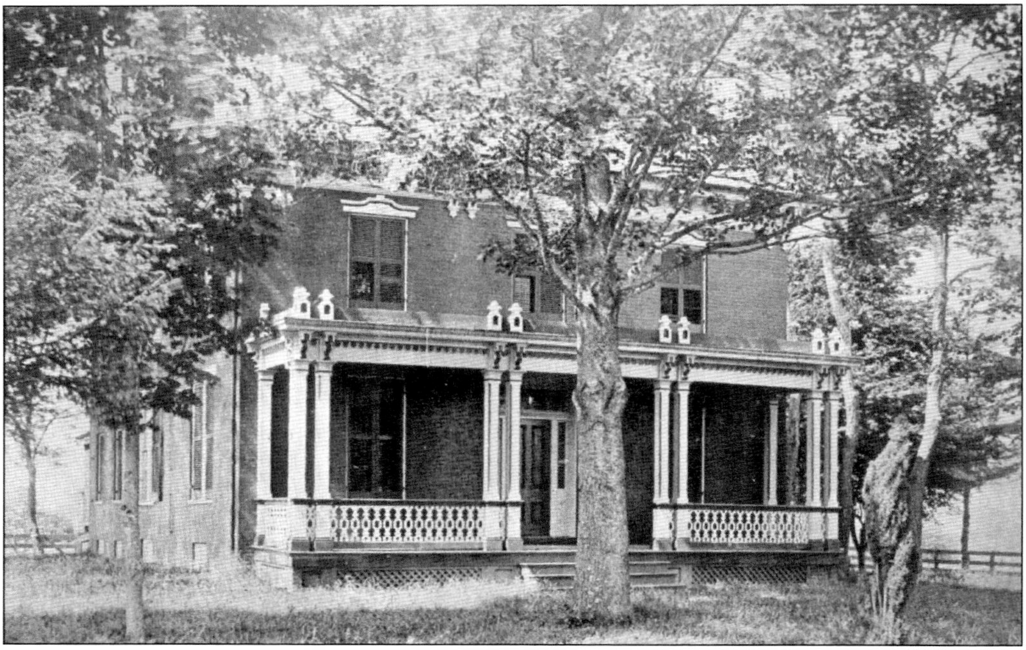

First known as the Rice House, Tallwood, at 708 East Broad Street, earned notoriety during World War II, when Dr. Milton Eisenhower and his wife, Helen, made the 1870s-era brick residence their home from 1938 to 1943. The Eisenhowers were responsible for turning the house white (below) from its natural brick (above). Dr. Eisenhower, a high-ranking official in President Roosevelt's administration, was the older brother of Gen. Dwight D. Eisenhower, who spent many nights in his brother's home. General Eisenhower maintained secrecy about his assignments, even from his wife; however, Milton learned of an important announcement ahead of time. On November 8, 1942, Milton, Helen, and Mamie Eisenhower were playing cards in the Eisenhowers' recreation room. Knowing his brother would announce the invasion of North Africa by radio at 9:00 p.m., Milton kept the radio on during the card game. Mamie's eyes filled with tears after hearing General Eisenhower's personal statement, but she was grateful she had not been told ahead of time.

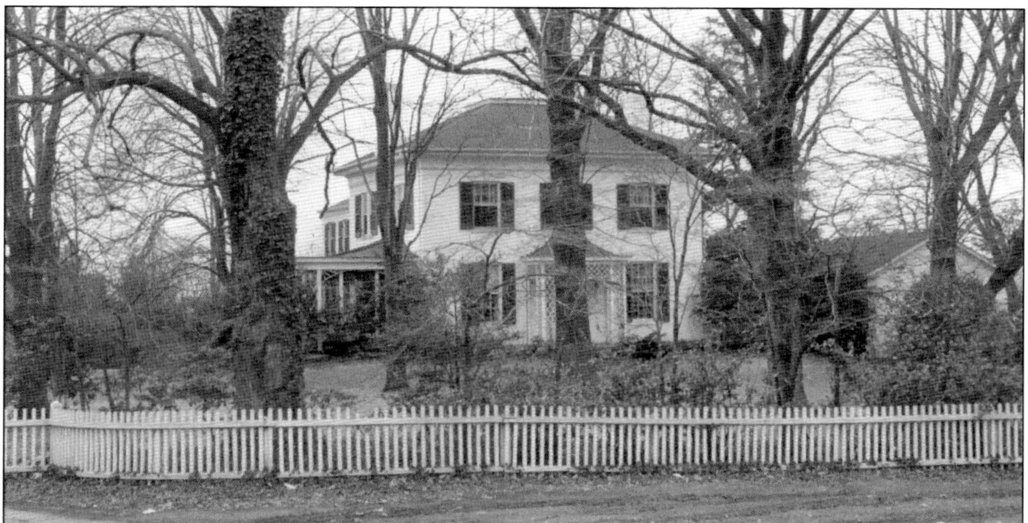

Three

Evolving Trails and Rails

In order to keep pace with the local industry, the village required top-notch transportation for local merchants and farmers to take their crops into Washington to sell. Town leaders also wanted western goods to easily find their way into town. Therefore, the sometimes-impassible dirt carriage tracks required upgrading, and a toll was established on Leesburg Pike.

With the advent of trains in the mid-1850s, tracks were laid through the heart of town, acquiring property through several farms. The train revolutionized travel for local citizens and further improved with the addition of an electric trolley line. However, the mass production of automobiles marked the beginning of the end for the financially unstable railway and further evolution of the roads connecting what had previously been remote villages requiring a day's ride to reach.

Ultimately, the Northern Virginia Regional Park Authority acquired the land the tracks ran through and turned it into a recreation path. Falls Church was the first city to pave over the tracks to see how residents would use it. The Washington & Old Dominion (W&OD) trail system now carries more people than it ever did during its heyday as a railroad. What the trains did do, however, was turn sleepy Falls Church into a main commuter suburb of Washington, allowing more people to discover its fresh air and open land while maintaining federal jobs in the city.

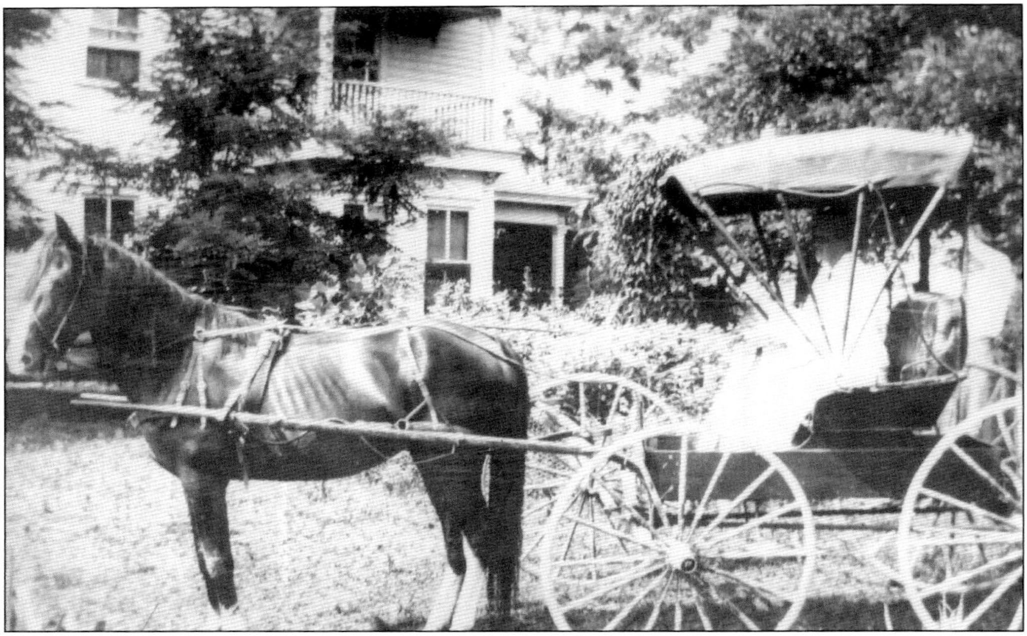

As a rural farming village, residents rode in uncomfortable horse-drawn buggies even as late as 1914. If the weather turned foul, the roads became rutted and impassable. The wealth of a family could be gleaned by how many carriages they owned and the particular models they had.

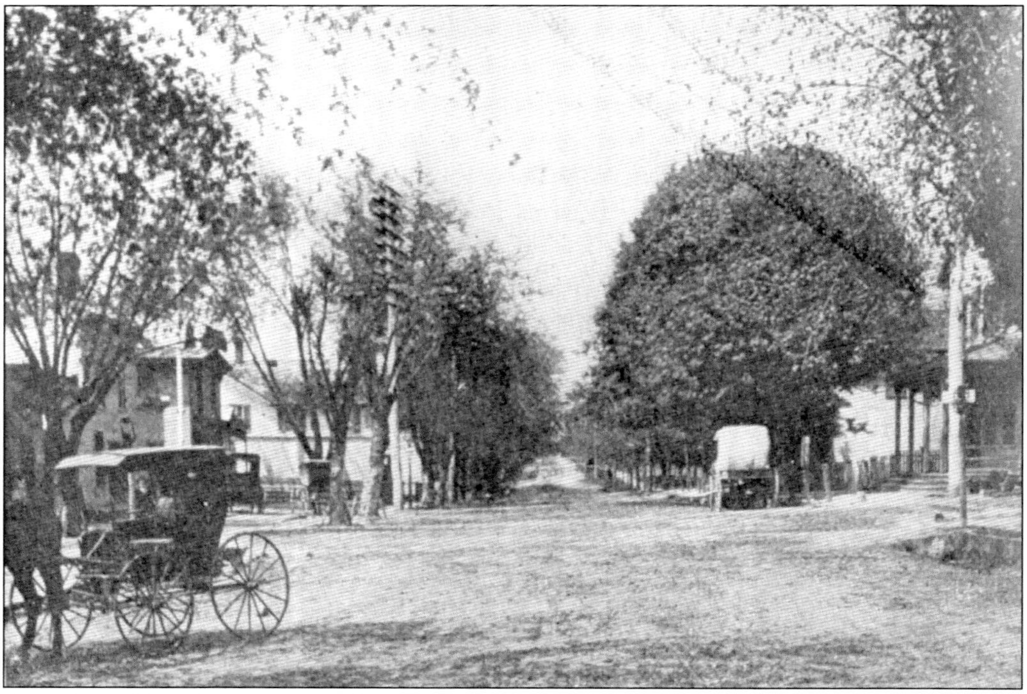

Since Falls Church was settled, the intersection at what is now Broad and Washington Streets has been the main intersection, with a tavern and merchants on the corners. An early ordinance prohibited letting any cow, horse, or hog loose to graze on the sidewalks or highways of town.

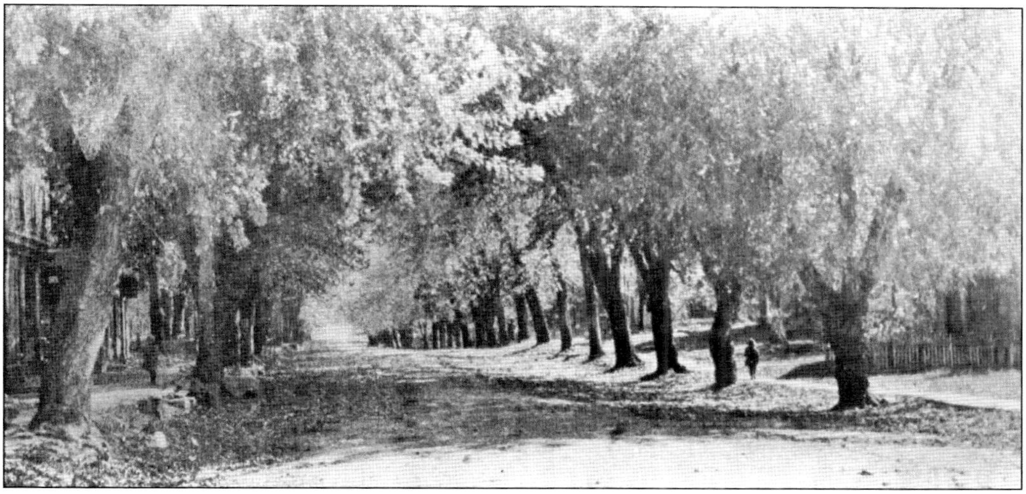

The beauty of tree-shaded Broad Street in the horse and buggy days was in many ways thanks to the organization of the Village Improvement Society in 1885, modeled after the Laurel Hill Society of Stockbridge, Massachusetts. The society's main objective was the adornment of streets and improvement of the roads, with fine shade trees planted on the main roads.

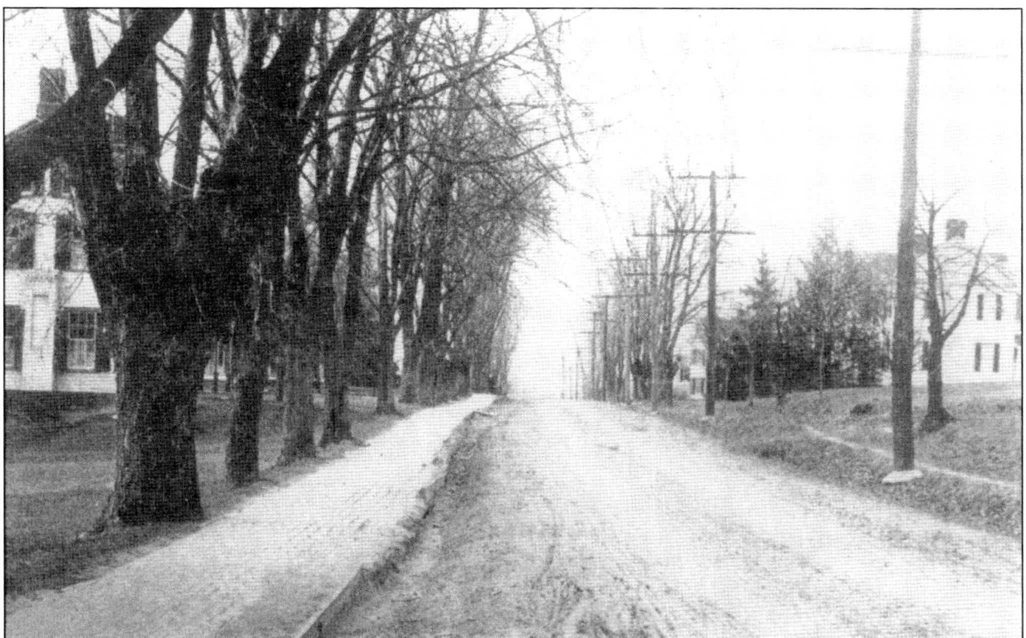

The main roads through town went by different names early on. Leesburg Pike was first called New Church Road, later Middle Pike, and then Leesburg & Alexandria Turnpike. Broad Street was originally known as Ridge Road, because it followed a natural ridge in the landscape, before becoming Falls Church and Fairfax Courthouse Road. Little Falls Street was also known as Rolling Road, because it was used to roll tobacco to warehouses.

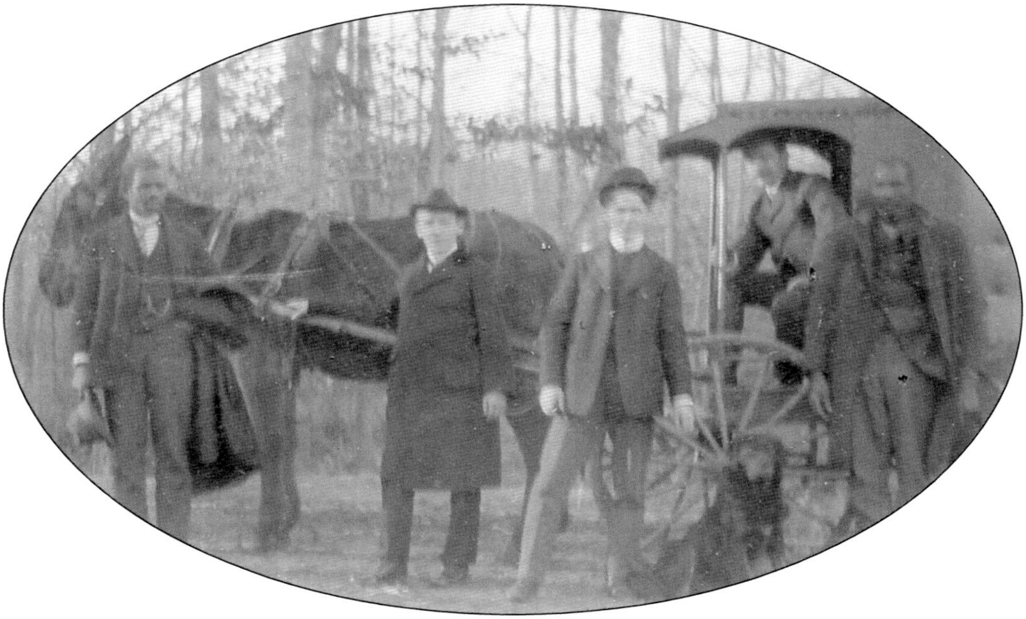

Routes to trade centers traversed through Falls Church, and as the suburbs around Washington grew, roads became of prime importance. Merchants needed to get their wares and services to ports and warehouses. The more traffic that was enticed through Falls Church, the better it was for businesses and residents, such as Wilbur Speakman. (Courtesy of Catherine Speakman.)

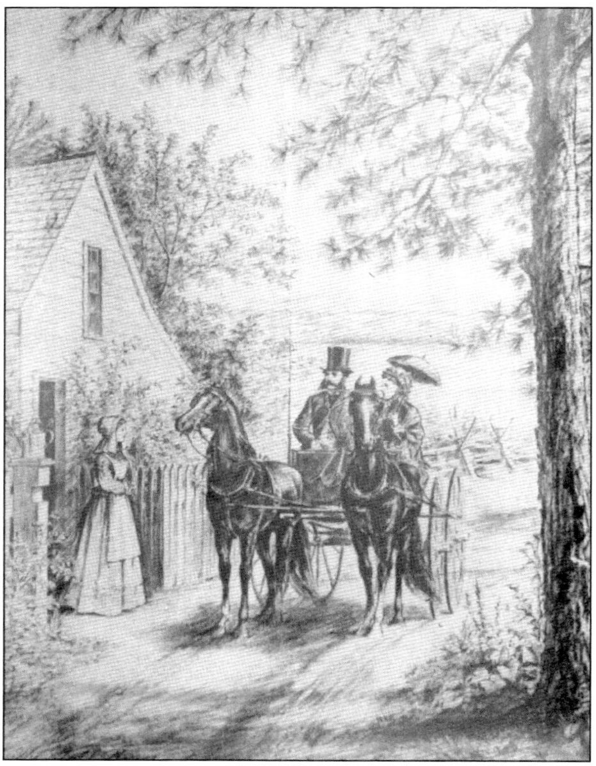

Leesburg Pike was made into a corduroy road by laying logs across it, and the earliest tollgate in the area was set up to help pay for the improvement. In this 1874 sketch, Nancy Williams is shown collecting the toll. Local agricultural economy depended on reliable roads. The turnpike, chartered in 1813 and completed in 1839, carried most of the freight between Alexandria's port and inland markets until railroads assumed the role in the 1850s.

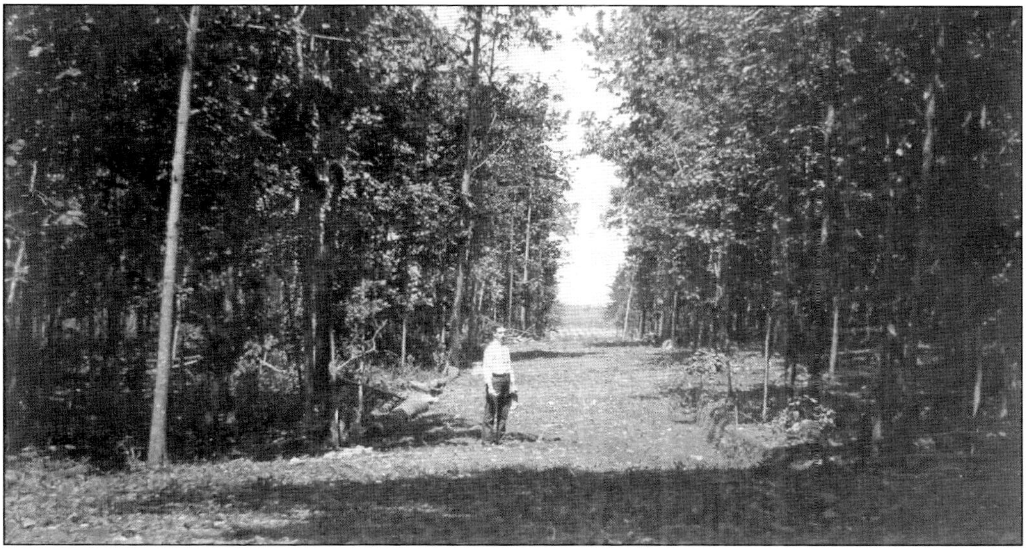

Alexandria, a prime port in Colonial days, was losing its footing, with Washington just north on the Potomac and Baltimore on the Chesapeake Bay owning better waterways and a brand new railroad pushing toward Ohio. Realizing this in the 1840s, Alexandria decided to take the leap into rail as well. After a few false starts, the Alexandria, Loudoun & Hampshire Railway Company received its charter in 1853 to build a line from Alexandria over the Blue Ridge past the Shenandoah Valley and Winchester. Forward-thinking townspeople lobbied for the train to pass through Falls Church in order to bring in more visitors, and residents sold strips of their land to the railroad company to facilitate a route for the tracks. A DePutron family member stands in a clear-cut strip for future train tracks above. Work began in 1855, the tracks through Falls Church were laid in 1857, the first sections opened in 1858, and the first train ran the full line in the spring of 1861. (Both, courtesy of Catherine Speakman.)

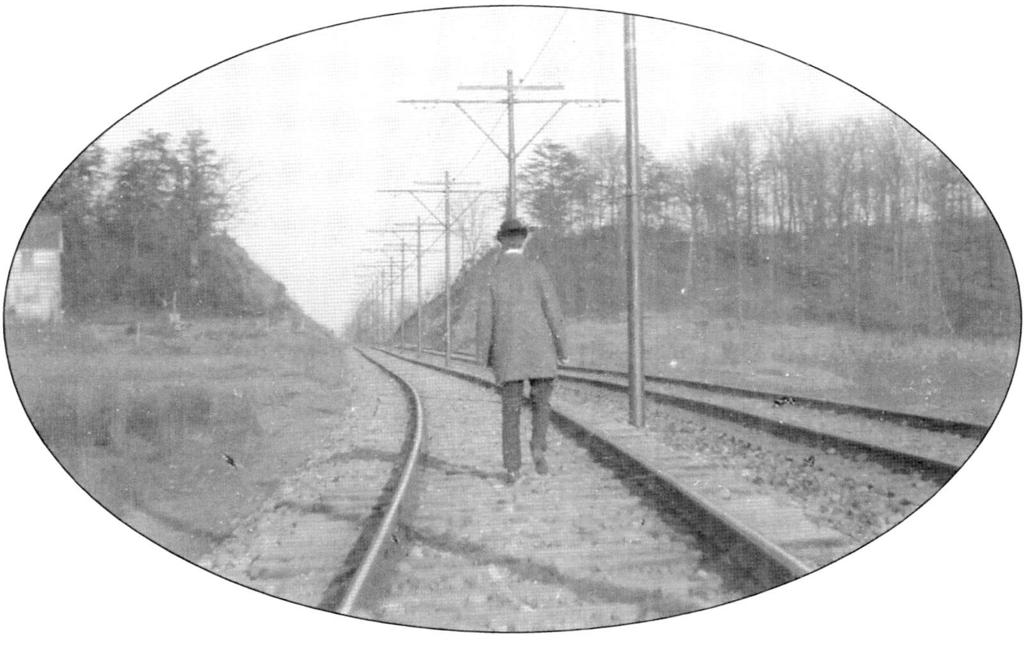

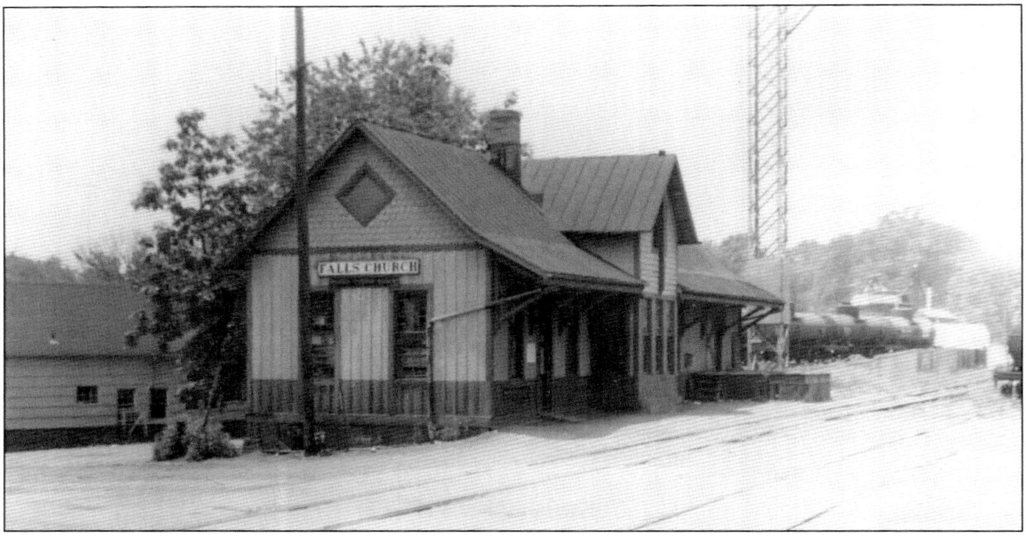

The railroads were constructed with industry in mind, owning far more freight trains than passenger trains with the goal of reaching the coalfields beyond the Blue Ridge Mountains. However, in Falls Church, the focus was on commuting. Three railway stops were in the Falls Church town limits: East Falls Church on the east end at Washington and Fairfax Streets, Rothsay Station in the center of town, and West Falls Church on the western edge. (NVRPA.)

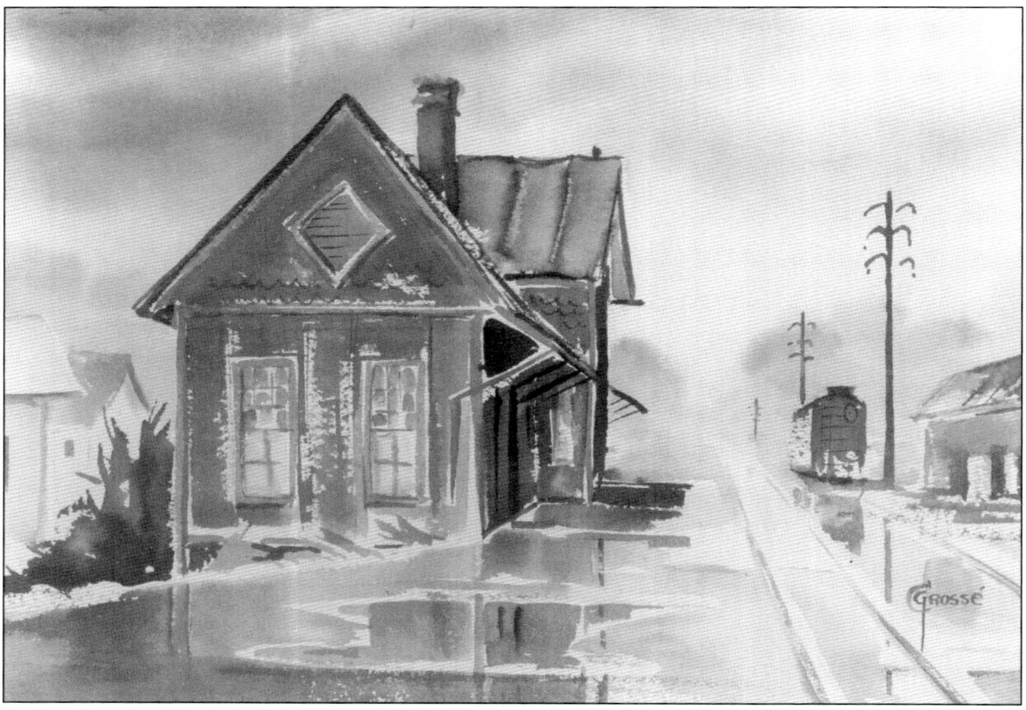

East Falls Church, on the edge of Alexandria County (pre-Arlington County), became a bustling center of activity. The trains provided passenger service to Alexandria, where passengers could change cars and take another line into Washington. However, trains were slow—called "Virginia Creeper" by riders—and the schedule was not reliable.

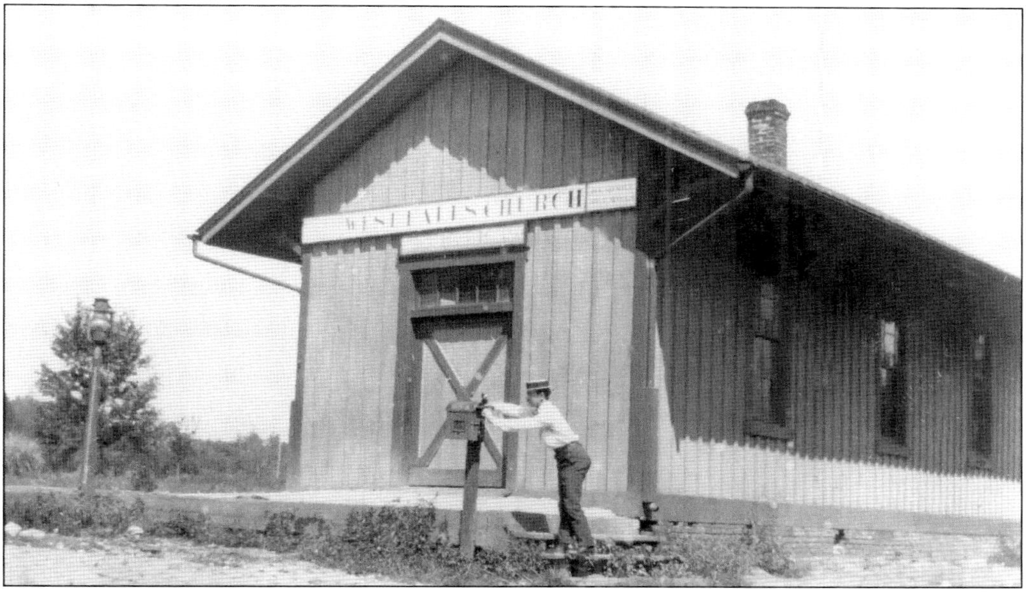

The East Falls Church and West Falls Church (or West End) stations were only a mile apart. Wood-burning trains preceded the coal engines. Residents planted flowers along the tracks and paid $25 to erect a waiting shed at their property line, after which the train would stop there and the station would be named for them. During the Civil War, the tracks west of Vienna were destroyed by the Confederates. The military took over the railway from Alexandria to Vienna, re-lettering the only remaining locomotive, *Clarke*, the *U.S. Military Railroad*. The train only met battle once, when a cavalry ambushed the military train outside Vienna and it became accidentally uncoupled by a cannonball. The engineer fled at full speed towards Falls Church, leaving the cars behind. The Confederates withdrew, believing the train would return with reinforcements, but it did not. The outnumbered Union troops wearily trudged on foot back to Arlington after the Confederates burned the remaining abandoned train cars. (Both, NVRPA.)

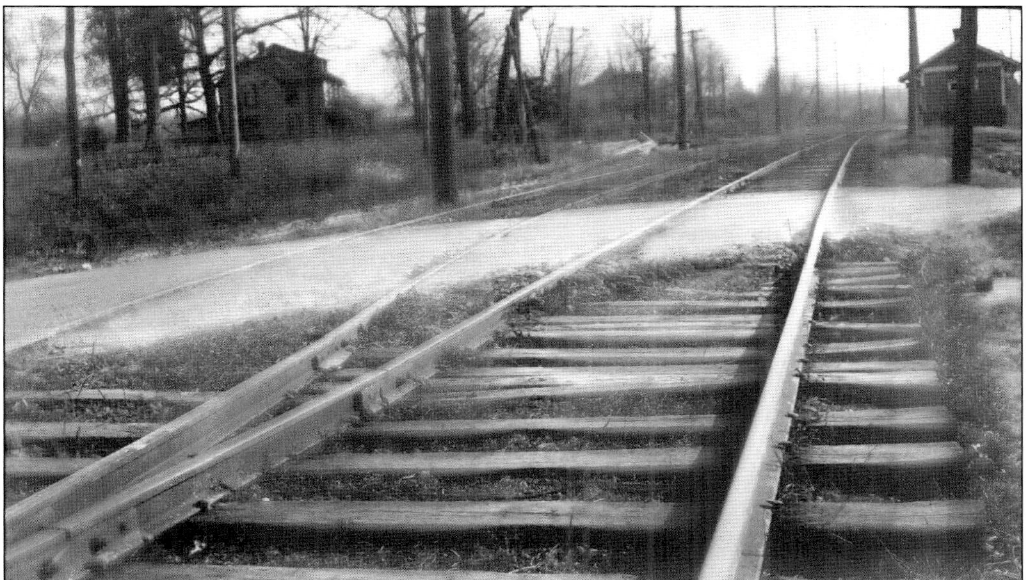

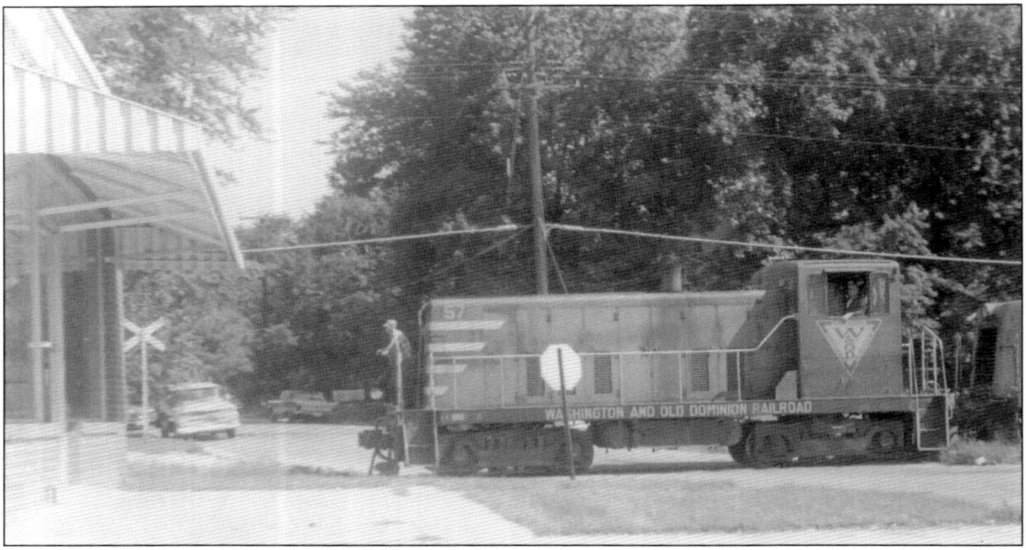

With much of its system in shambles after the Civil War, the railway was slow to recover. By the time it was once again functioning, it was renamed the Washington & Ohio Railroad. Pres. Ulysses S. Grant and members of his cabinet rode the train through Falls Church in 1873. Early in the 1870s, two government clerks drove over the rough and hilly road from Washington and looked around the little hamlet of a dozen houses scattered along the Leesburg Turnpike from the old brick church to the railroad station at West End. They were impressed with its inviting hills as the ideal situation for country residences. Real estate agents and others had the same thought, and with the train, access to and from Washington was much more easily accomplished and less dependent on good weather and roads. The town and the railway subsequently experienced a period of intense growth in the years after the Civil War.

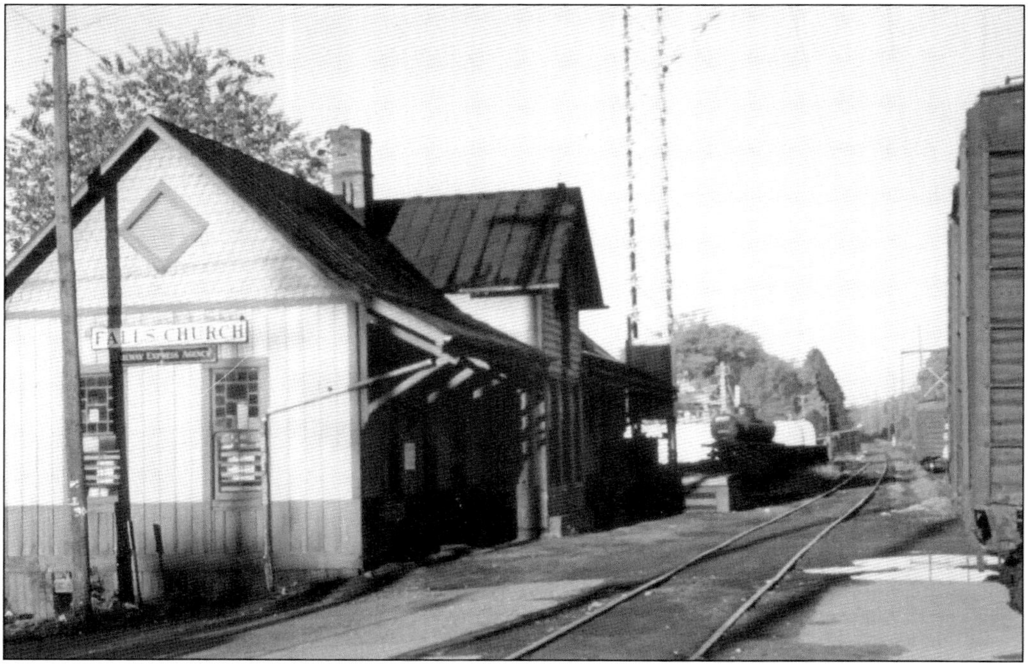

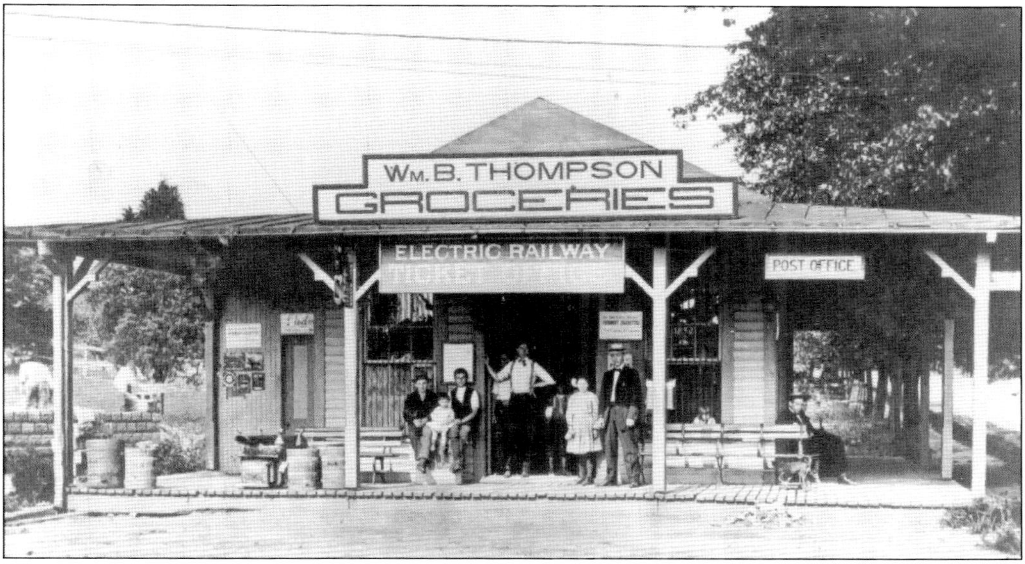

The trains were still slow and cumbersome with the junction change at Alexandria, but electric railway tracks were laid parallel to the train tracks in town, reaching East Falls Church in 1897 and extending along Lincoln Avenue to West End by 1901. Wm. B. Thompson Groceries also housed the electric railway ticket depot and post office.

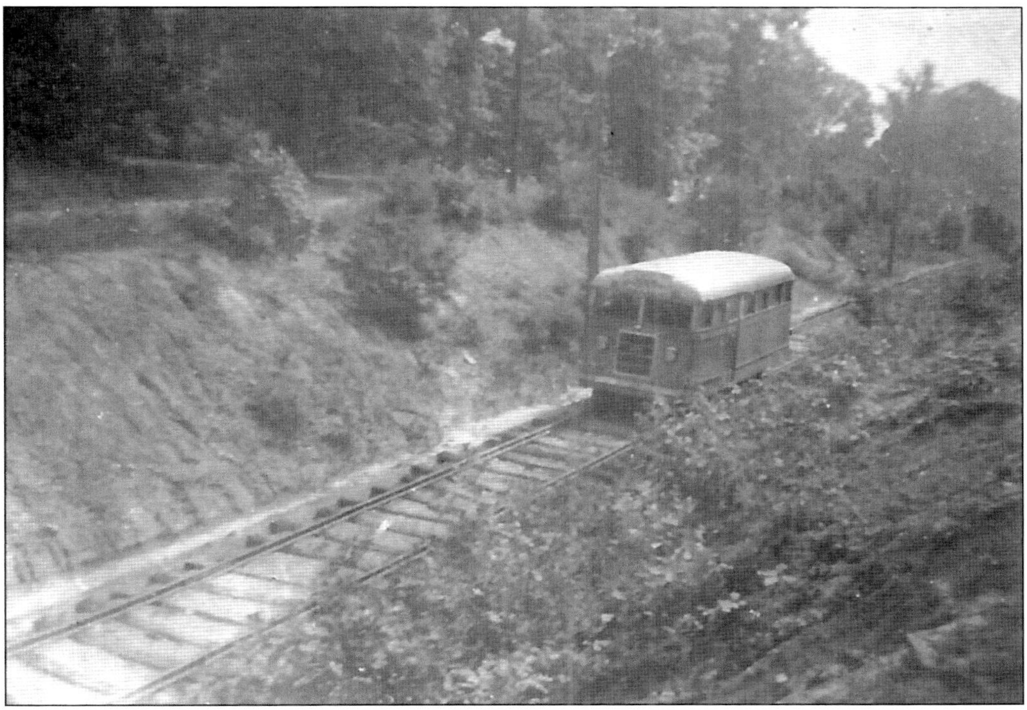

The trolley ran in a ravine along Lincoln Avenue in which children enjoyed playing. The electric train to Washington gave excellent service, running every half-hour from early in the morning until midnight. The trolley provided many more stops in the suburbs of Washington, making transportation even easier. (Courtesy of Donna Jean Bonner.)

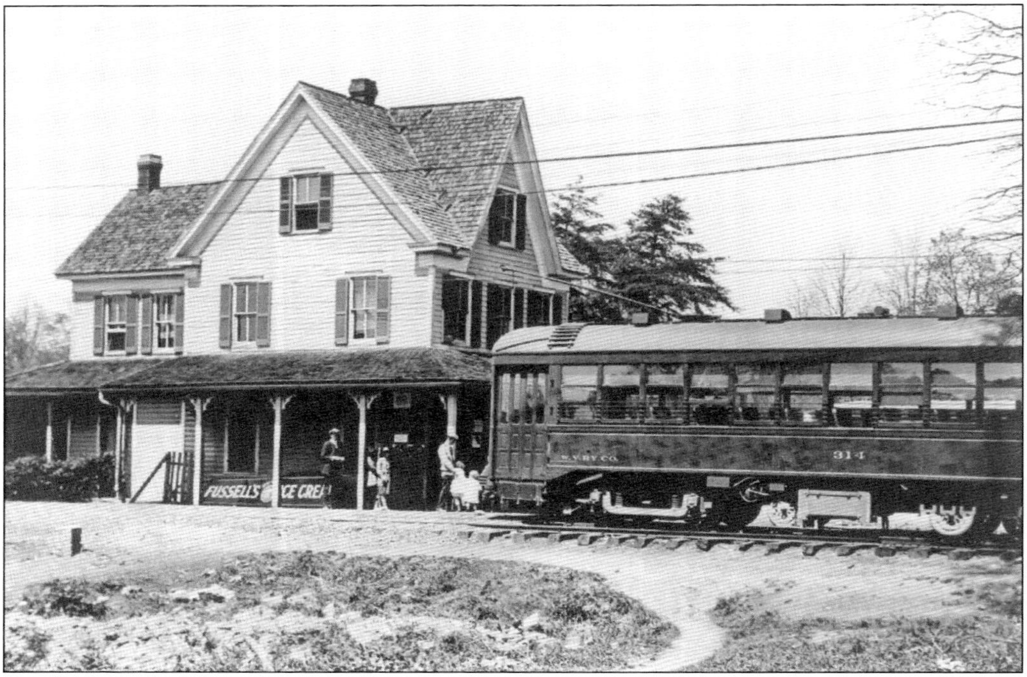

Shephard House, at 1101 West Broad Street, served as both a station and stationmaster's residence on the West End. By 1903, real estate agents, subdivision developers, and potential residents of Falls Church were using the trolley services extensively, seeing development and promotional opportunities with the service providing flexible access to previously remote locales.

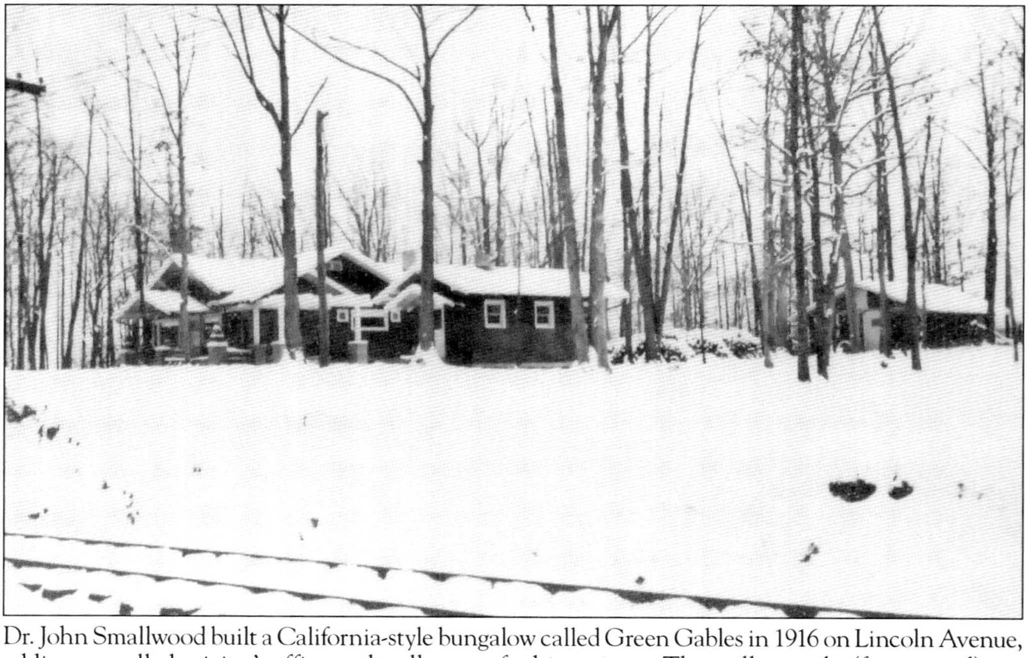

Dr. John Smallwood built a California-style bungalow called Green Gables in 1916 on Lincoln Avenue, adding a small physician's office and trolley stop for his patients. The trolley tracks (foreground) ran in front of the house, while the railway tracks ran behind it. (Courtesy of Donna Jean Bonner.)

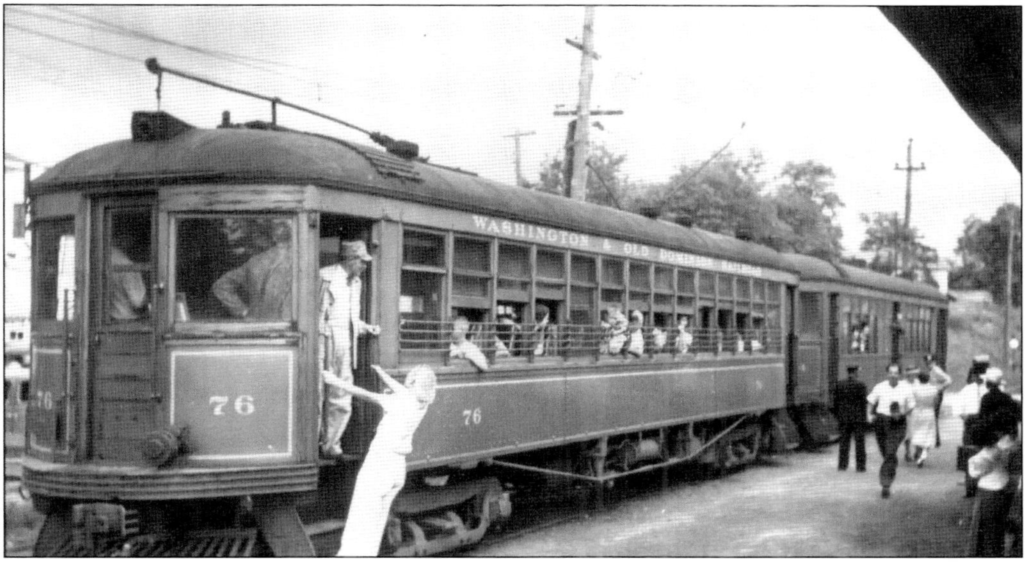

Devastated by the Civil War, the Alexandria, Loudoun & Hampshire Railway Company, only ever having reached Leesburg, did not fulfill the financial export bounty dreamed up at its inception. Once back up and running in 1867, the railway enthusiastically embraced extending the line over the mountains, aiming for Ohio, but the project quickly ran out of steam, and by 1878, the railway changed to the Washington & Ohio Railroad. (NVRPA.)

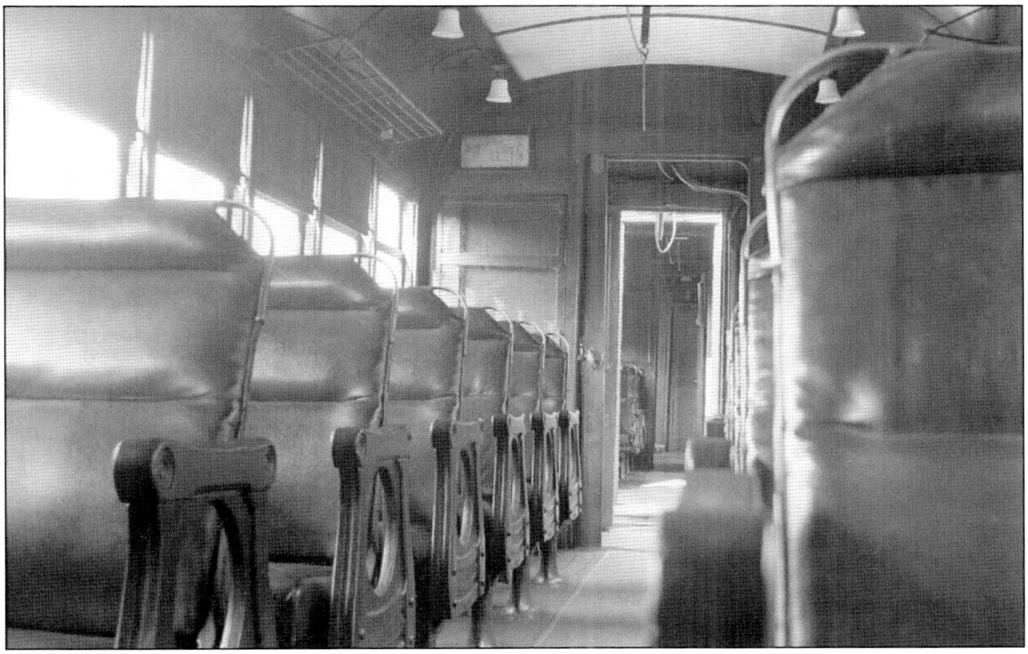

The Southern Railway bought the line in 1894, and by 1900, the rail ended as far west as Bluemont. Residents of Falls Church pleaded with the town council to enact a noise abatement law regarding the Southern Railway trains in 1899. A small new railway connecting Rosslyn at the Potomac River to Great Falls wanted to acquire more lines, leasing the Southern Railway line and giving it the name recognized today, Washington & Old Dominion. (NVRPA.)

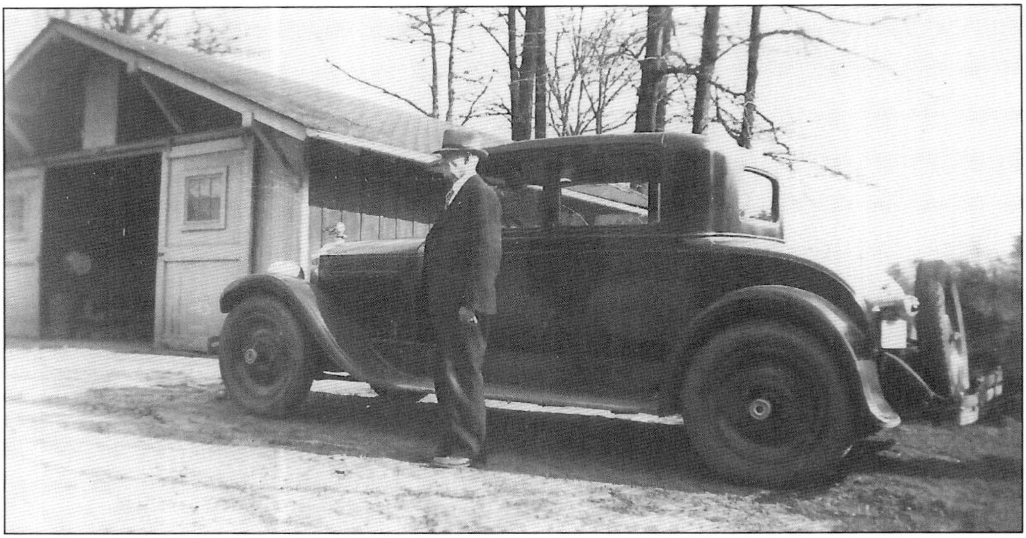

Dr. John Smallwood of Green Gables poses with his new car, as many did after automobiles began making an appearance in 1907. The new machines revolutionized transportation in the village of Falls Church and elsewhere. The trains and trolleys were less relevant, as residents now had a mode of transportation they could use on their own schedule. (Courtesy of Donna Jean Bonner.)

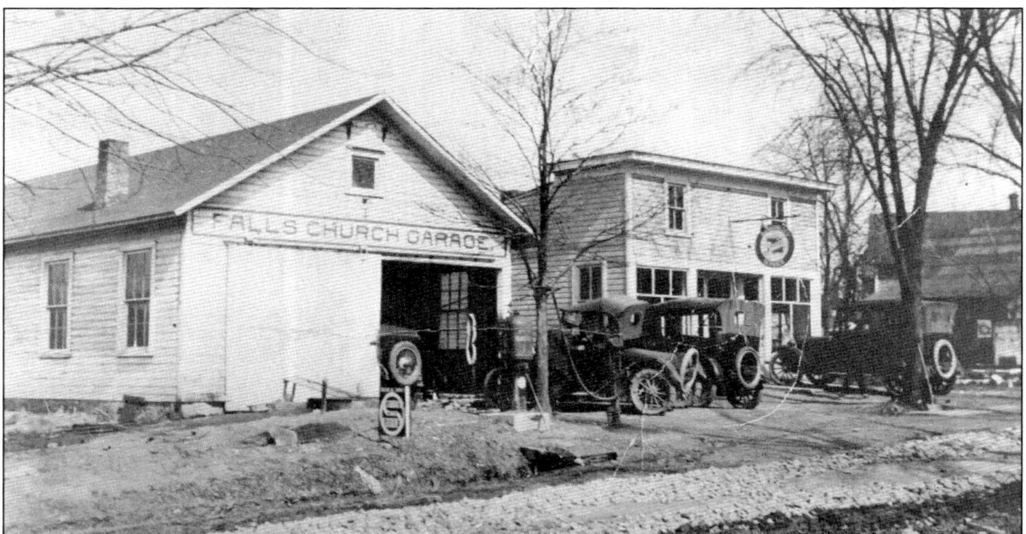

Automobiles also brought the need for new businesses, and the Falls Church Garage opened to service the new machines. Only during World War II did the use of automobiles suffer a decline, when rationing made it impossible to replace tires. Maintenance and expansion of roads became more pressing than that of railway beds.

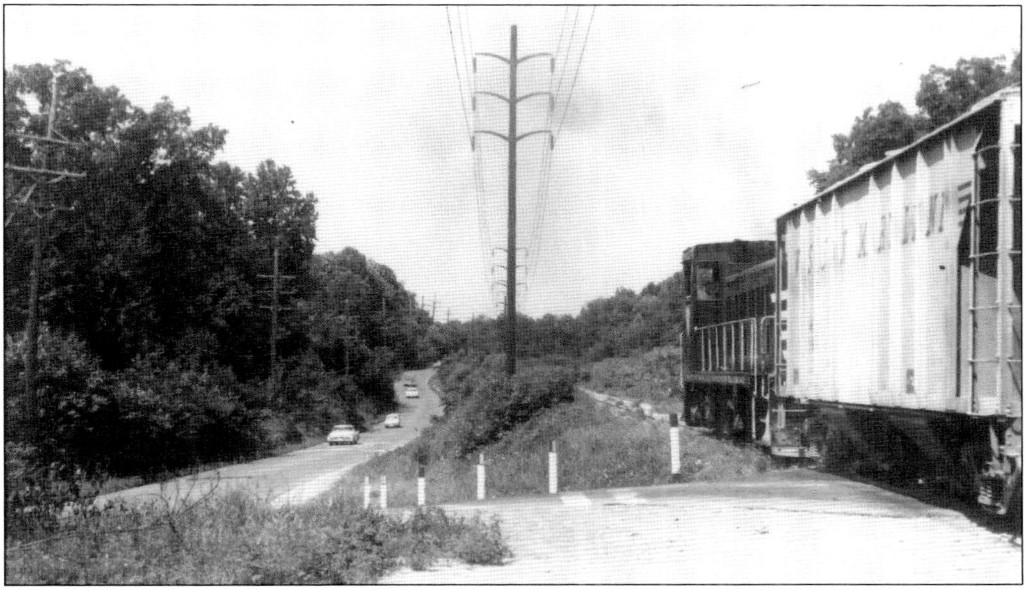

The number of cars continued to increase, and trains took a back seat. This freight train barreling past the crossroads with Shreve Road is still a familiar sight—minus the train—because the tracks were among the first converted in the Rails to Trails program. (NVRPA.)

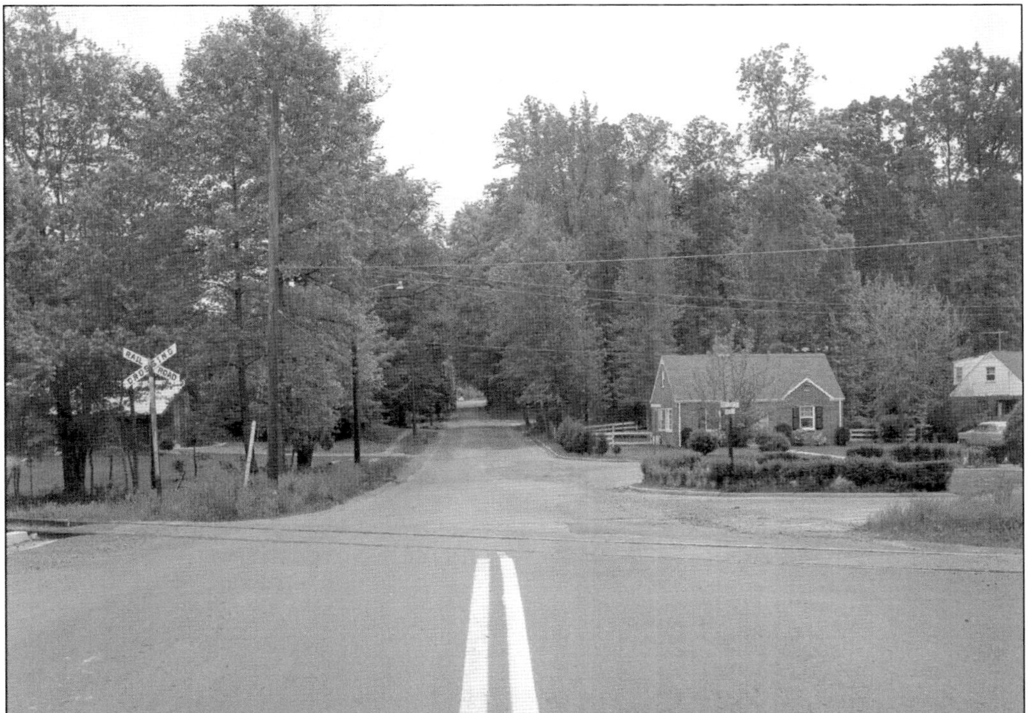

The crossing on Great Falls Street looking east from Lincoln Avenue is another popular point on the current recreation trail used by cyclists, joggers, and walkers. The system is now under the authority of the Northern Virginia Regional Parks Authority and connects to other branches in the system.

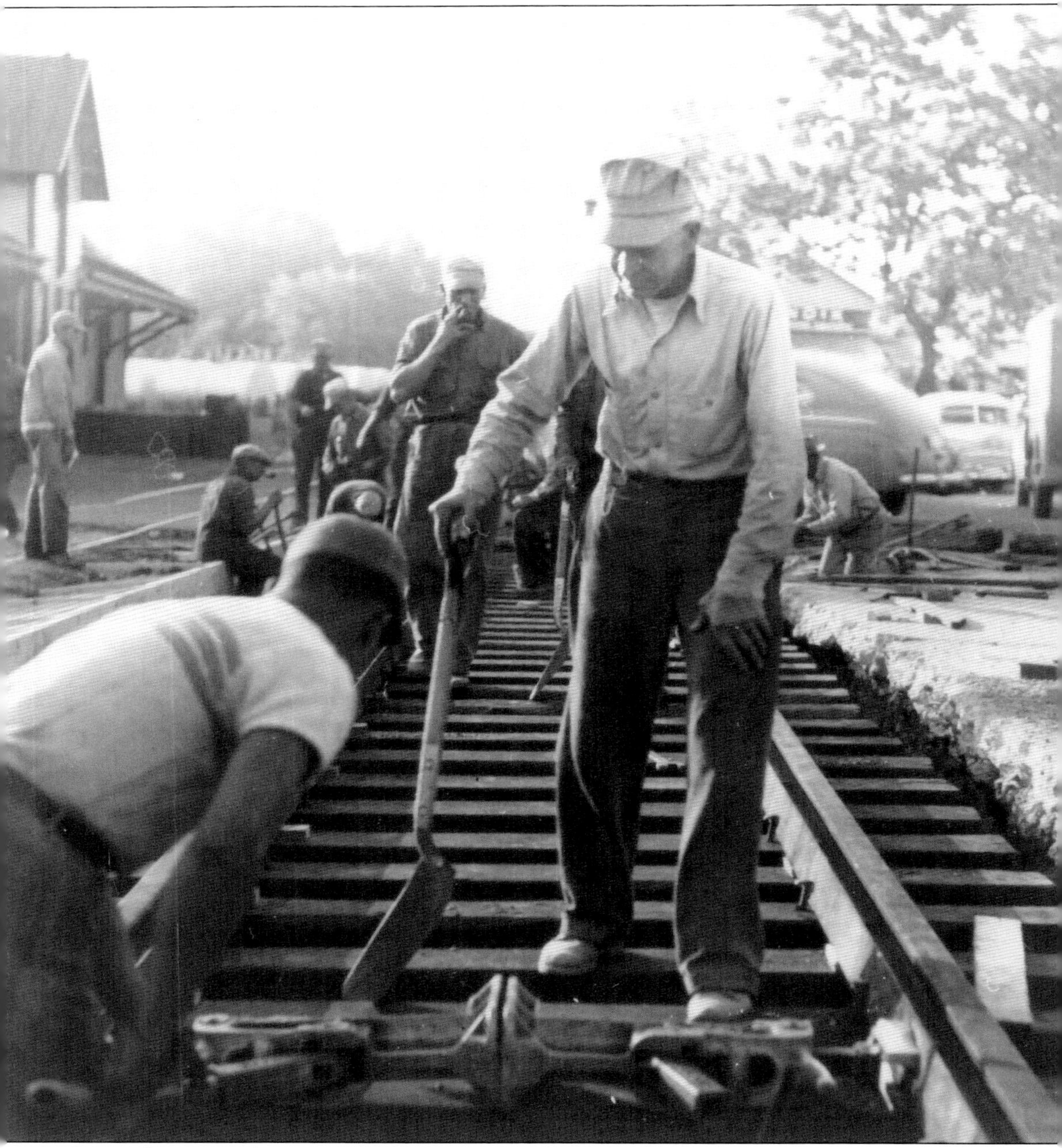

Workers repair the crossing at Washington Street near the East Falls Church station. As automobile use grew, so did the roads, and crossing repairs were costly for the railway company and disrupted traffic flow to both trains and vehicles. By the 1930s, the railway cut service on the seldom-used passenger line between Purcellville and Bluemont. Passenger service had become a money-losing venture, and the writing was on the wall that train service was heading toward the end of the line. For those who did not trust the new machines and preferred the train and those who had ridden it their whole life, the closing of railway passenger service caused much grief. (NVRPA.)

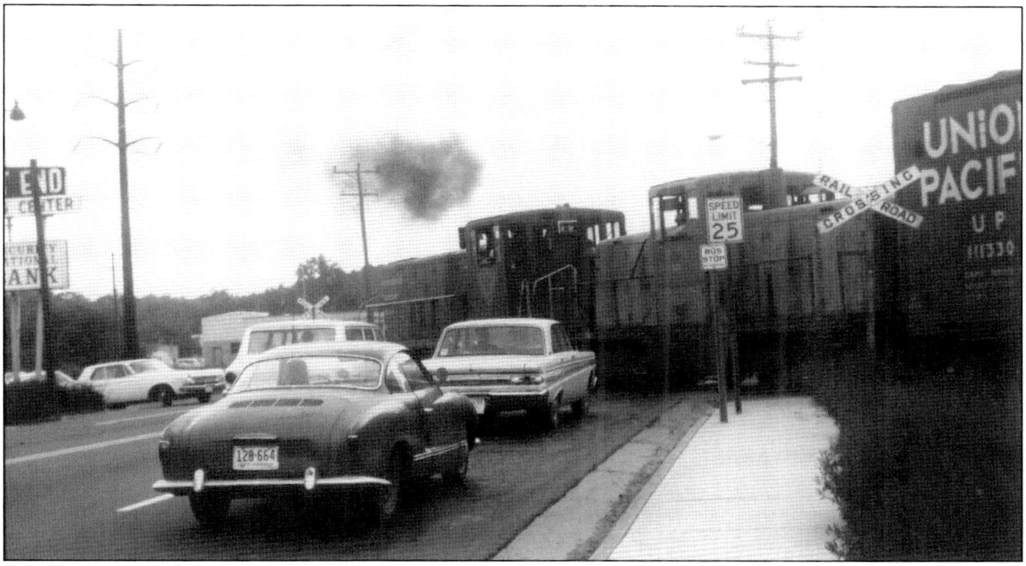

Cars and trains did not work well together, and railways already possessed a long-suffering financial history. The Washington-Virginia Railway electric trolley line entered a period of steep decline and was liquidated in 1927. Falls Church resident Merton E. Church tried to save it until his death four years later, but the railway lost its right-of-way to Washington and closed for good in 1939. Ownership and responsibility for the main railway line changed hands several times over its life. Washington & Old Dominion Railroad, unable to compete with the flexibility of the new interstate highways and burdened by the need to upgrade its many surface-grade crossings of major thoroughfares, ended all service in 1968. The twice-daily round-trip passenger train line was closed and the last train through Falls Church, Train 45, made its last run in the late spring of 1951, drawing media and fanfare for the event. (Both, NVRPA.)

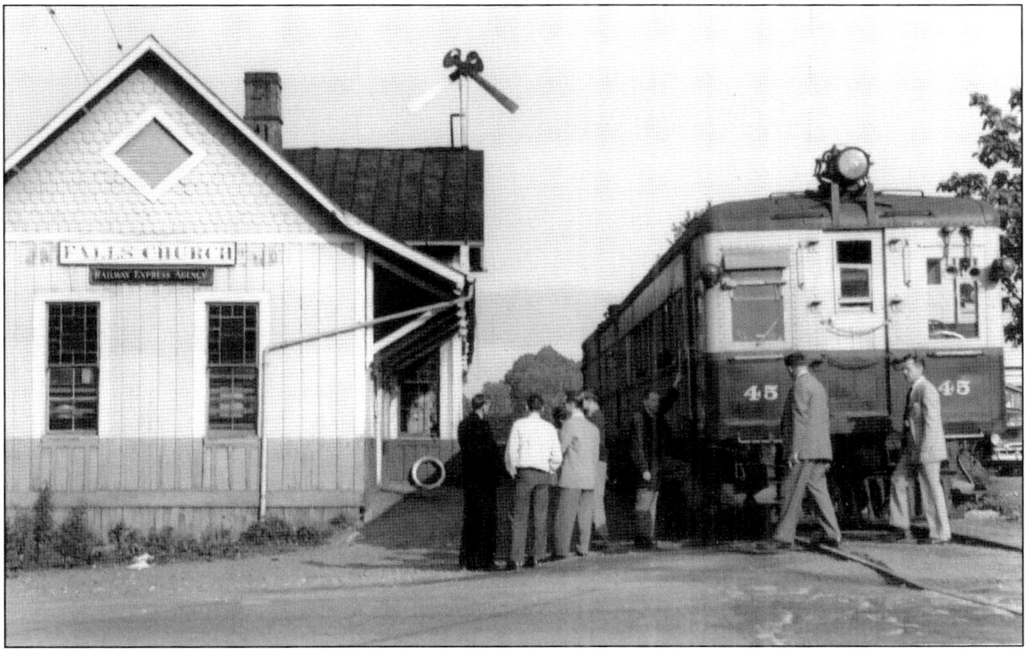

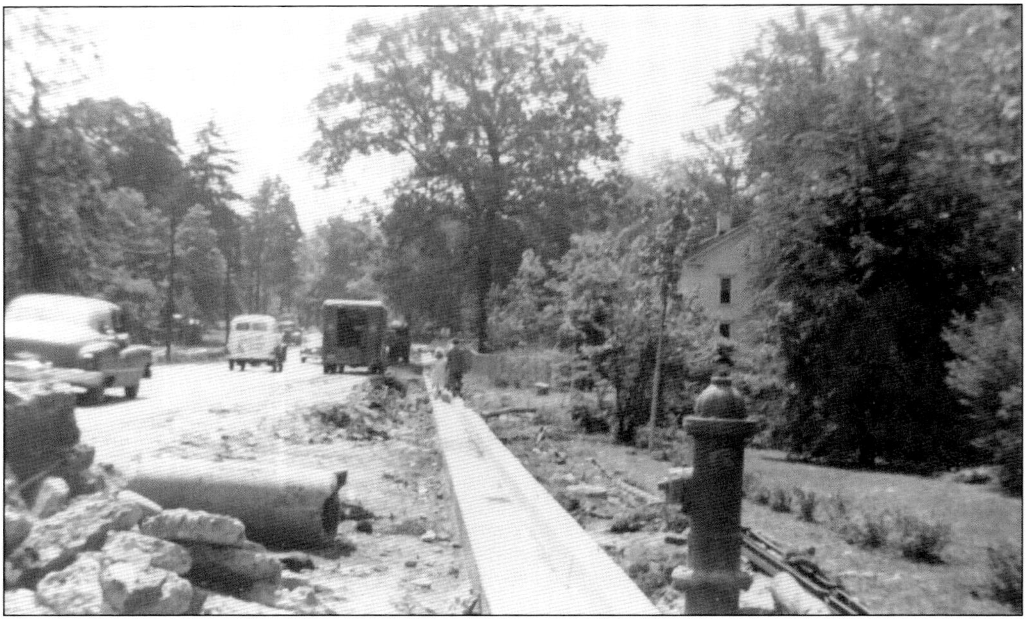

As the town grew, so did the need for better roads with larger capacity. During early widening of Broad Street, the trees lining the borders were replanted. However, subsequent enlarging left out the trees.

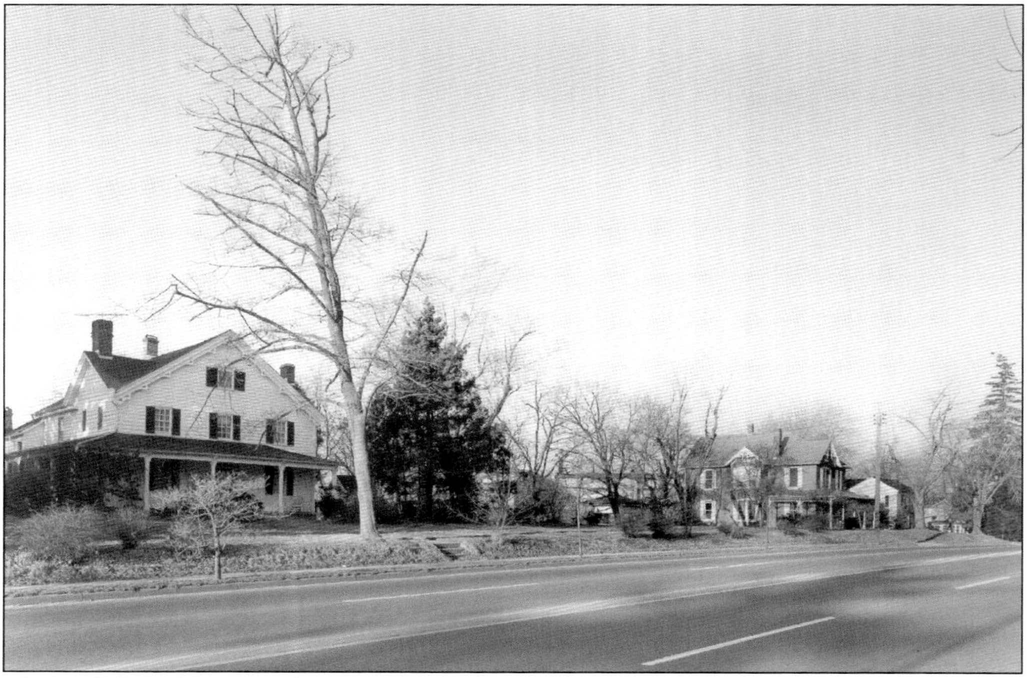

Thoroughfare edges crept closer to the front porches of homes as Broad Street became more of a main highway through town toward Washington. Eventually, the shade trees gave way to ever-expanding pavement in order to accommodate increasing traffic. The sleepy village of yesteryear was no more, though Falls Church managed to maintain its small-town charm.

Four

Blazing the Civil Rights Trail

While the trails and dirt-packed crossroads transformed into turnpikes and railway networks, another trail was blazed in the Falls Church community. Thanks to the strength and local efforts of both free and enslaved African American citizens of Falls Church, the path to equality was fought and earned locally and carried influence nationally.

A local Columbia Baptist pastor's belief that his black followers should have enough education to enrich their lives ultimately led to his death at the hands of Mosby's Raiders. However, the Baptist pastors left the community empowered enough to create their own churches. Enslaved men braved death to escape and fight for freedom during the Civil War, returning to Falls Church as free, land-owning citizens.

Many of the descendants of those first families still reside in the city, which was transformed thanks to the nationally reaching efforts of the Tinner and Henderson families. The times were not without struggle, and the town and county leaders did not always put the interests of the African American community first, at one point gerrymandering the boundaries of the town to shift the bulk of Lincoln supporters outside the town voting district.

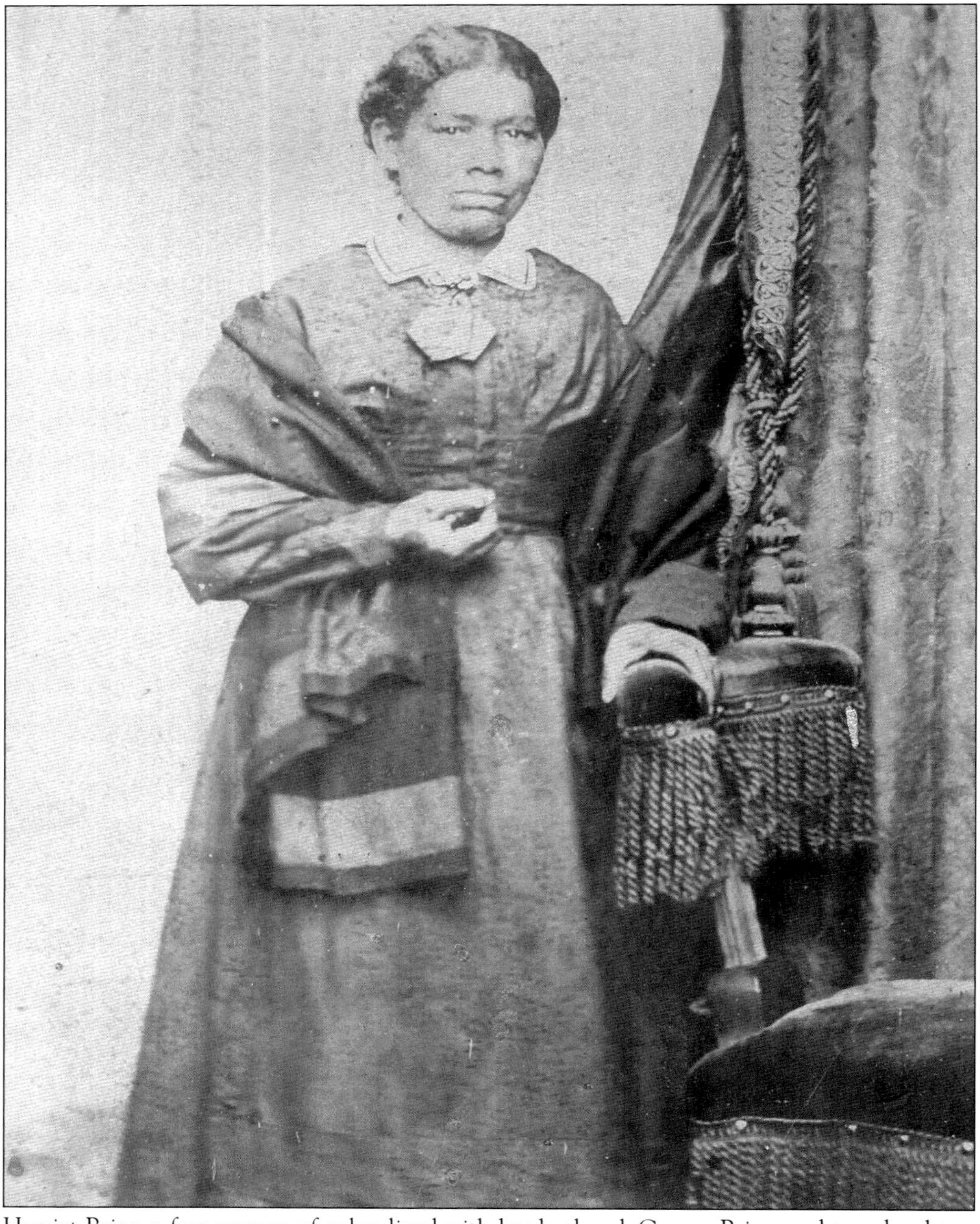

Harriet Brice, a free woman of color, lived with her husband, George Brice, and two daughters near Falls Church on her own property purchased in 1864. While she was free, her husband was a slave up until the Civil War, but he escaped and joined the Union army during the Civil War, serving in the 6th Regiment, US Colored Troops, and seeing action in the siege at Petersburg and Richmond. In 1867, Harriet Brice donated land for the establishment of Galloway Methodist Church, and in 1871, the couple sold a lot to trustees for the building of Second Baptist Church. Both churches are still active and played important roles in the struggle for equality. (Courtesy of the Ferguson Family Collection.)

Upon his return from war, George Brice arranged with absent local landowners still away at war to farm their property in exchange for a portion of the crops. Soldiers destroyed most of the crops Mr. Brice raised, and after the war, the Brices filed a claim for compensation of the lost crops. It is unclear if they were ever compensated. Harriet Brice's Southern Claims testimony from 1871 read as follows: "I am the wife of the claimant. In 1864–65 I lived at Falls Church. . . . He lived on the piece of land I bought of mine. We had 12 acres of corn destroyed by Sheridan's cavalry. . . . We didn't accumulate anything after they came along and took possession." (Both, National Archives.)

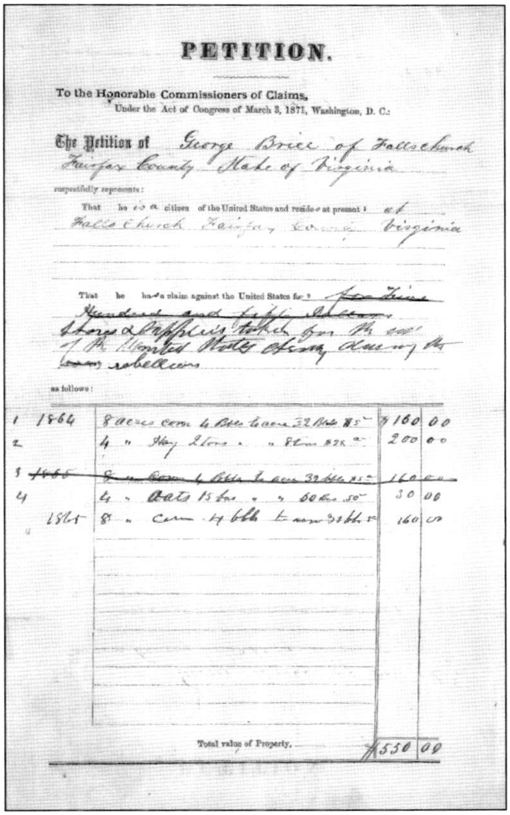

PETITION.

To the Honorable Commissioners of Claims,
Under the Act of Congress of March 3, 1871, Washington, D. C.:

The Petition of George Brice of Fallschurch Fairfax County State of Virginia

respectfully represents:

That he is a citizen of the United States and reside at present at Falls Church Fairfax County Virginia

That he has a claim against the United States for Five Hundred and fifty Dollars Stores & Supplies taken for the use of the United States Army during the rebellion

as follows:

1	1864	8 acres corn 4 Bbls to acre 32 Bbls $5	$160 00
2		4 " Hay 2 tons " " 8 tons $25	200 00
3	~~1865~~	~~8 " corn 4 Bbls to acre 32 Bbls $5~~	~~160 00~~
4		4 " Oats 15 bu " " 60 bu 50	30 00
	1865	8 " corn 4 bbls to acre 32 bbls $5	160 00
		Total value of Property,	$550 00

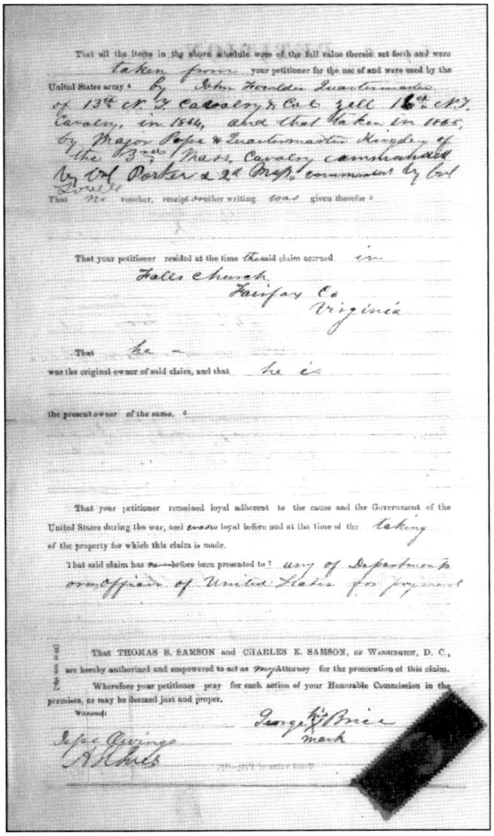

That all the items in the above schedule were of the full value therein set forth and were taken from your petitioner for the use of and were used by the United States army by John Howlden Quartermaster of 13th N.Y. Cavalry & Col. Gell 16th N.Y. Cavalry, in 1864, and that taken in 1865, by Major Pope & Quartermaster Kingsley of the 3rd Mass. Cavalry commanded by Col. Porter & 2d Mass. commanded by Col. Lowell

That no voucher, receipt or other writing was given therefor.

That your petitioner resided at the time the said claim accrued in Falls Church Fairfax Co Virginia

That he was the original owner of said claim, and that he is the present owner of the same.

That your petitioner remained loyal adherent to the cause and the Government of the United States during the war, and was loyal before and at the time of the taking of the property for which this claim is made.

That said claim has not before been presented to any of Departments or officer of United States for payment

That THOMAS S. SAMSON and CHARLES E. SAMSON, of Washington, D. C., are hereby authorized and empowered to act as my Attorney for the prosecution of this claim.

Wherefore your petitioner pray for such action of your Honorable Commission in the premises, as may be deemed just and proper.

Witness:

Isaac Ewings
A. White

George his mark Brice

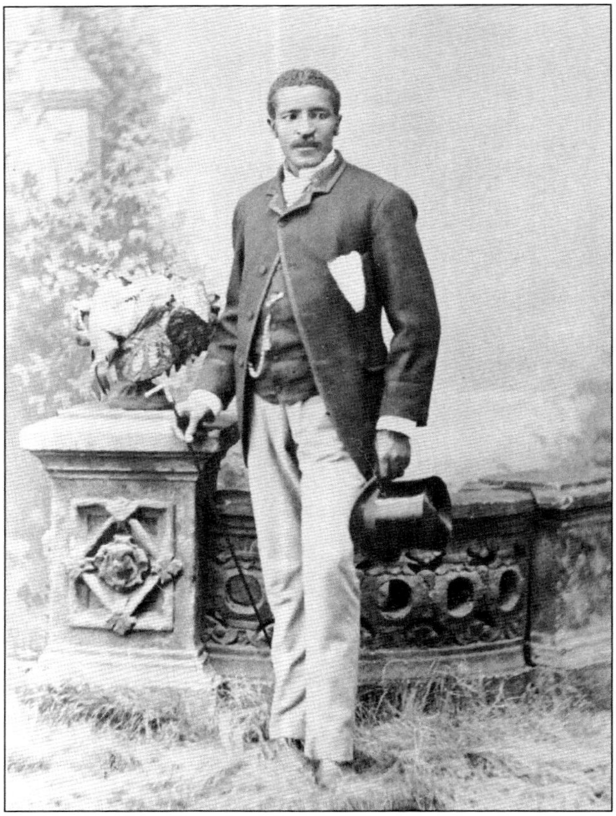

A former slave, Frederick Foote Sr. purchased about 39 acres from the Minor family following the Civil War with money he had earned working as a blacksmith for Union troops. A respected black businessman in the community, Foote served Falls Church for 10 or more years, first as town sergeant from 1876 to 1880 and then as a town councilman from 1880 to 1889. Foote's land, originally known as Fort Buffalo, was freed for development only after Foote's descendants convinced a court to invalidate his last will and testament, which had forbidden them to allow his 39 acres to leave the family, in 1956. The land became Seven Corners, one of the region's first suburban malls, and a little country orchard transformed overnight into the large Seven Corners shopping center.

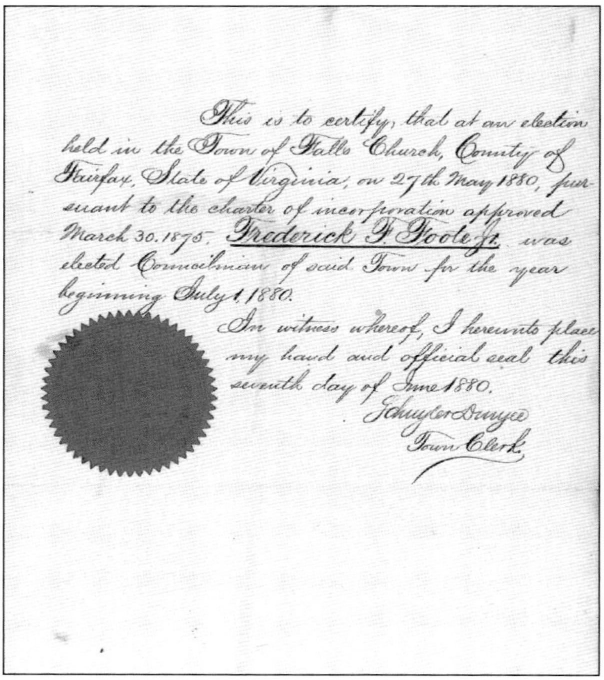

This is to certify, that at an election held in the Town of Falls Church, County of Fairfax, State of Virginia, on 27th May 1880, pursuant to the charter of incorporation approved March 30. 1875. Frederick F. Foote Jr. was elected Councilman of said Town for the year beginning July 1, 1880.

In witness whereof, I hereunto place my hand and official seal this seventh day of June 1880.

Schuyler Duryee
Town Clerk

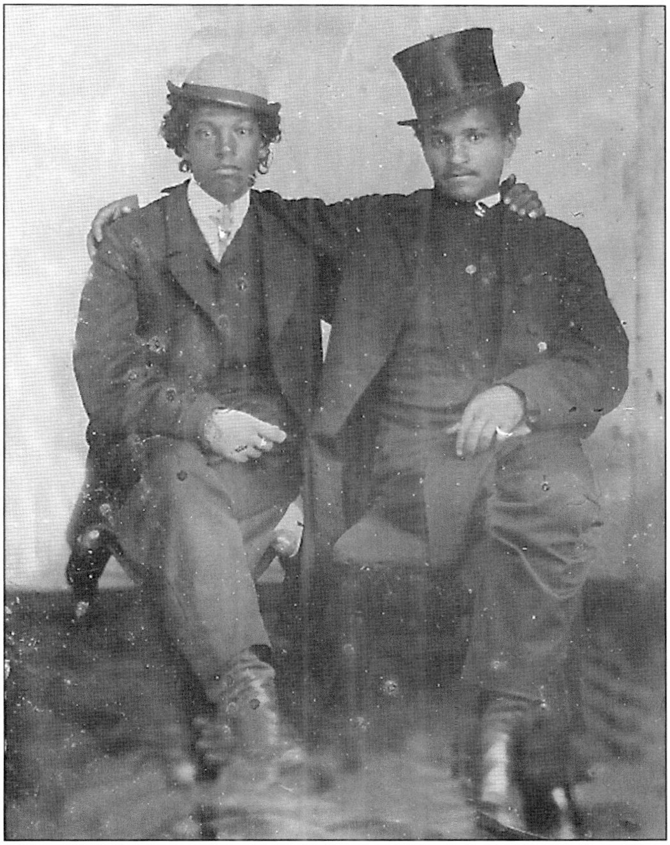

George Thomas (left) and Frederick Foote Jr. (right) were both respected black leaders and businessmen in the community in the 1880s. Thomas owned a shoe shop (below, small building in the forefront) attached to the Star Tavern on the corner of Broad and Washington Streets. (Right, courtesy of the Henderson Foundation.)

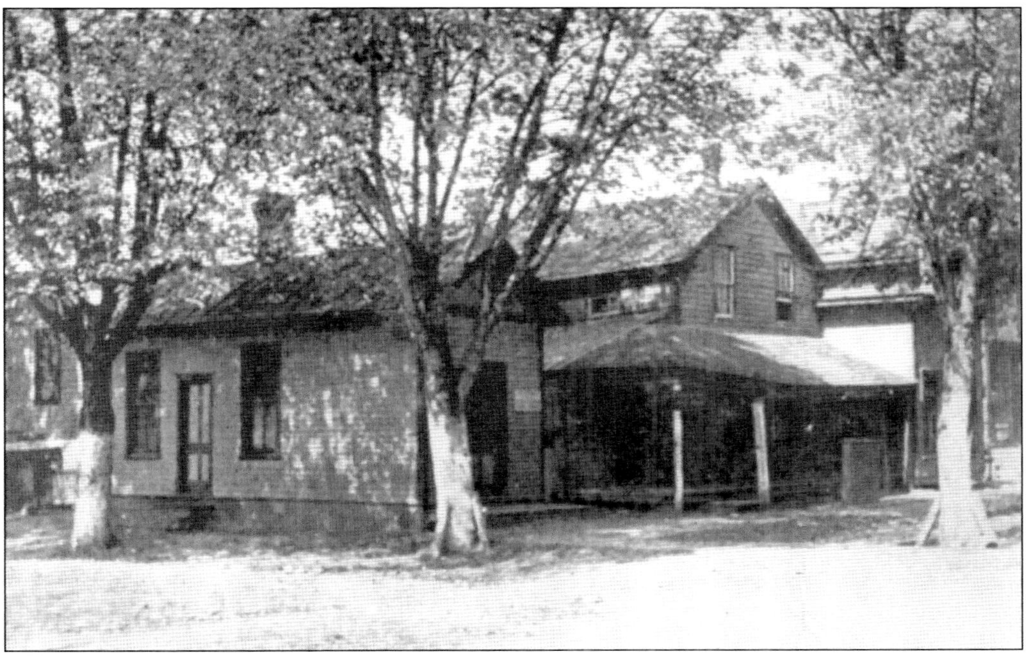

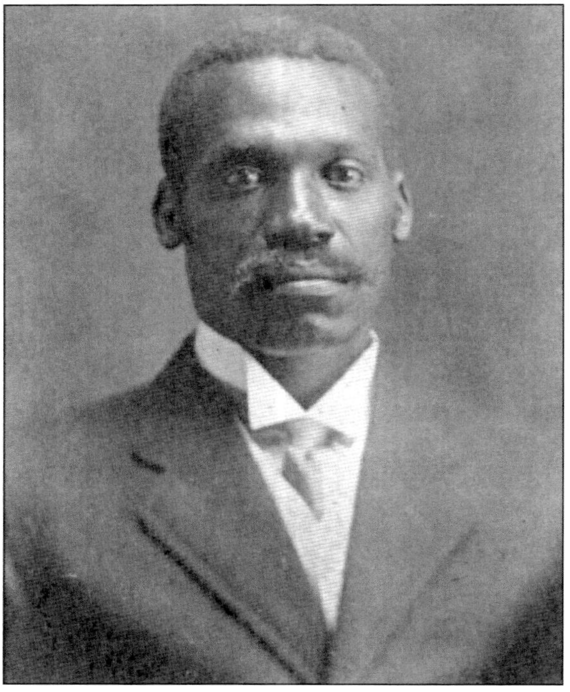

On December 14, 1914, the town council adopted the Virginia Senate act approved on March 12, 1912, providing for designation of segregated districts for whites and blacks. Joseph B. Tinner (left), E.B. Henderson, and others spoke on the subject. The ordinance was enacted, and the council's segregation committee was instructed to prepare a map showing the boundaries of segregation districts. (MRSPL, Joseph B Tinner.)

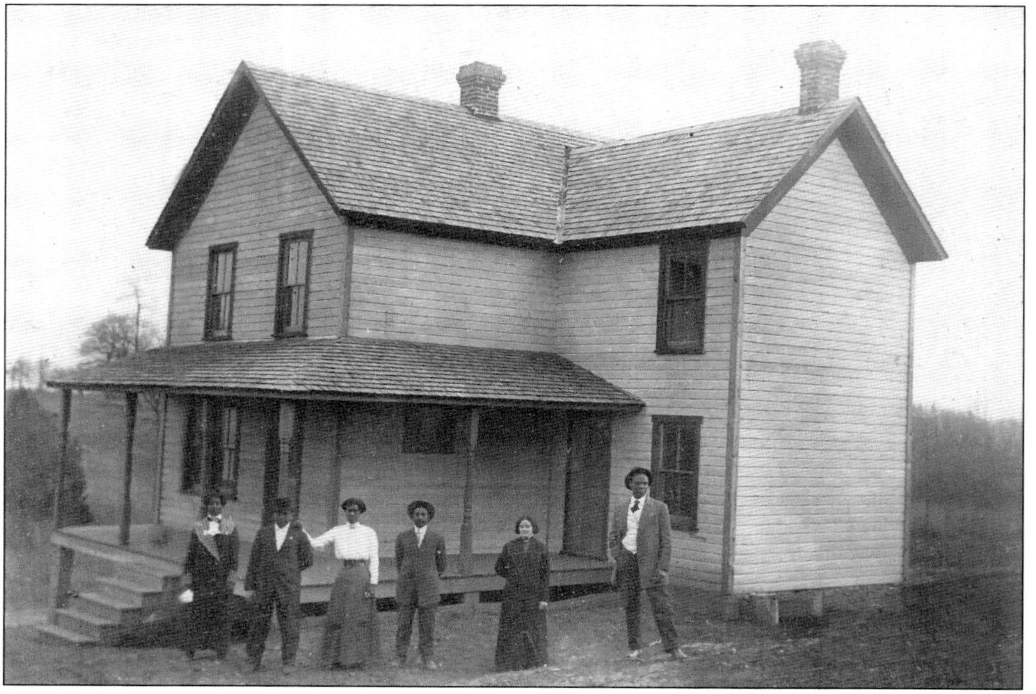

Joseph B. Tinner and his family, of Tinner Hill, were known for their fine stonemasonry, examples of which still exist in Falls Church. Charles Tinner, a stonemason and the son of Joseph Tinner, fought in the Home Guard during the Civil War. Charles Tinner is buried at Galloway Methodist Church. (Courtesy of the Tinner Hill Heritage Foundation.)

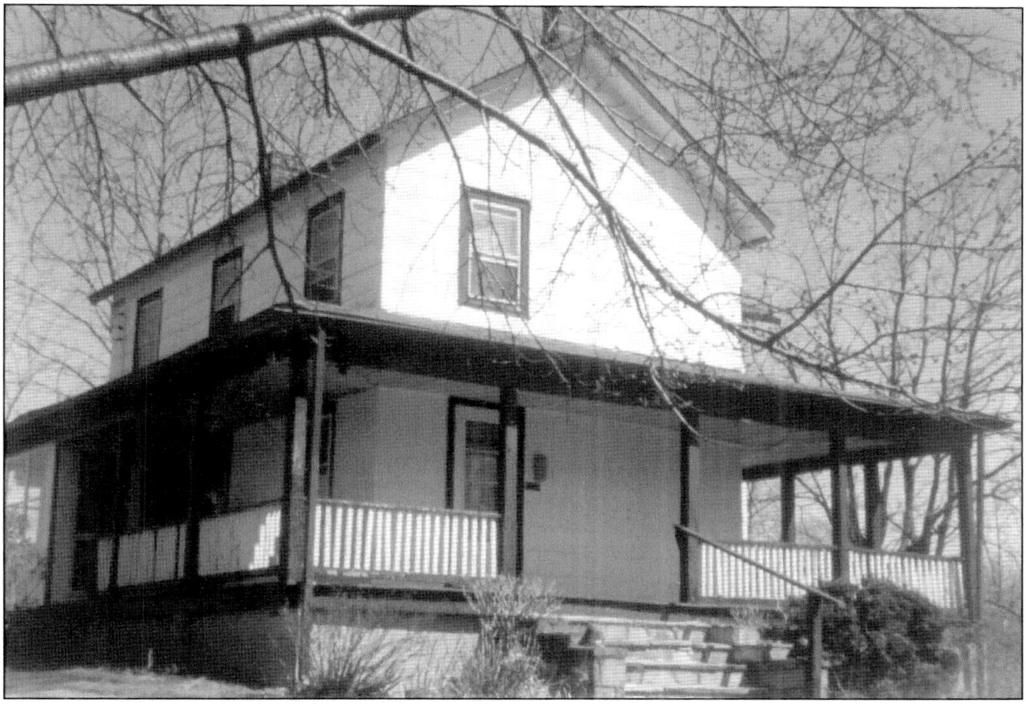

African Americans continue to be counted among Falls Church's notable citizens, and Tinner Hill, settled by blacks after the Civil War, is home to descendants of those original families today, including the Tinners and the Hendersons. The settlement was a short distance south of the town limits, described in Charles Stewart's *A Virginia Village* in 1904 as "consisting of probably a hundred cottages with a population of between four and five hundred. They have a school building and three churches." Joseph Tinner became an important figure in the National Association for the Advancement of Colored People (NAACP) at the encouragement of Edwin Bancroft "E.B." Henderson. Henderson and Tinner founded the Colored Citizens' Protective League (CCPL) with Tinner, a great speaker, serving as president. The CCPL succeeded in defeating the segregation ordinance and advanced numerous civil rights endeavors. The organization later became the first rural branch of the NAACP.

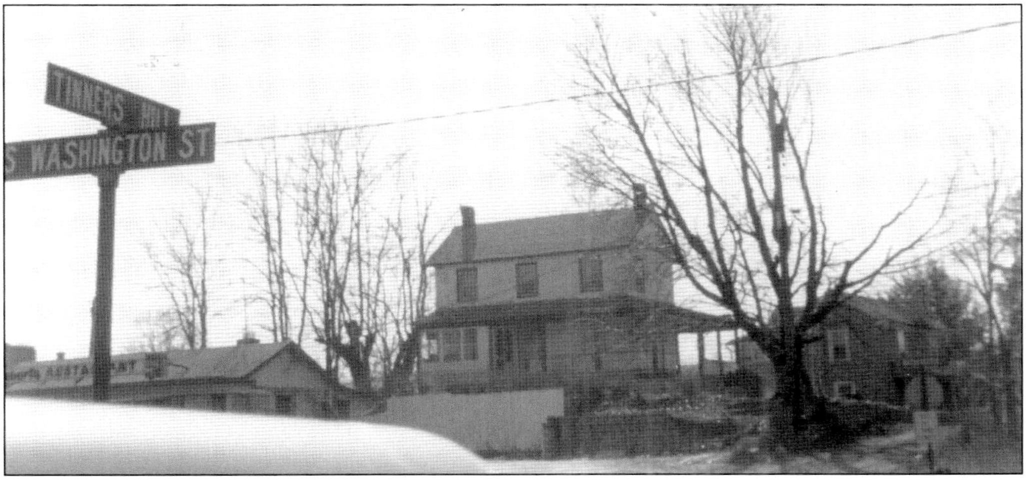

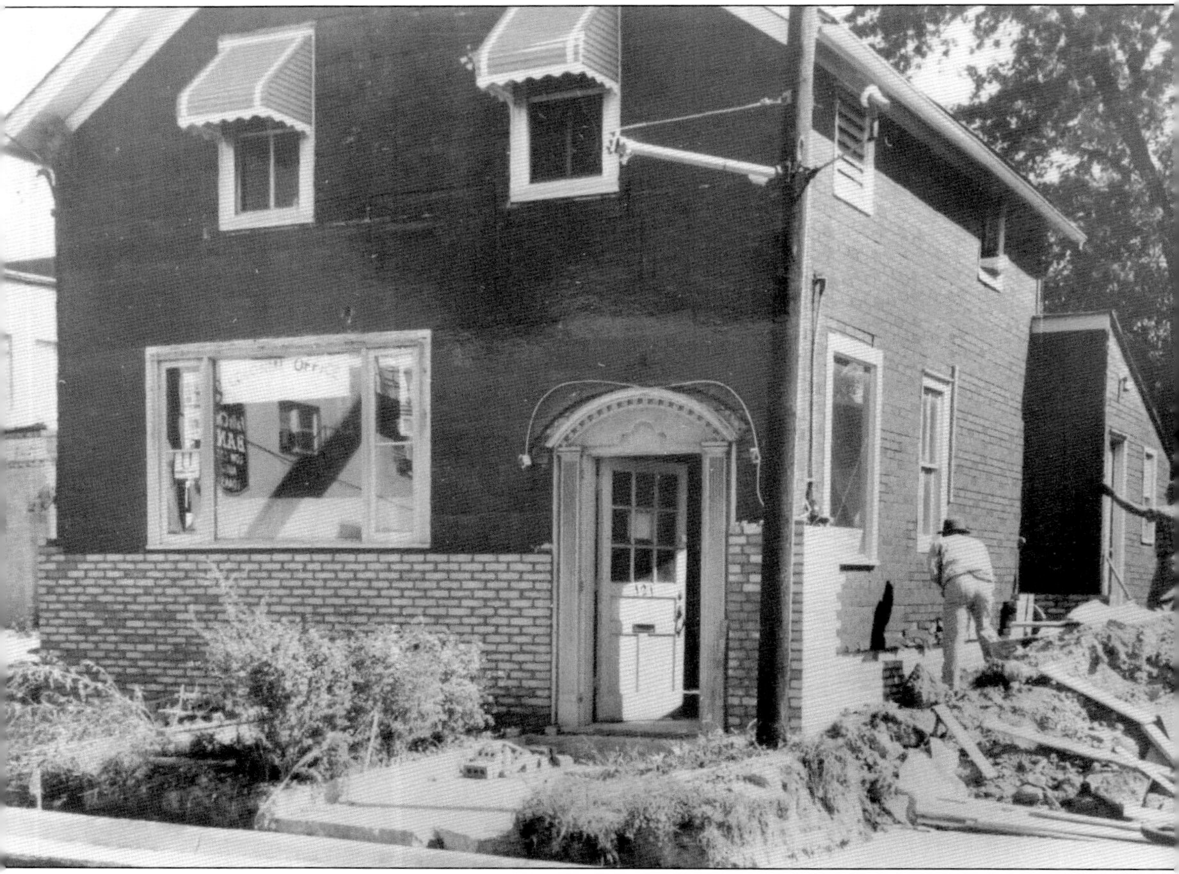

E.B. Henderson's original home stood at 121 South Washington Street. He was critical to the early and continued success of Falls Church's African American community in the fight for educational opportunities and civil rights. He became nationally known after writing *The Negro in Sports*. Edwin dedicated his life to fighting for equality in athletics as well as education. For three summers, he attended the Sargent Dudley School of Physical Training at Harvard University, where he became the first black male to receive certification in physical education in 1907.

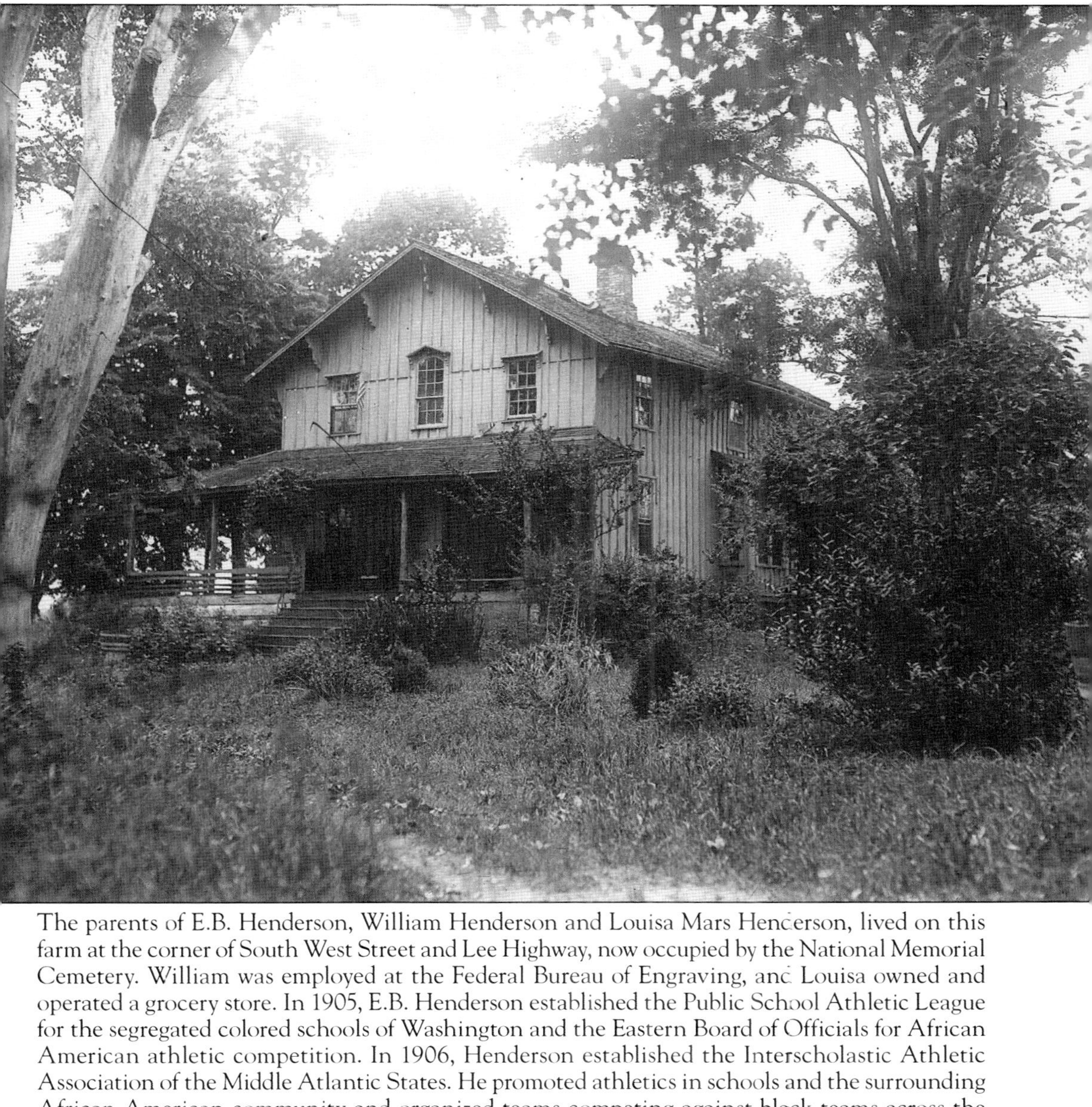

The parents of E.B. Henderson, William Henderson and Louisa Mars Henderson, lived on this farm at the corner of South West Street and Lee Highway, now occupied by the National Memorial Cemetery. William was employed at the Federal Bureau of Engraving, and Louisa owned and operated a grocery store. In 1905, E.B. Henderson established the Public School Athletic League for the segregated colored schools of Washington and the Eastern Board of Officials for African American athletic competition. In 1906, Henderson established the Interscholastic Athletic Association of the Middle Atlantic States. He promoted athletics in schools and the surrounding African American community and organized teams competing against black teams across the country, culminating in the best teams competing in the Colored Basketball World Championship. As captain of the Washington 12th Streeters in the 1909–1910 season, Henderson led the team to win the championship. After petitioning Howard University to accept the 12th Streeters as its varsity team the following year, they again won the Colored Basketball World Championship without Henderson as a player. (Courtesy of the Henderson Family Collection.)

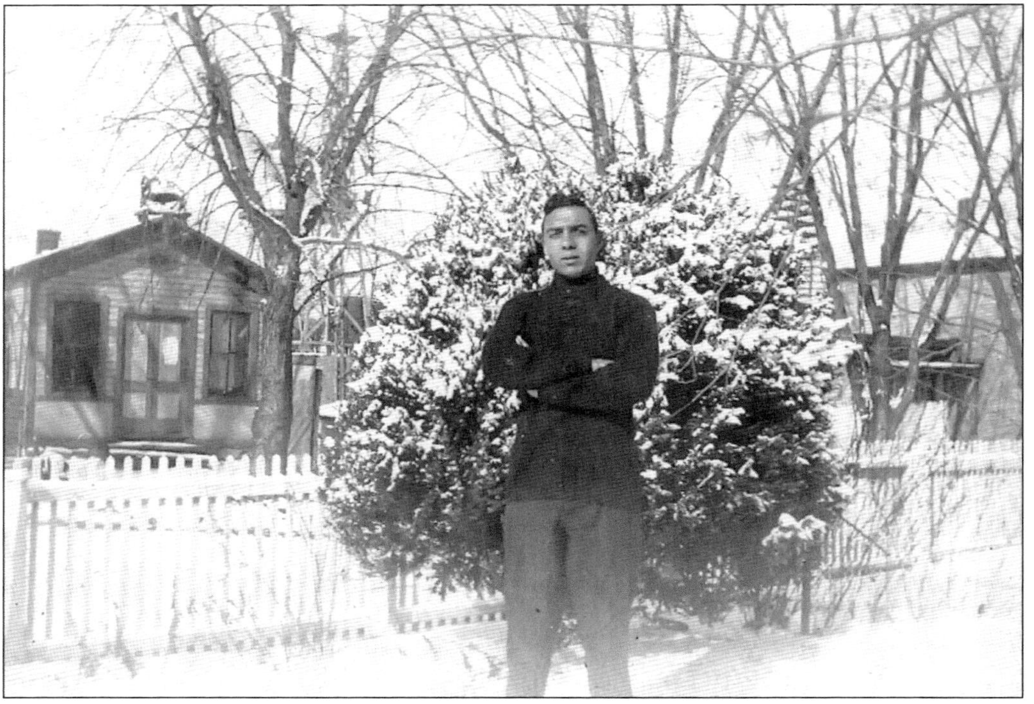

A prolific and persuasive writer, E.B. Henderson earned notoriety for penning over 3,000 editorial letters in an effort to fight segregation and discrimination published in newspapers across the country. He also authored several books spreading awareness about the emergence of black sports and became the first African American certified to teach physical education in a public school. In 1933, he earned a master's degree from Columbia University. (Courtesy of the Henderson Family Collection.)

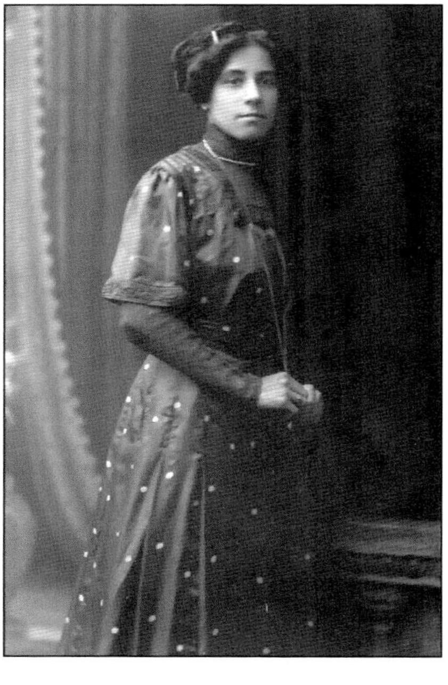

An outstanding educator and civil rights activist, Mary Ellen Meriwether Henderson, born in Washington, DC, left the District classroom she taught in to tend to the family farm and their two sons after her marriage to Edwin Henderson. At that time, married women were not permitted to teach in the District. In 1919, the black community implored Mary Ellen to re-open the local school for blacks. The school had been closed due to lack of a teacher. (Courtesy of the Henderson Family Collection.)

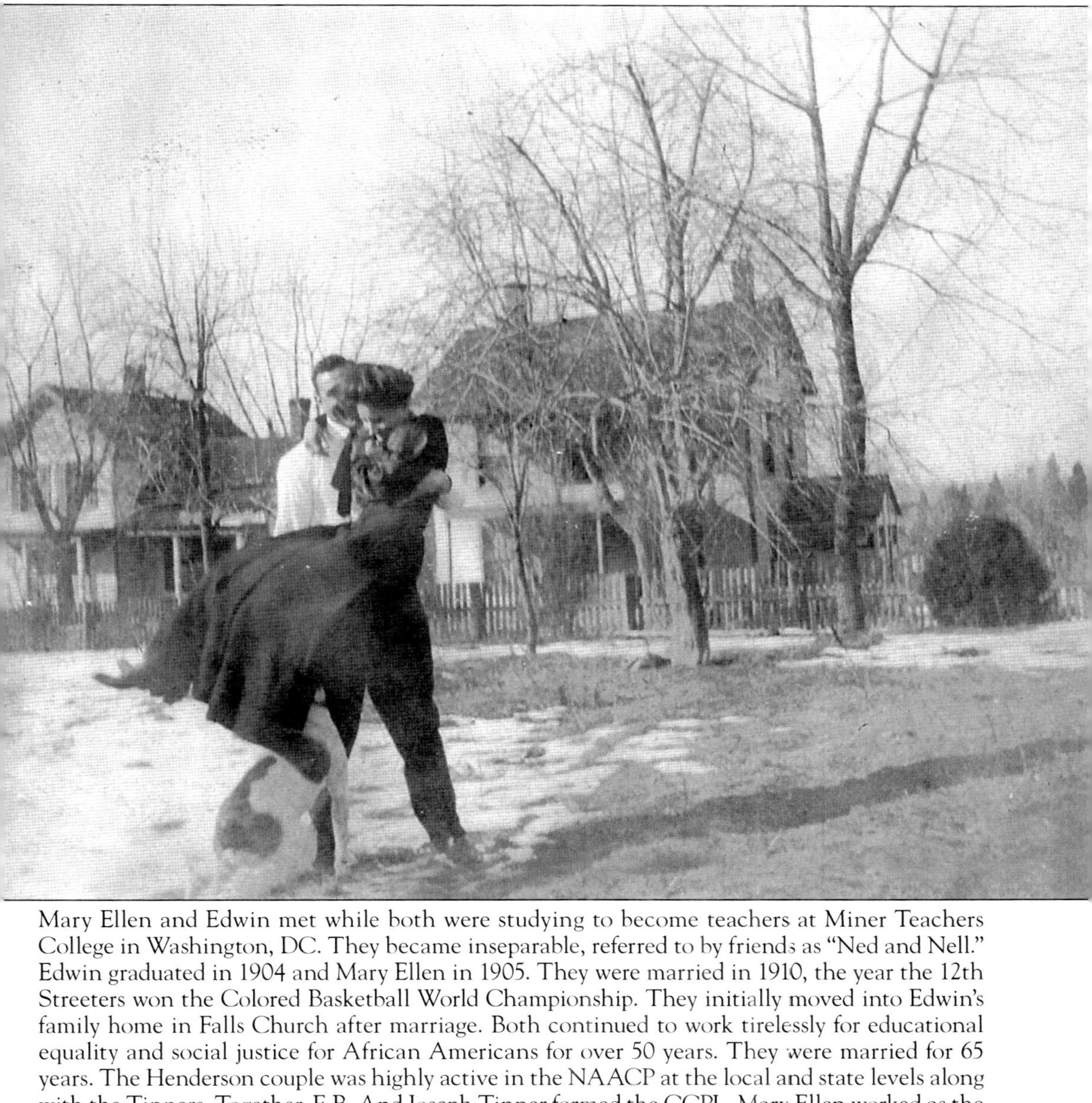

Mary Ellen and Edwin met while both were studying to become teachers at Miner Teachers College in Washington, DC. They became inseparable, referred to by friends as "Ned and Nell." Edwin graduated in 1904 and Mary Ellen in 1905. They were married in 1910, the year the 12th Streeters won the Colored Basketball World Championship. They initially moved into Edwin's family home in Falls Church after marriage. Both continued to work tirelessly for educational equality and social justice for African Americans for over 50 years. They were married for 65 years. The Henderson couple was highly active in the NAACP at the local and state levels along with the Tinners. Together, E.B. And Joseph Tinner formed the CCPL. Mary Ellen worked as the leading state recruiter for the eventual branch of the NAACP that the CCPL became. (Courtesy of the Henderson Family Collection.)

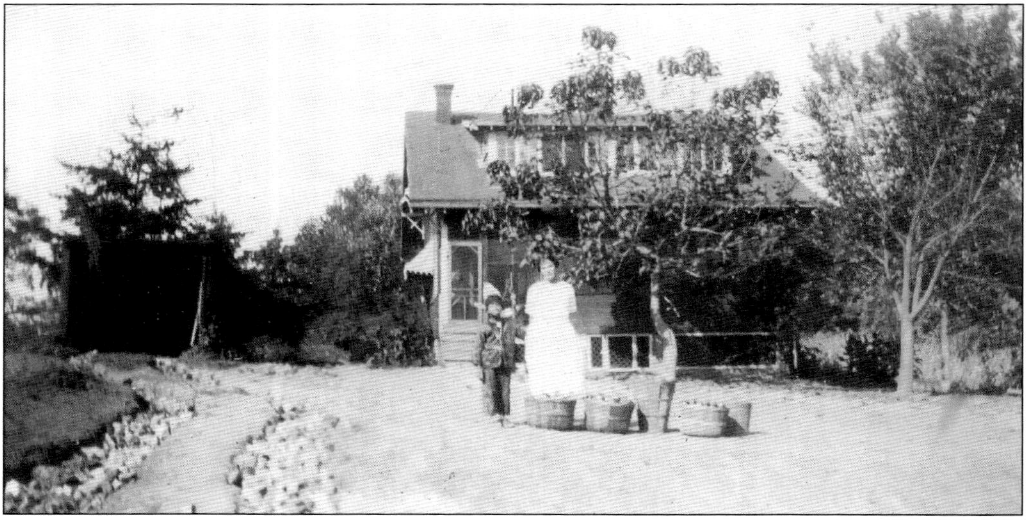

Due to their activism, the Hendersons became the target of threatening phone calls, letters, and a burning cross on their front lawn. Despite the threats against them, their efforts not only affected their community but also helped shape the nation. Mary Ellen was principal of the Falls Church Negro School and later the James Lee Elementary School, which provided quality education to Falls Church–area minority students until local schools were desegregated. Older pupils were bused to school in Manassas. E.B. and Mary Ellen bought and moved into this Sears kit house on land on South Maple Avenue in Falls Church where they raised their two sons. At one point, the house had a barn a distance behind it. Lee Highway was built between the house and barn, so E.B. moved the house closer to Maple Avenue and added a carport. (Both, courtesy of the Henderson Family Collection.)

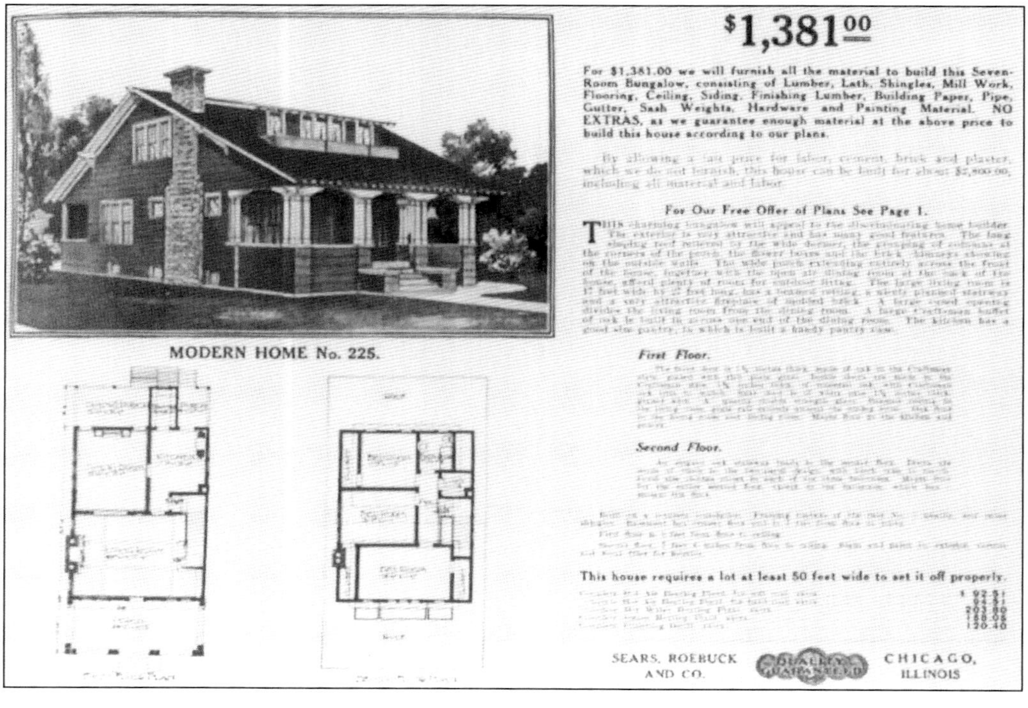

Five

Village to Town to City

Pastoral tobacco plantations on hundreds of acres of British-granted land patents slowly gave way to divisions of property into smaller farms as the initial families settled into Falls Church. The community growing up around the brick church and Wren's Tavern bonded. Still relatively sparsely populated through the Civil War, families began finding Falls Church a highly desirable location to settle in after the war, including many soldiers who passed through the town during their tours.

Federal employees who wanted to live outside the boundaries of Washington, DC, saw Falls Church as the perfect country village full of fresh air and abundant trees on gently rolling hillsides, ideal for residences and close enough to get to their jobs. The commuter suburb began evolving around that era. As the community grew, so did the yearning for its own governing body separate from Fairfax County, particularly since the population in Falls Church outnumbered that of any other Fairfax community at one point. Several characters stand out as the anchors and catalysts in Falls Church's path to independence, namely Joseph S. Riley and Merton Church.

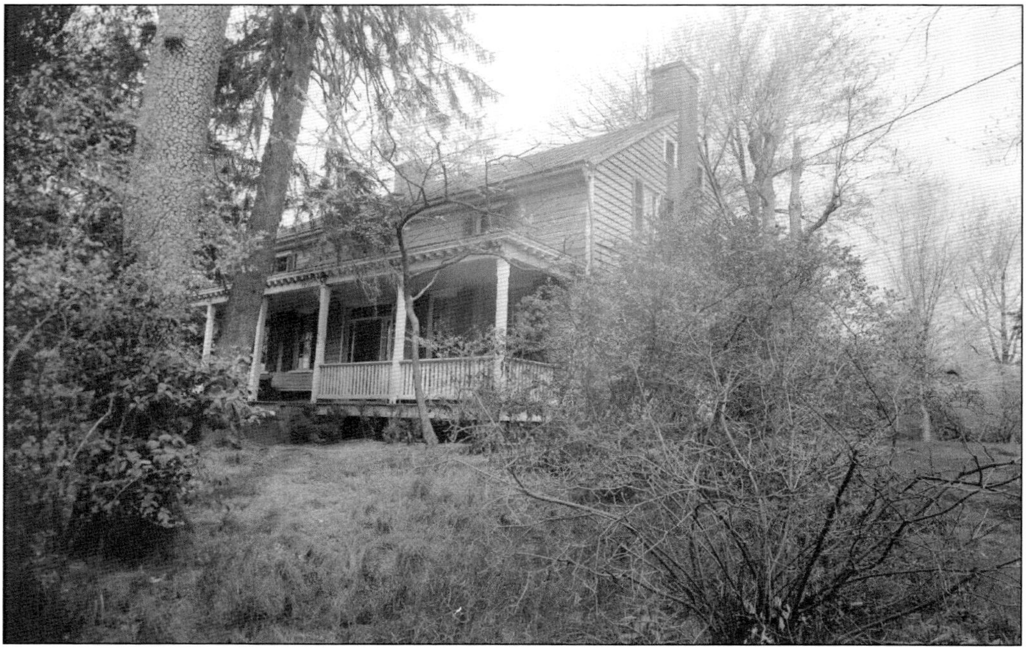

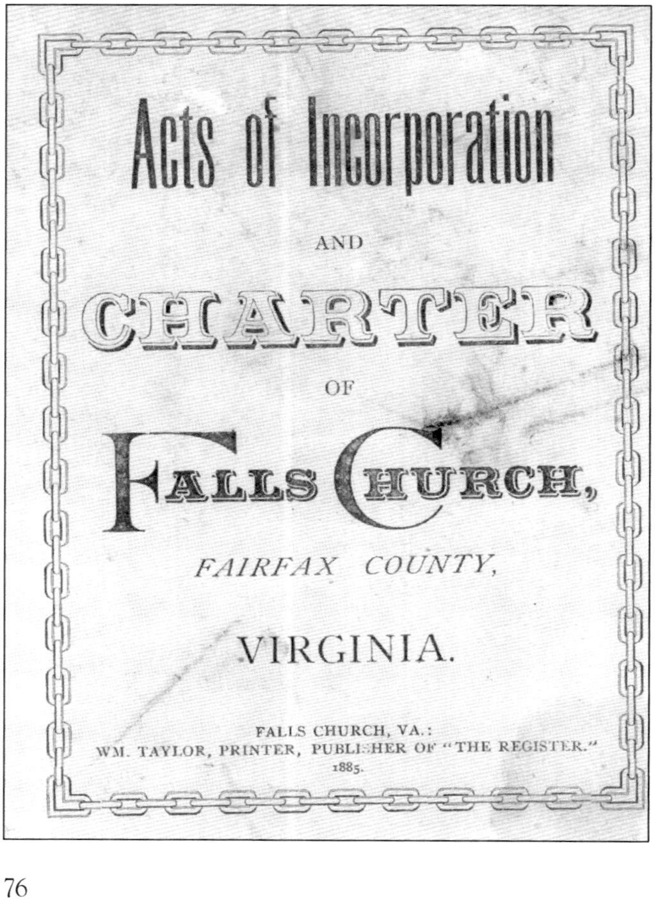

Acts of Incorporation

AND

CHARTER

OF

FALLS CHURCH,

FAIRFAX COUNTY,

VIRGINIA.

FALLS CHURCH, VA.:
WM. TAYLOR, PRINTER, PUBLISHER OF "THE REGISTER."
1885.

Joseph S. Riley of Cherry Hill Farm is widely credited with the incorporation of Falls Church as a town in 1875. Riley traveled to Richmond on his own dime to usher the act successfully through the legislature. Riley was also appointed to the first town council along with Isaac Crossman, Joseph Edward Birch, George Ives, and others. The Acts of Incorporation in 1875 outlined the boundaries of the newly formed town and included land south of Lee Highway, then known as the "colored settlement." In 1887, the township of Falls Church retroceded that land back to Fairfax County. Borders varied over time, shrinking the town's limits with the giving back of the colored land on the south side of town to Fairfax County and the eventual loss of East Falls Church to Arlington.

The office of the auditor sent letters to Joseph Riley, Esq., addressing one as "Dear Friend," to keep him apprised of the progress of the bid for incorporation. On April 14, 1875, he wrote, "The Charter of Falls Church was passed exactly in the form you devised and approved by the Governor on 30th March, 1875, and is a law from that date. I am very busy or I would send you a copy, but I repeat, it was passed in the exact shape you desired it." With education at the forefront of his priorities, G.A.C. Merrifield presented a petition signed by taxpayers to the council to levy a tax for the purpose of sustaining free public schools. A public meeting was held to devise a means of continuing the schools while being relieved from the Fairfax County tax for schools. Mayor George B. Ives appointed Riley to a committee on schools whose action led to the opening of the Jefferson Institute Elementary School.

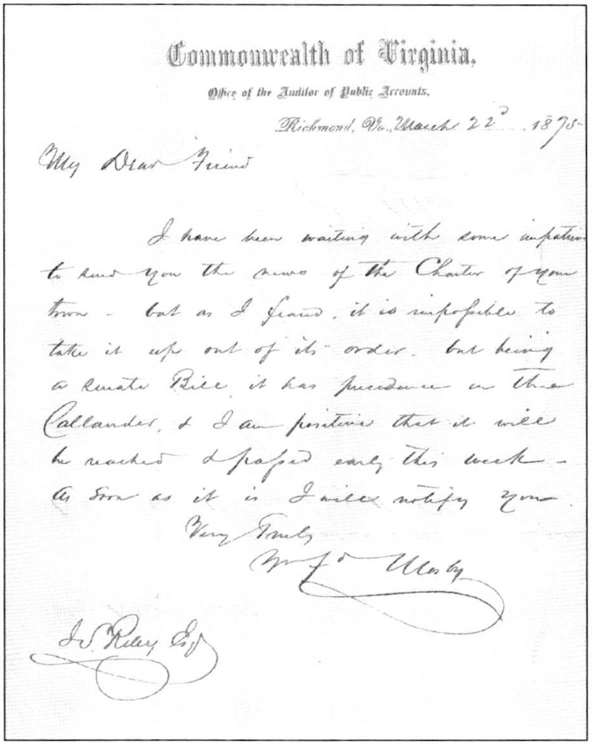

Commonwealth of Virginia,

Office of the Auditor of Public Accounts,

Richmond, Va., March 22d 1875

My Dear Friend

I have been waiting with some impatience to send you the news of the Charter of your town - but as I feared, it is impossible to take it up out of its order. but being a Senate Bill, it has precedence in the Callander, & I am positive that it will be reached & passed early this week - As soon as it is I will notify you.

Very Truly

[illegible] Mosby

J. S. Riley Esq

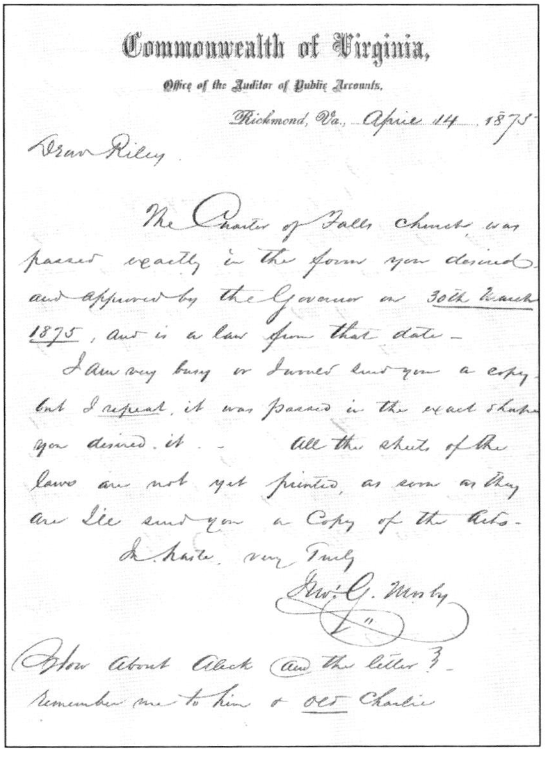

Commonwealth of Virginia,

Office of the Auditor of Public Accounts,

Richmond, Va., April 14 1875

Dear Riley.

The Charter of Falls Church was passed exactly in the form you desired and approved by the Governor on 30th March 1875, and is a law from that date -

I am very busy or I would send you a copy. but I repeat, it was passed in the exact shape you desired it. - All the sheets of the laws are not yet printed, as soon as they are I'll send you a Copy of the Acts.

In haste, very Truly

Jno. G. Mosby

How about Aleck and the letter? - remember me to him & Old Charlie

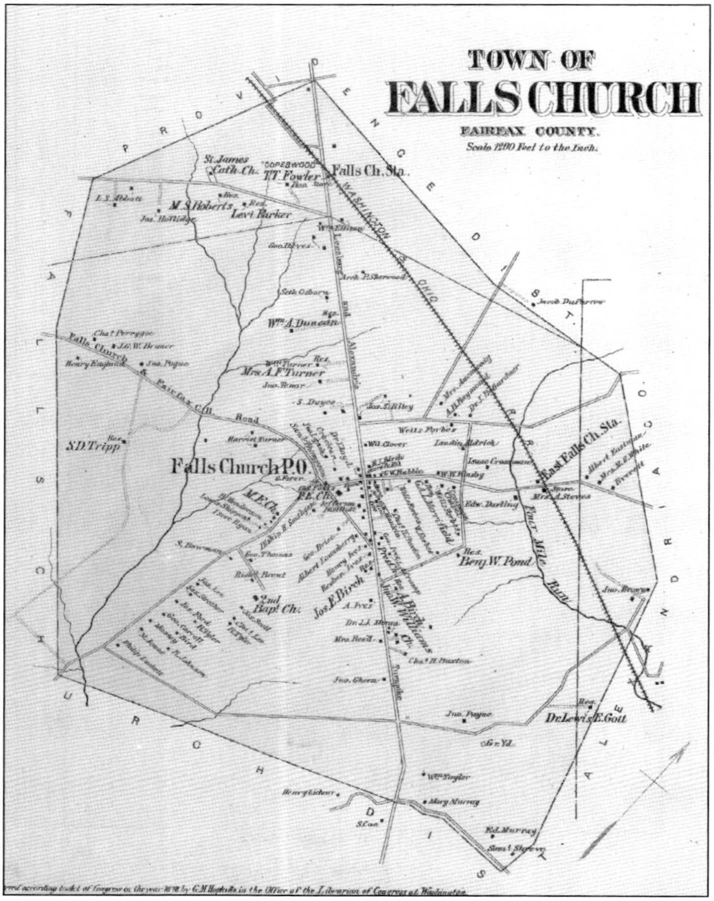

The G.M. Hopkins postal map of 1878 shows that during the burgeoning growth period after the Civil War, Falls Church had three postal stops. The boundaries of the town limits varied slightly over the years, and the African American section of town was gerrymandered out due to their Democratic leaning at one point, making the front of the Second Baptist Church in Falls Church and the property behind it outside the town limits. (LOC.)

Prior to 1849, Mount Hope, the home of Amzi Coe on South Oak Street, served as the early postal stop for the village before trains ran through town. Mail may have also been left at the Big Chimneys Tavern near The Falls Church.

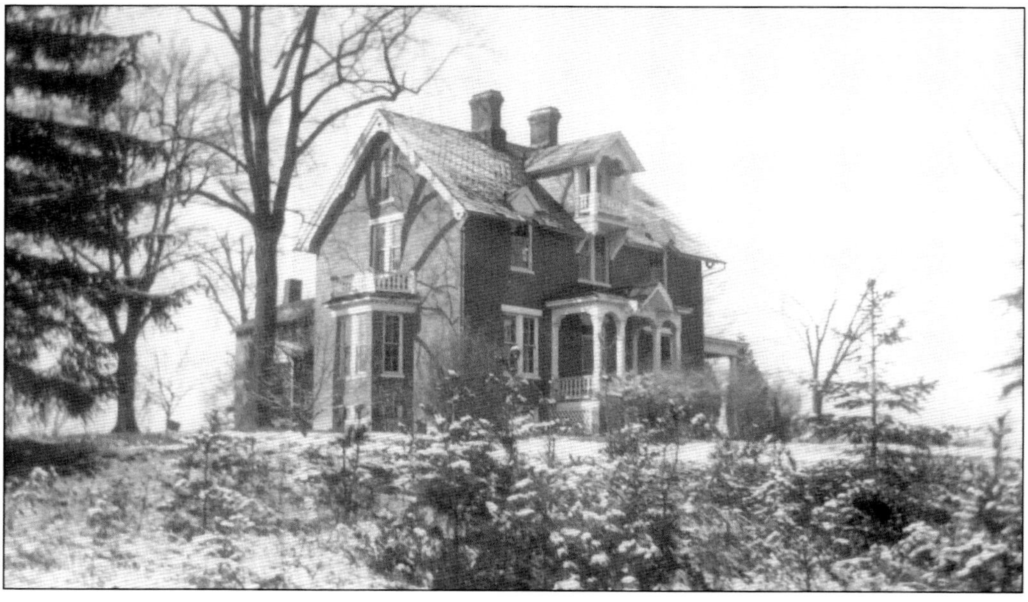

Concurrent with its opening service to Leesburg in 1861, the railroad received its first mail contract, the beginning of a regular service that—with a break during the Civil War—continued for 90 years. At first, the mail was carried only three days a week. Baggage and mail were held in a compartment of the car, while passengers rode elsewhere, as seen in this 1940 photograph. (NVRPA.)

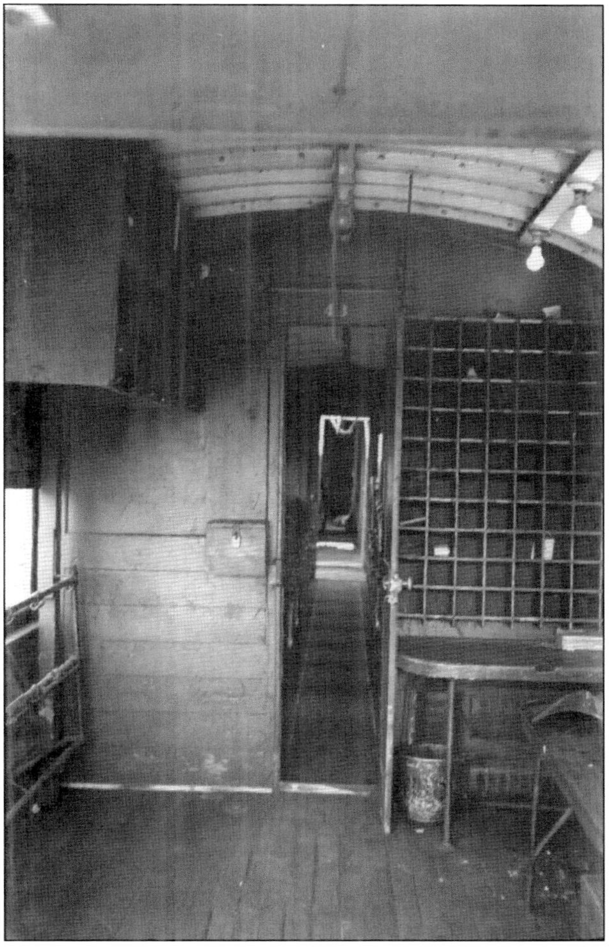

Residents, particularly on the west end of town, met the train to fetch their mail on a regular basis. The mail contract was canceled in 1951 and passenger fares were not sufficient to sustain the railway, leading to the ultimate shutdown of passenger service not long after this 1945 photograph of the US Mail Railway Post Office. (NVRPA.)

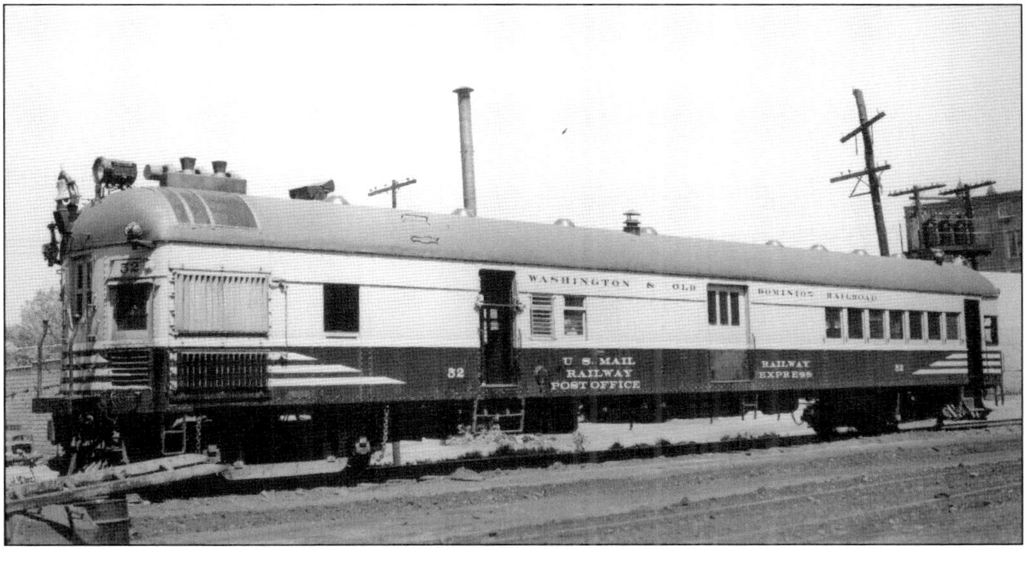

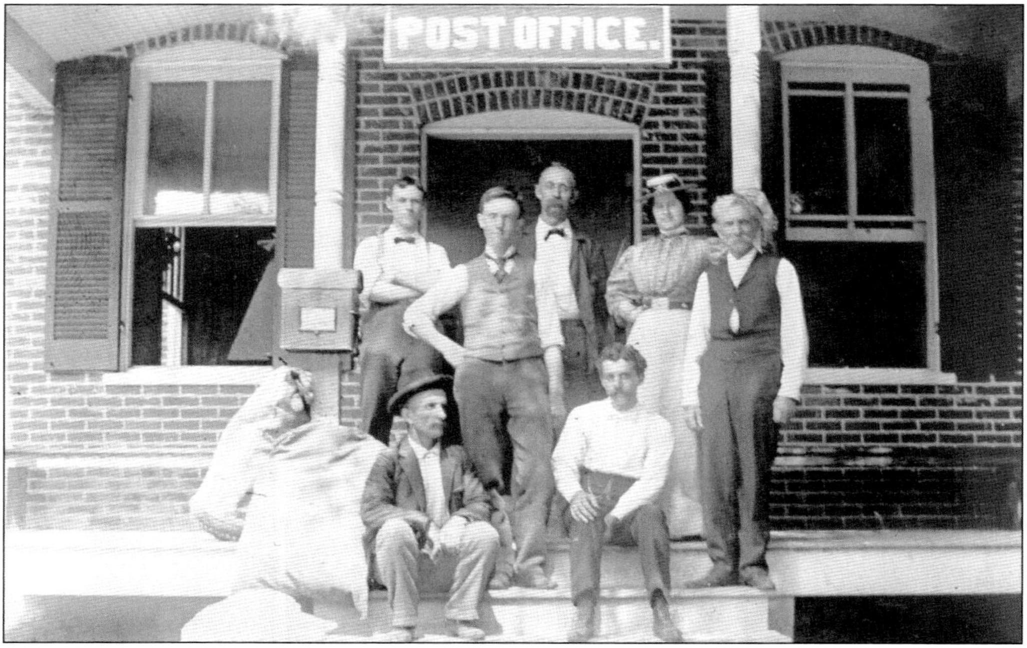

Post offices occupied various town businesses over the years, including the Star Tavern and Brown's Hardware. In 1895, Charles Mankin opened the first building erected solely for use as a post office. Ella Lynch served as assistant postmaster, as she had in Brown's Hardware. The above post office, seen in 1939, was in the 100 block of East Broad Street next to William Nathan Lynch's store.

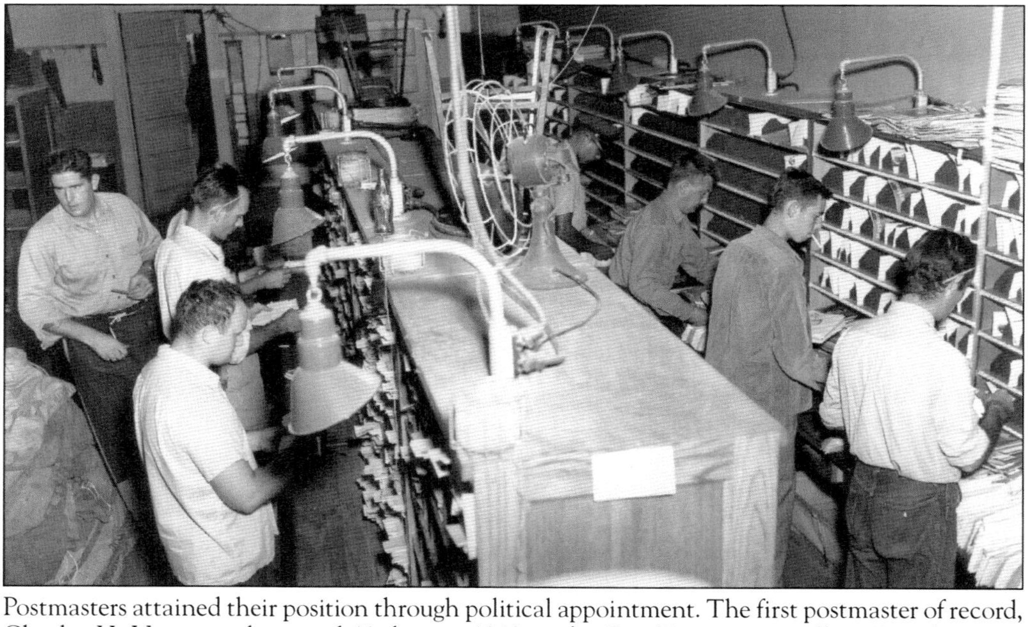

Postmasters attained their position through political appointment. The first postmaster of record, Charles H. Upton, only served 11 days in 1849 at the Star Tavern post office. Postal service was consolidated from three branches—West End, East Falls Church, and Town Center—in 1942. In 1952, the post office moved into quarters on West Broad Street, where it served 70,000 addresses.

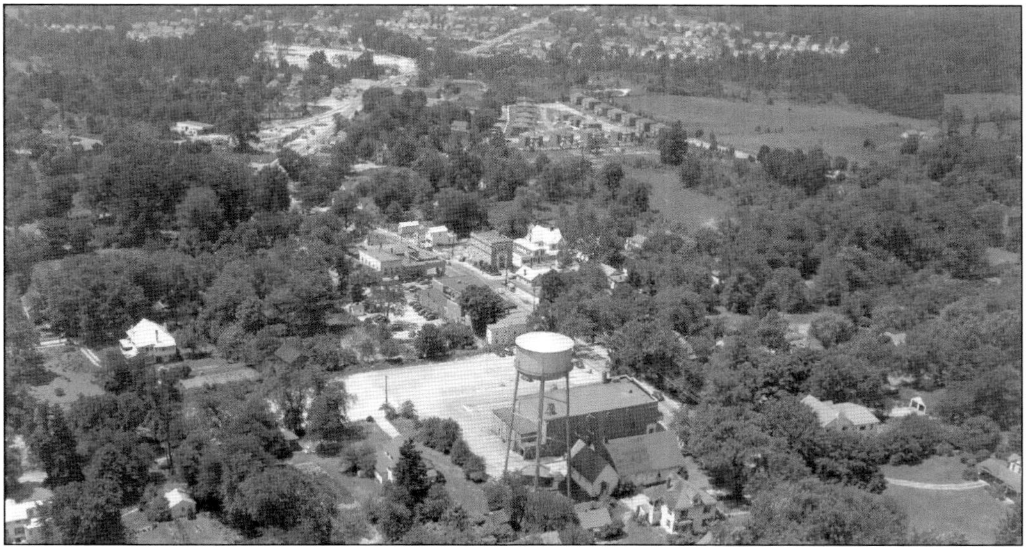

The town's population more than doubled between 1900 and 1930, from 1,007 to 2,109. Without a city water system, a drought plaguing the area ran most wells dry, so the mayor and council took the steps to provide the needed water from town-drilled wells into a new central piping system. The first of four wells was drilled around 1931 on a lot behind the old First Congregational Church where the town's first water storage tank was built. The town decorated the tank with a star during the winter holiday season each year. By the mid-1940s, water was piped to Falls Church and Fort Buffalo (Seven Corners) via a connection made with Arlington near Chain Bridge. Falls Church completed its own Potomac River crossing and a direct connection to the Dalecarlia treatment plant in Maryland in the 1950s, ensuring a steady supply of water to the city in the face of rapid growth following World War II.

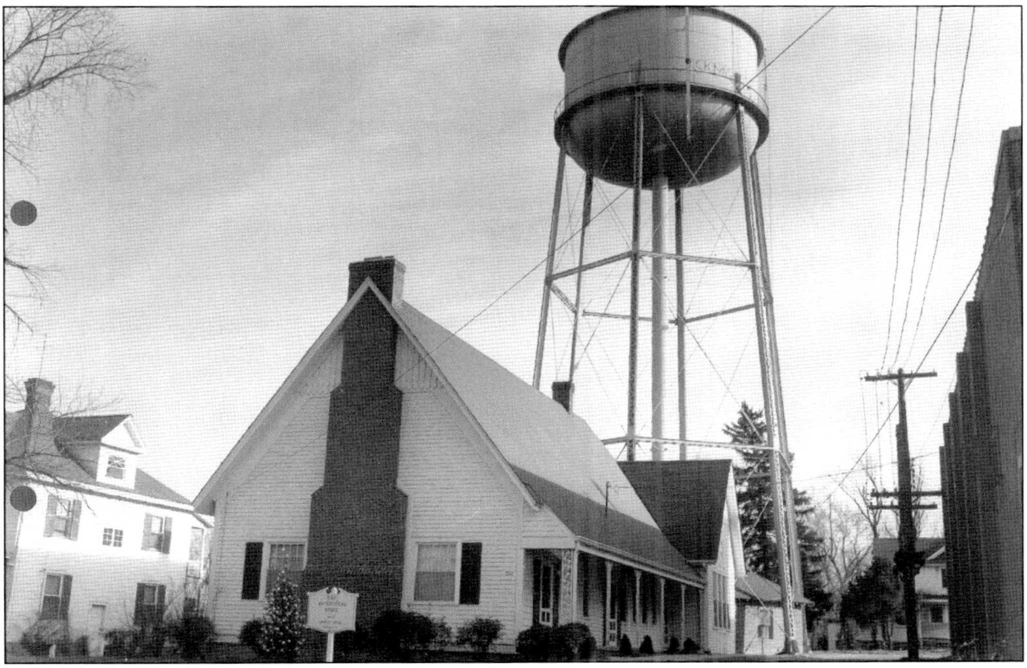

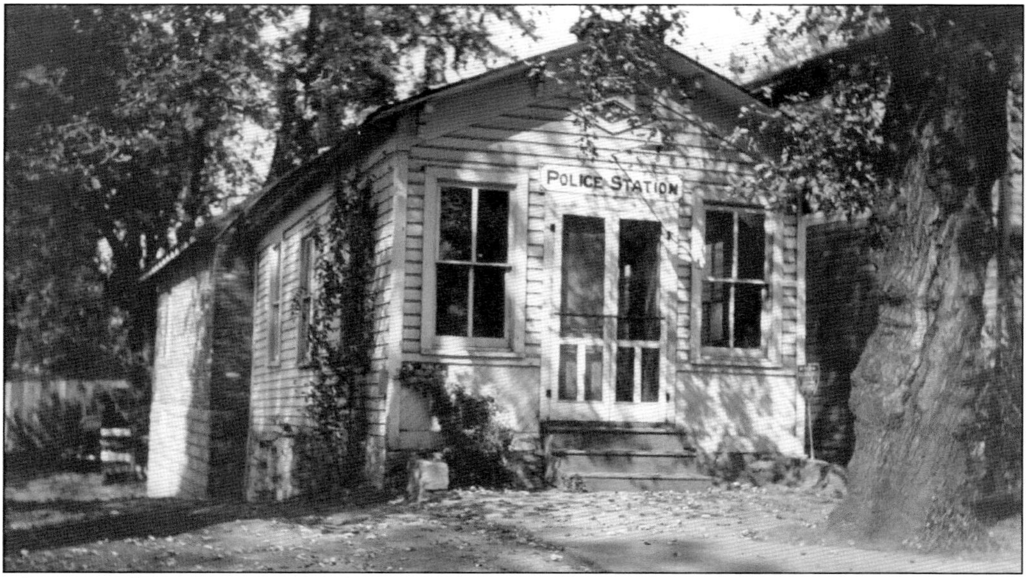

The tiny police station on South Washington Street in 1939 also served as a jail. The building was originally erected to house the municipal offices of the new town of Falls Church in 1875. At the time, the police force was completely comprised of Caucasian males. The more diverse police force is now based out of city hall.

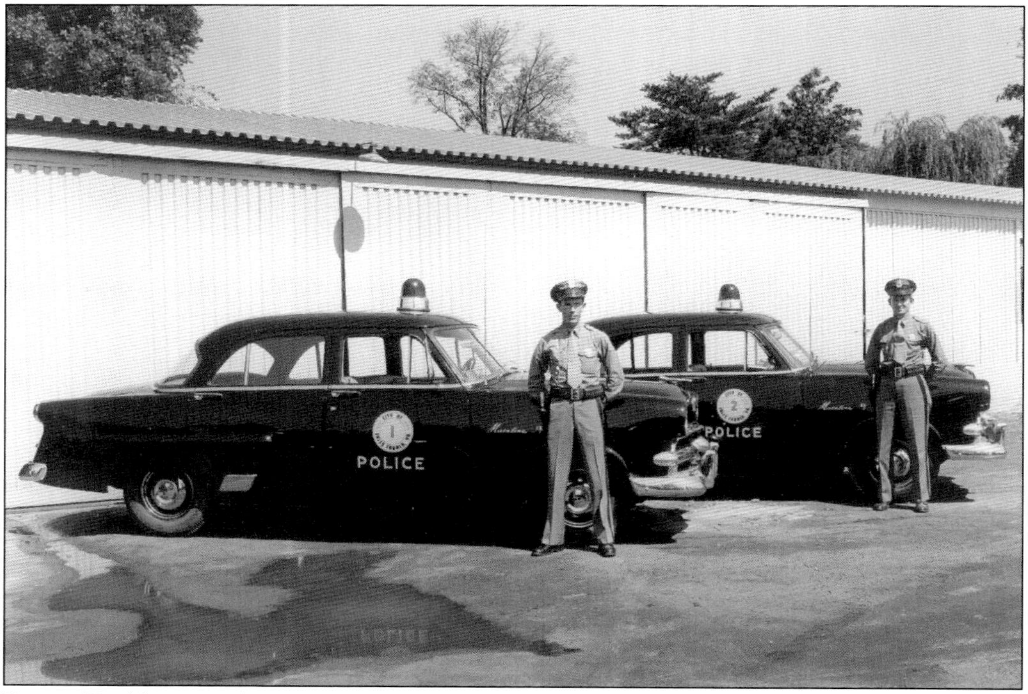

During World War II, the town council chartered a civilian defense committee to assist in managing the aftereffects of an enemy attack on Washington, including policing, traffic control, directing refugees, and reporting sabotage or espionage. Fairfax County's air raid warden headquarters were established in the Falls Church police station.

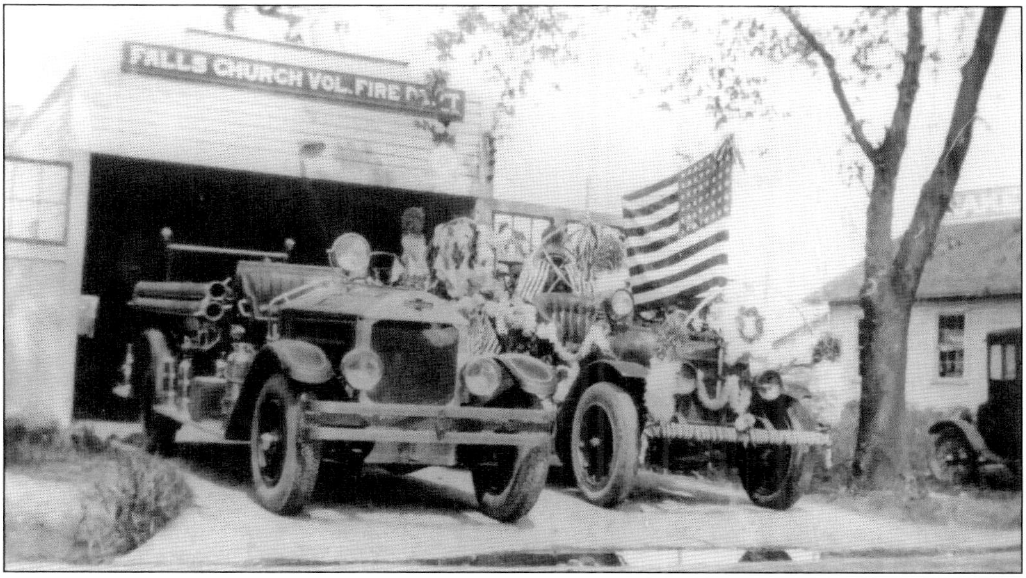

The fire department organized in 1898 with one small truck at the East Falls and West End sides of town and a larger truck in the center of the village. George T. Mankin served as the first ward fire warden. The Falls Church volunteer fire department was incorporated in 1925 and decked out for the Labor Day parade at the North Washington Street station in the 1930s.

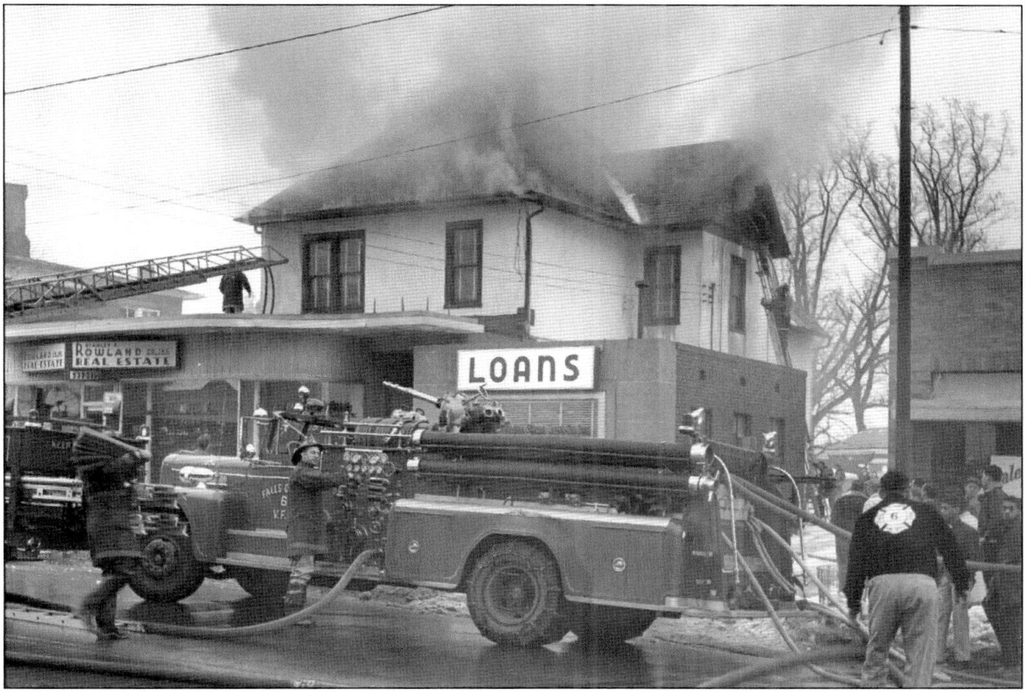

Doug Royston was born three days after his parents moved into their home on part of the subdivided Isaac Crossman property, where his father was Mrs. Crossman's carpenter. He joined the fire department in 1925 at the age of 15 and served as chief from 1931 to 1956. Here, the fire department puts out the fire at the Rowland Realty office at 120 East Broad Street.

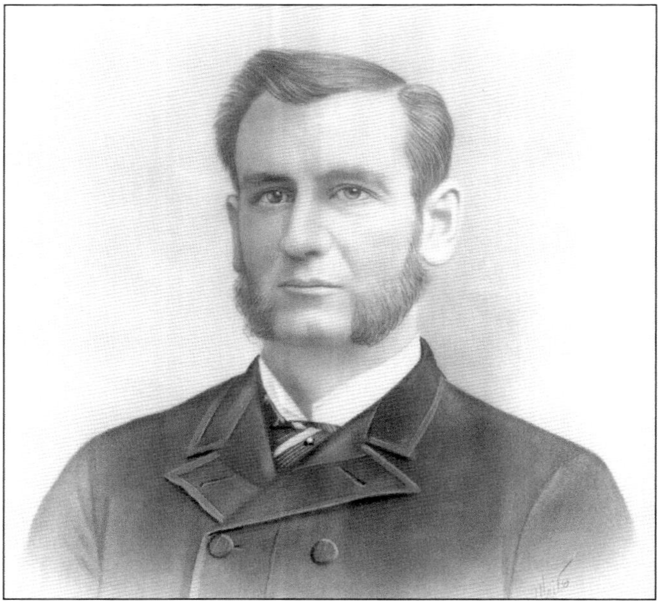

Merton Elbridge Church, born in Vermont in 1858, arrived in Virginia as a child with his mother and stepfather, George S. Spofford, whom his mother married after Church's father died serving in the Union army. He was about 32 in this photograph and beginning a diverse and accomplished career that impacted Falls Church immensely.

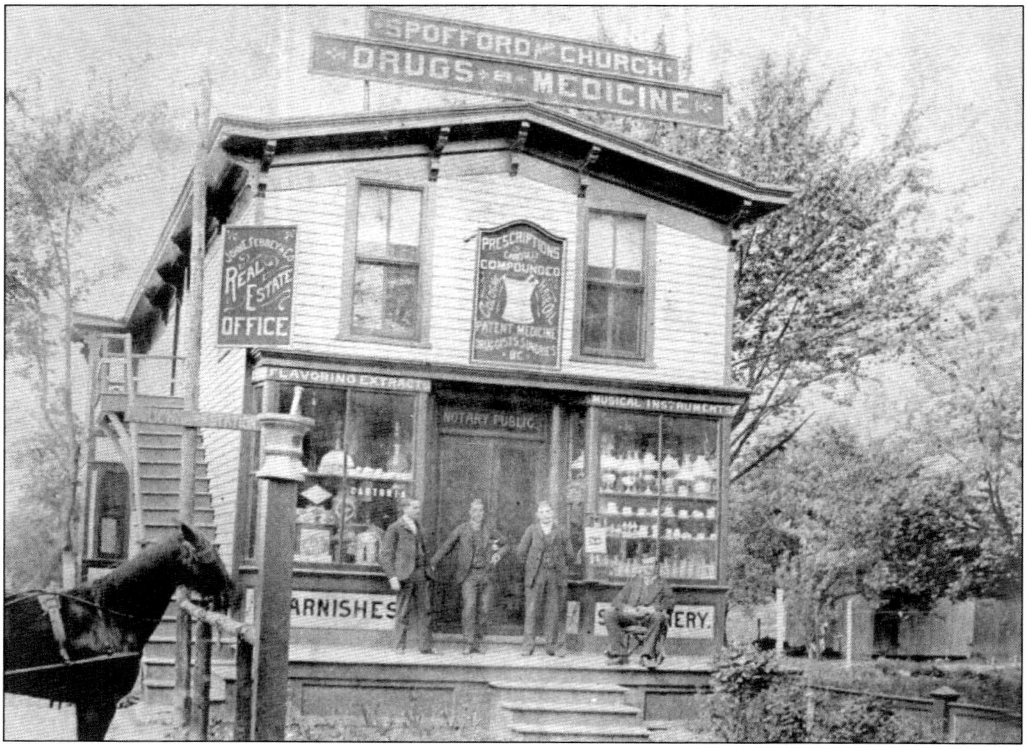

Church co-owned Spofford & Church Drugs on West Broad Street with his stepfather for 12 years. He trained several young pharmacists and was unanimously elected president of the state pharmaceutical association. He spring-boarded from there to become the town's leading businessman and innovator, helping to advance Falls Church in almost every facet of the infrastructure, from electricity to roads to telephones.

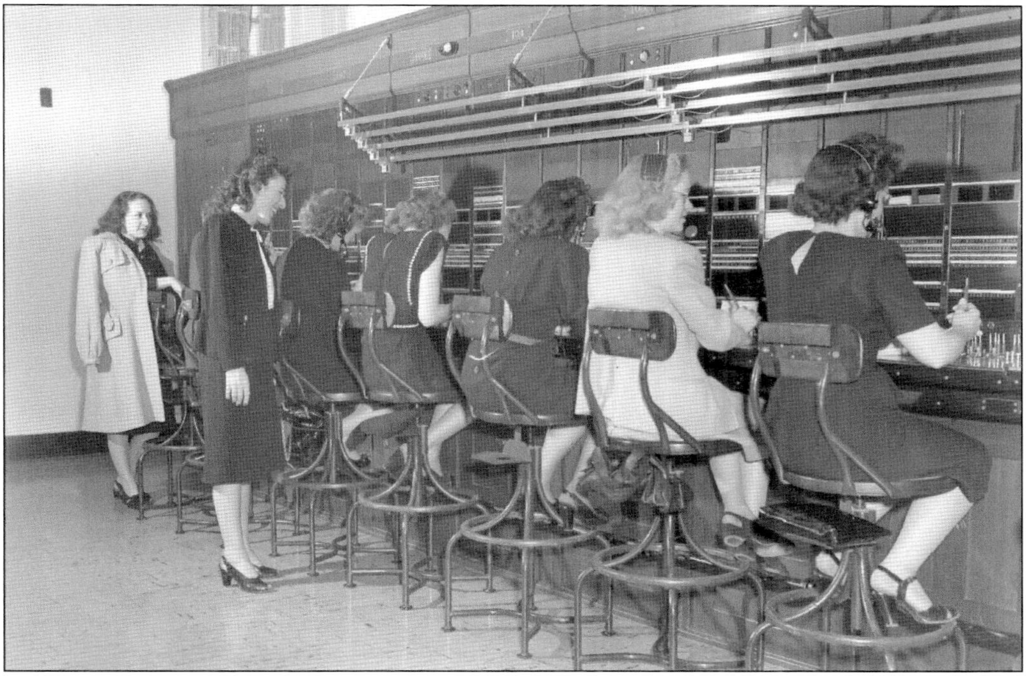

Falls Church Telephone Company was incorporated in 1888 by forward-thinking citizens including Robert Morrison, W.H. Doolittle, Schuyler Duryee, E.J. Northrup, Dr. T.M. Talbott, D.D. Munson, and Dr. Merton E. Church. Church developed a telephone system for Northern Virginia, extending over Fairfax and Alexandria Counties and reaching to Bluemont in the Blue Ridge Mountains, which he eventually sold to the Chesapeake & Potomac Telephone Company in 1916. In 1898, he lobbied the War Department to situate a training camp for 30,000 soldiers—Camp Alger—just outside of town by promising to extend the telephone and telegraph wires to the camp. In 1904, Church was the editor of the town's one weekly paper, the *Falls Church Monitor*, an officer of the Village Improvement Society, and treasurer of the Oakwood Cemetery Association.

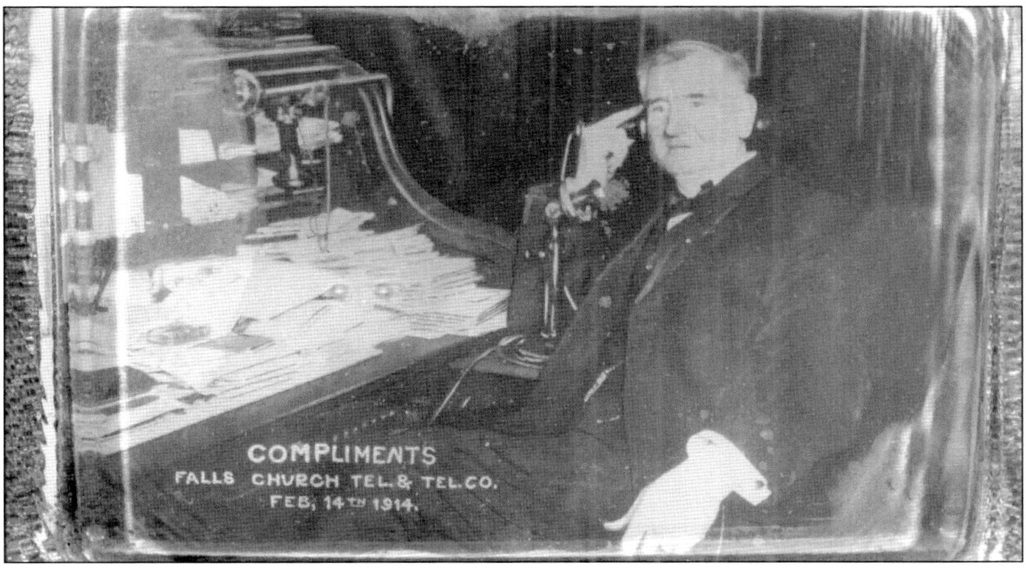

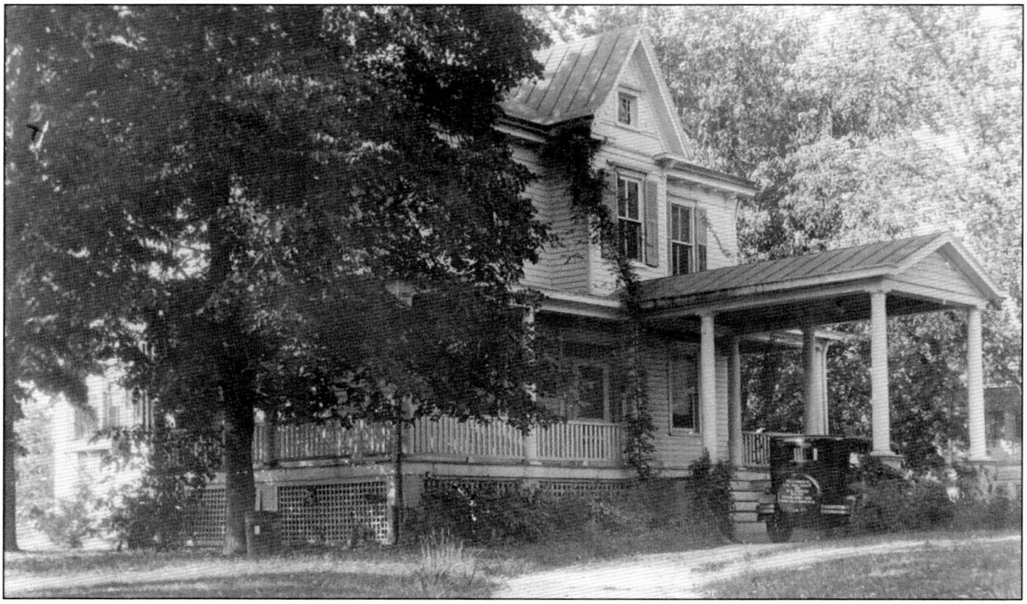

After the narrow, dirt Fairfax Courthouse Road, which was only reliable in dry weather, was turned into the paved present-day route of Lee Highway, real estate agents reported a 1,000-percent increase in sales and a 100-percent increase in the value of property along the new highway. Merton E. Church, with no prior experience, went into the real estate business himself, pioneering the novelty of auto advertising before it became mainstream.

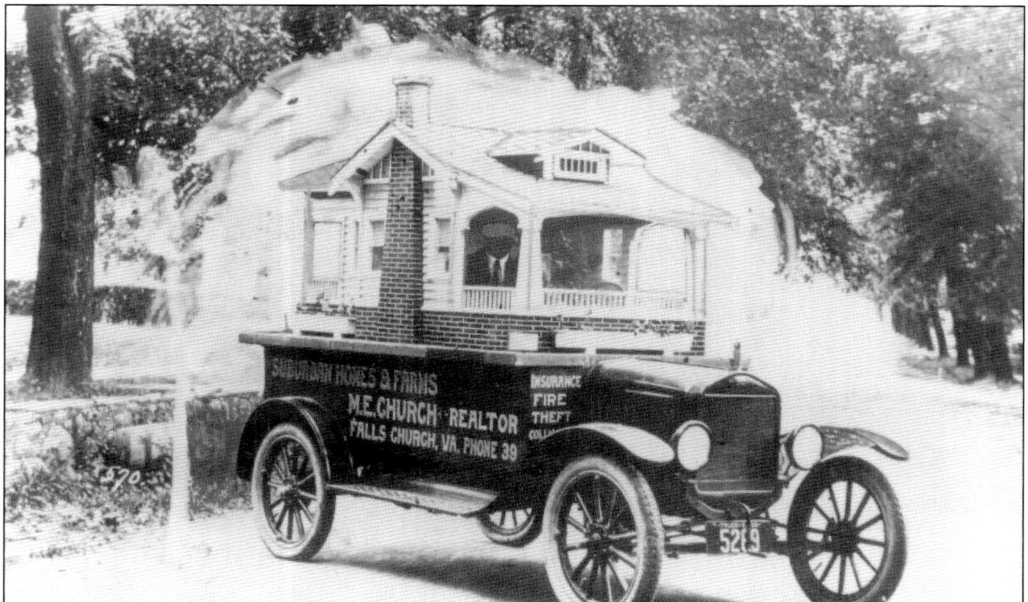

In 1918, with World War I over and improved mobility thanks to new roads and trains, Merton E. Church, the town banker, noted that with "the increased number of Government clerks and war activities in Washington the housing problem has become very acute. . . . Every house in Falls Church is rented and we could rent many more if we had them."

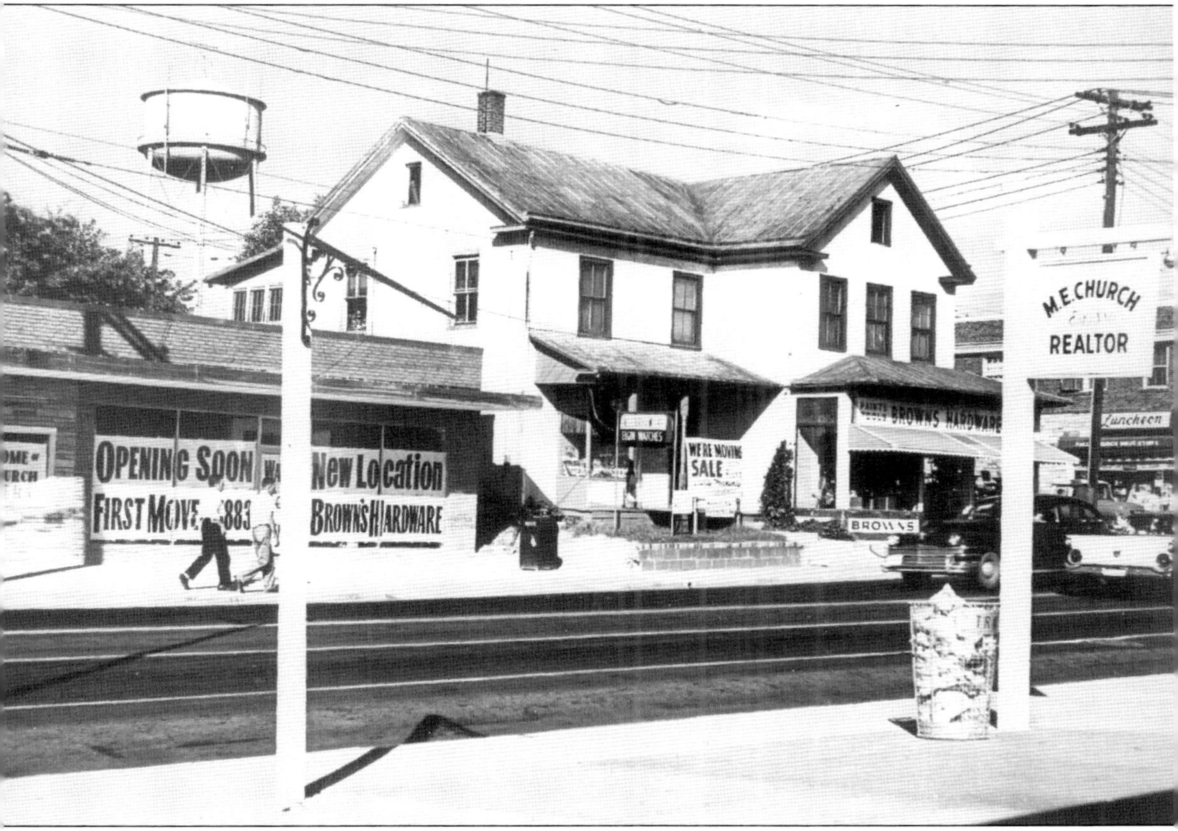

With its easy commute to Washington, Falls Church became a desirable locale for summer cottage visitors and federal employees. Lots south of the Rothsay station running down the east side of Woodland Road the length of Pennsylvania Avenue were sold in narrow 25-foot widths, with expectations of overnight cottages being built for weary train travelers. The cottages were never built, but the concept of the subdivision was not lost. The Sherwood family still owned a large tract of land around St. James Catholic Church north of Broad Street, and Merton Church headed the Falls Church Improvement Company, which managed the subdivision and development of the Sherwood property in 1891. Soon after, in another act of positive community involvement, Church saved the electric trolley line from insolvency.

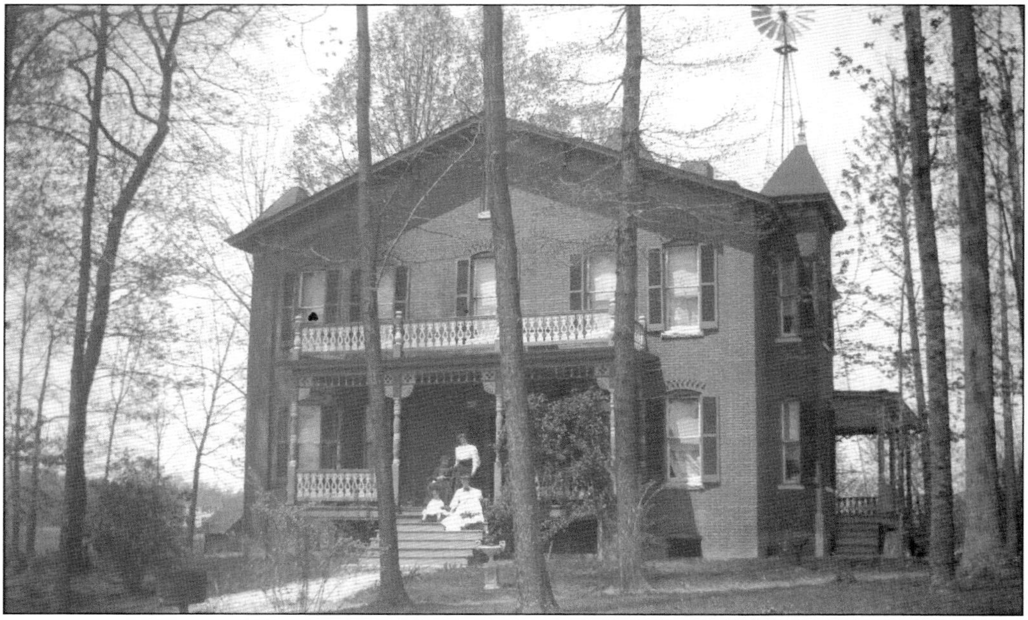

Jacob C. DePutron and Mary Sherwood DePutron were active in Falls Church before building their family home on 210 acres off Lincoln Avenue in 1893. Bricks were manufactured on the property for all but the front facade. Shortly after the city provided residents water, what is believed to be the first bathroom with indoor plumbing was installed on the second floor under a cistern in the attic. (Courtesy of Catherine Speakman.)

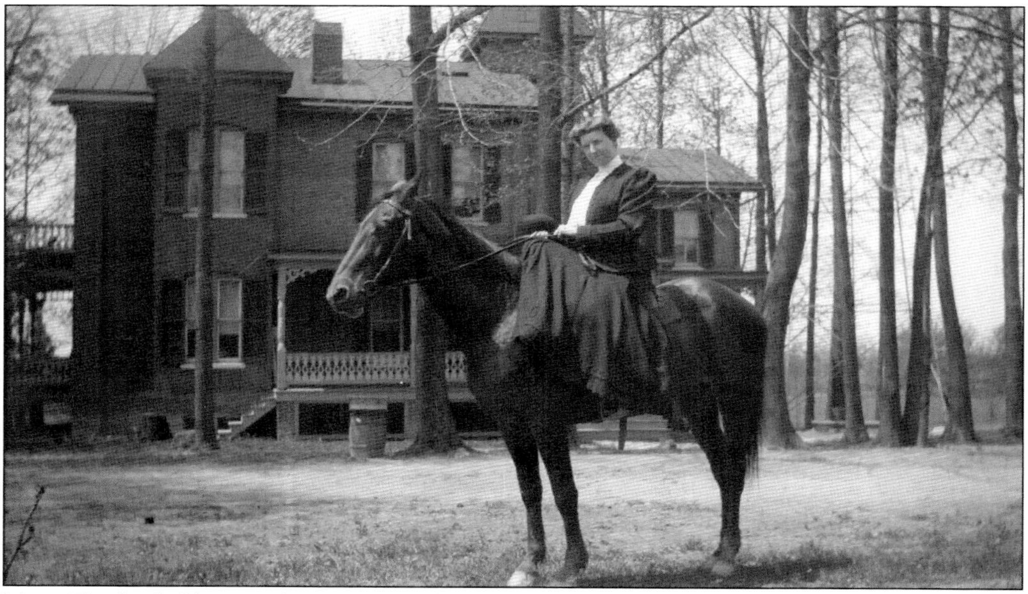

Mary Elizabeth Sherwood DePutron inherited the large tract of Sherwood property north of Broad Street and worked with Merton Church to subdivide and sell the property in lots as the first subdivision in Falls Church in 1891. Flyers were printed and distributed, and prospective buyers and real estate agents from all over arrived on the train for the successful sale of the lots. (Courtesy of Catherine Speakman.)

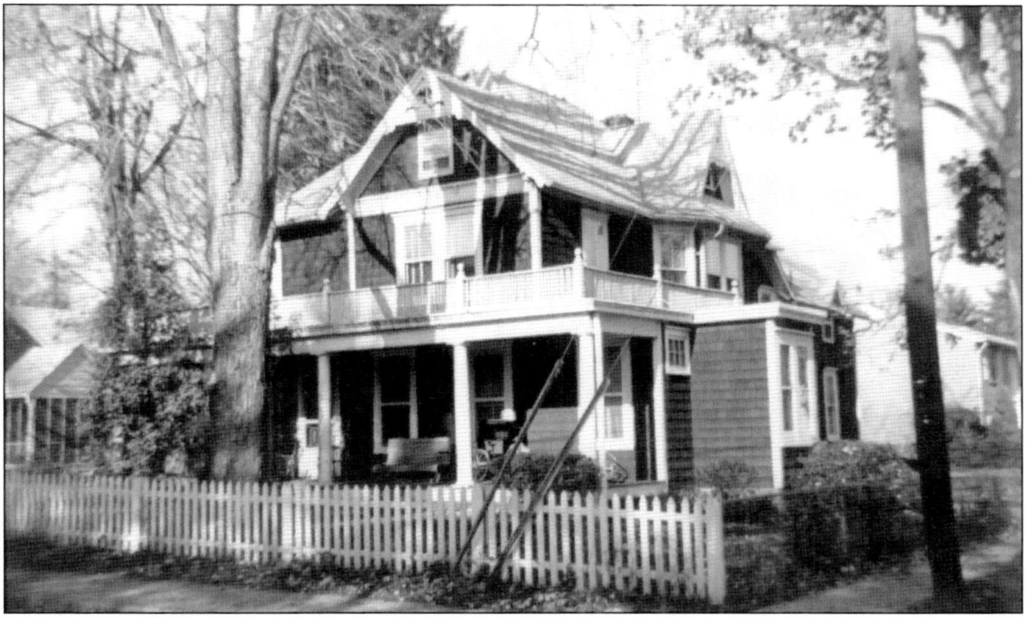

Judge Brophy believed his house at 900 Park Avenue, built in 1891, was the first house developed as part of Merton E. Church's Falls Church Improvement Society Sherwood subdivision. The house is on the corner of Park Avenue and Spring Street, across from the St. James Church.

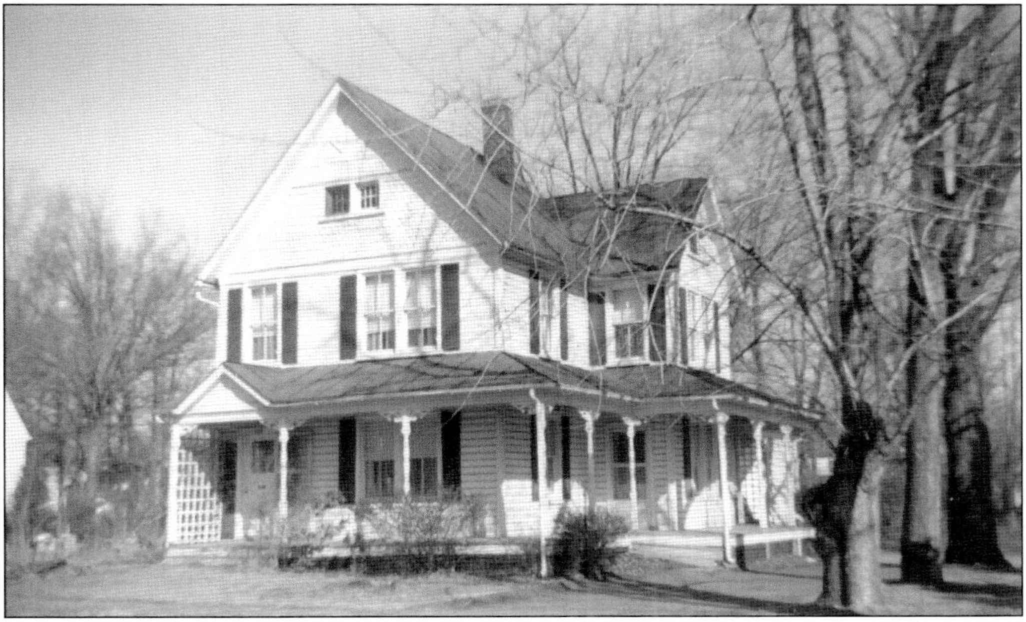

Washington attorney J.C. DePutron successfully defended E.B. Henderson's father, William, after an assault accusation on the trolley shortly after the Hendersons moved to Falls Church when a white segregationist demanded Henderson's seat, and DePutron was hanged in effigy at East Falls Church for his role in the case. After he divorced Mary Sherwood, DePutron bought two lots in the Sherwood subdivision at 502 North Oak Street and 704 Lincoln Avenue in 1905. He made 502 his home and remarried.

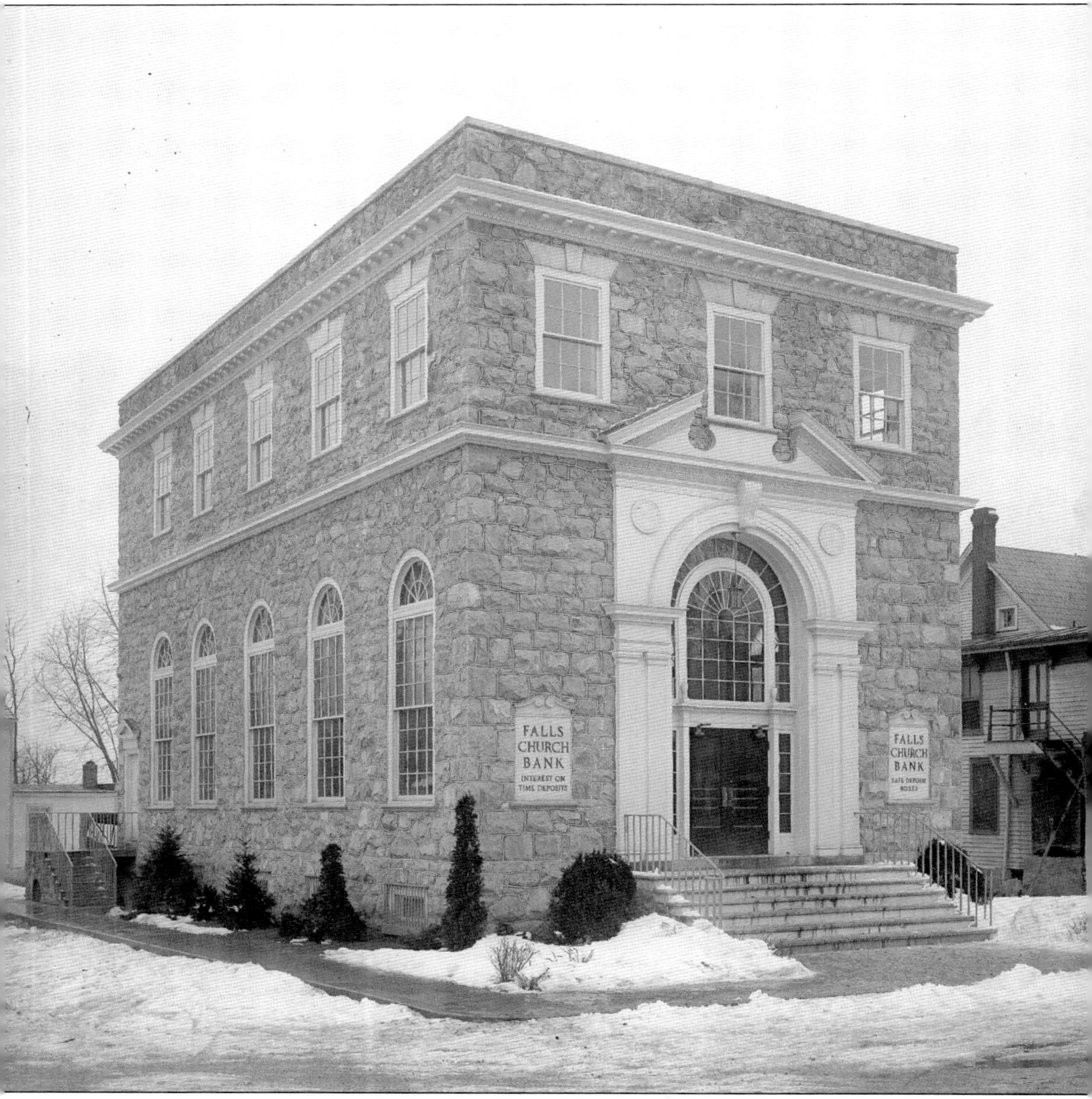

In 1911, the town council decided to electrify the town. The only response to the request for bids was made by Merton E. Church, general manager of the Arlington Electric Company. The council accepted his offer to buy the franchise for $10, and the city had electricity in 1912. As a banker, Church successfully sold Liberty Loans during World War I. In the 1920s, Church constructed the Falls Church Bank—the city's first—at the southwest corner of Broad and Washington Streets from native granite quarried locally on Tripps Run. He also loaned the money to build the new Second Baptist Church in 1924. Seeing the continued value of automobiles, he also built a gas station of the same quarried granite on the opposite side of South Washington Street. Since the roads were unfit for cars, Church headed a local good roads movement in the 1920s to have the new Lee Highway rerouted through Falls Church in order to boost the economy, leading the effort to privately fund its construction. (LOC.)

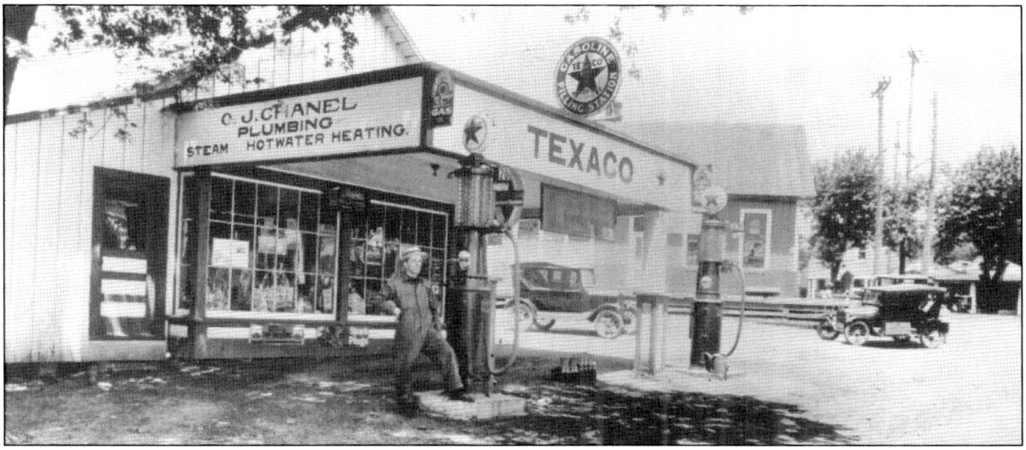

Frustrated and feeling that Fairfax County was not responsive to the educational needs of the town, Falls Church pushed further toward independence and separation from the county, but not without some preceding drama that hurt both parties in the long run. East Falls Church, a bustling business and residential district, first voiced the sentiment of separation from Falls Church in 1921. Falls Church and West Falls Church were in Fairfax County, and East Falls Church was in Arlington County but also bound to town mandates. Citing "intolerable confusion of overlapping governmental agencies," East Falls Church citizens successfully petitioned for permission to leave the town, officially withdrawing in 1936. Interestingly, the East Falls Church business district ended up largely eradicated by Interstate 66 in the 1970s. In 1948, Falls Church successfully earned independence from Fairfax County, and its charter was officially granted in 1950. (Above, NVRPA.)

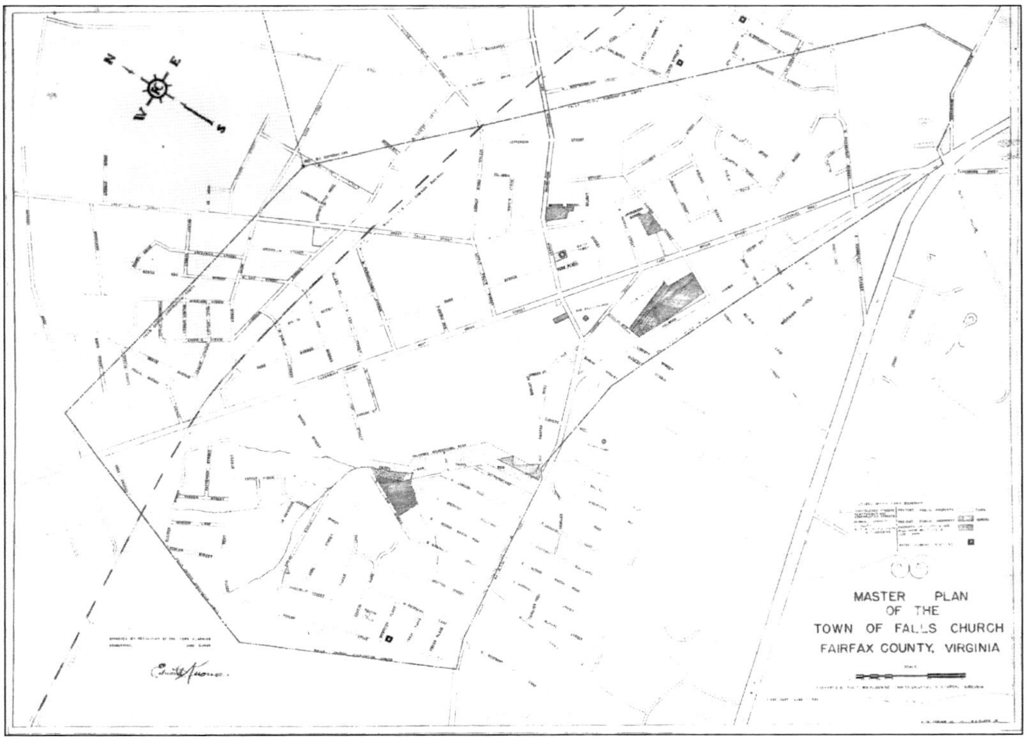

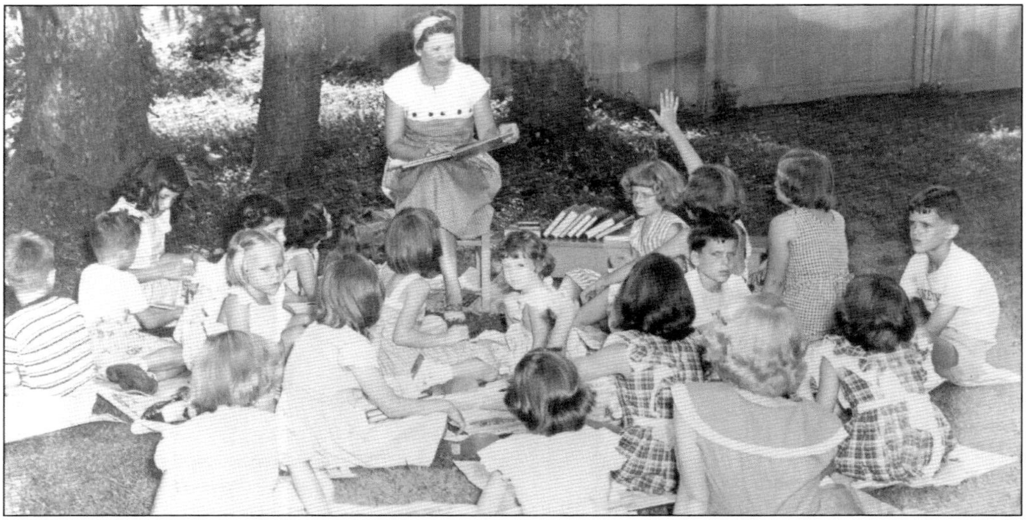

In 1899, shortly after her marriage to Samuel Styles, Mary Riley Styles, the daughter of Joseph S. Riley and Mary "Mollie" Edwards Pultz of Cherry Hill Farm, organized the Falls Church Library with a group of women. The first building was on Columbia Street near Washington Street, with George W. Hawxhurst serving as librarian. A frame farmhouse on West Broad at North West Streets housed the library in 1951. Here making the best of cramped facilities at the converted library, a librarian holds children's story time outside. Samuel Styles became a member of the town council and served on the school board for 15 years, while Mary Riley Styles was continually active maintaining a library in the city, giving unfailingly of her time and money. Her children, Elizabeth and Francis Styles, donated land across from their Cherry Hill farmhouse for the Falls Church Public Library, which opened in 1958.

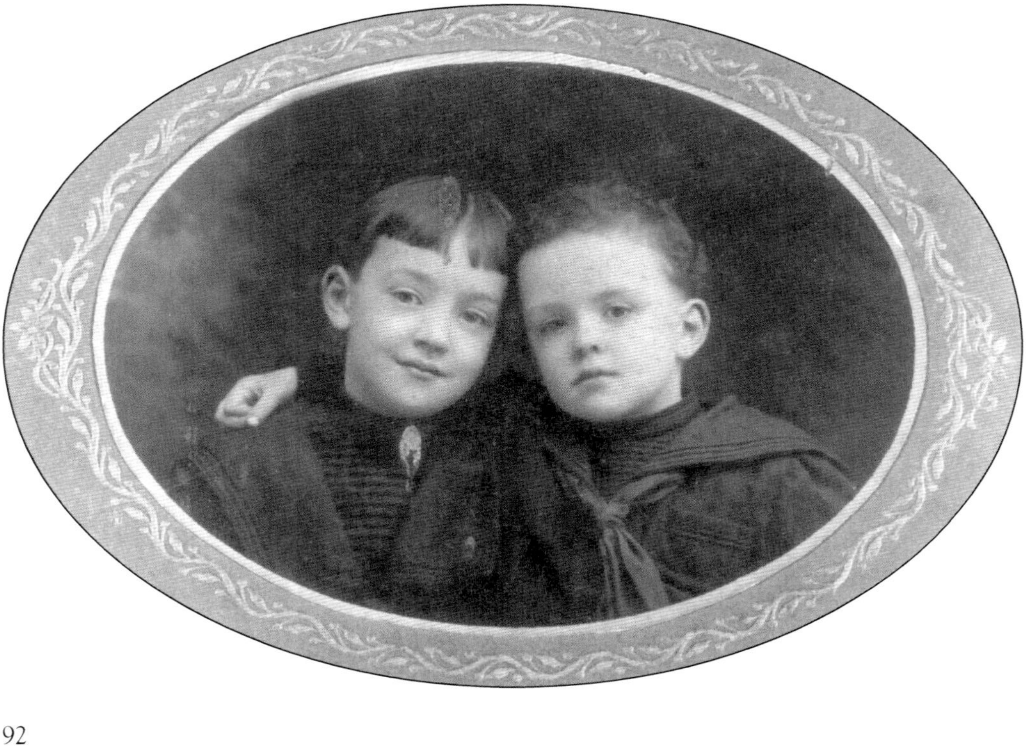

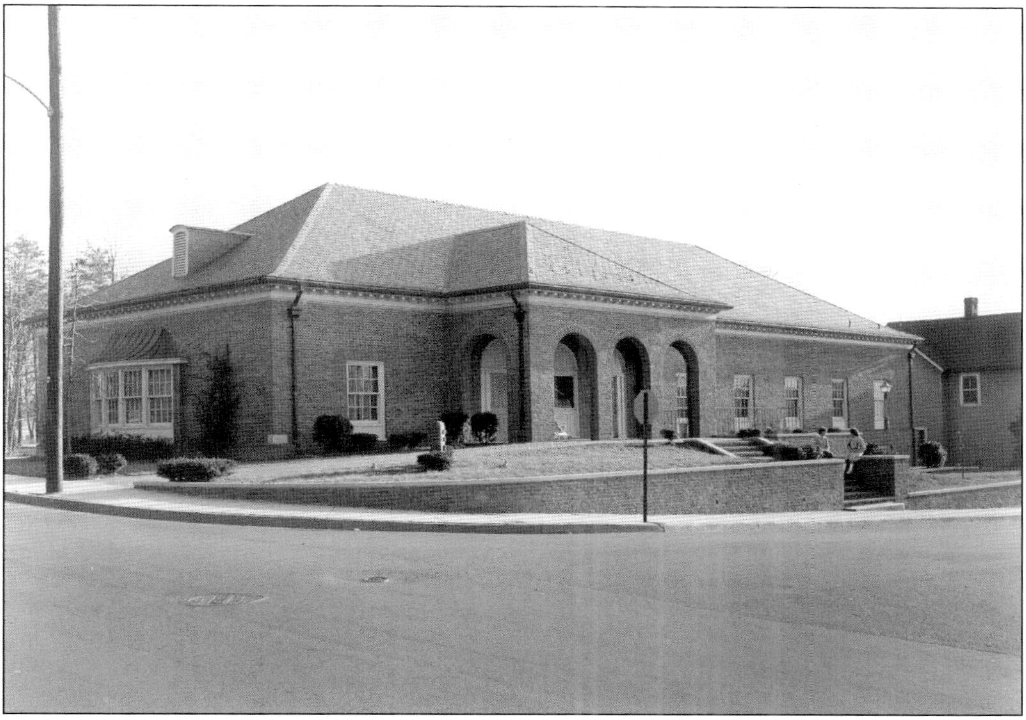

The new library built on land donated by Francis and Elizabeth Styles of Cherry Hill Farm was per their mother's express wish and named in her honor. The library was built in Georgian style to complement the foundation of the town, the Falls Church.

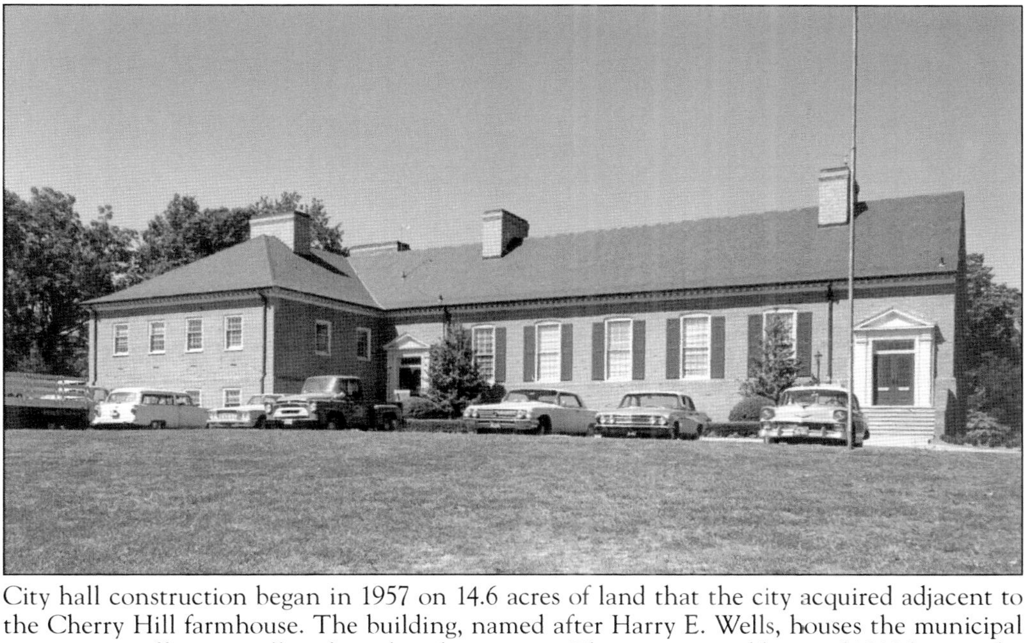

City hall construction began in 1957 on 14.6 acres of land that the city acquired adjacent to the Cherry Hill farmhouse. The building, named after Harry E. Wells, houses the municipal government offices as well as the police department. The east wing addition of 1982 houses the council chamber, circuit court, and administrative offices.

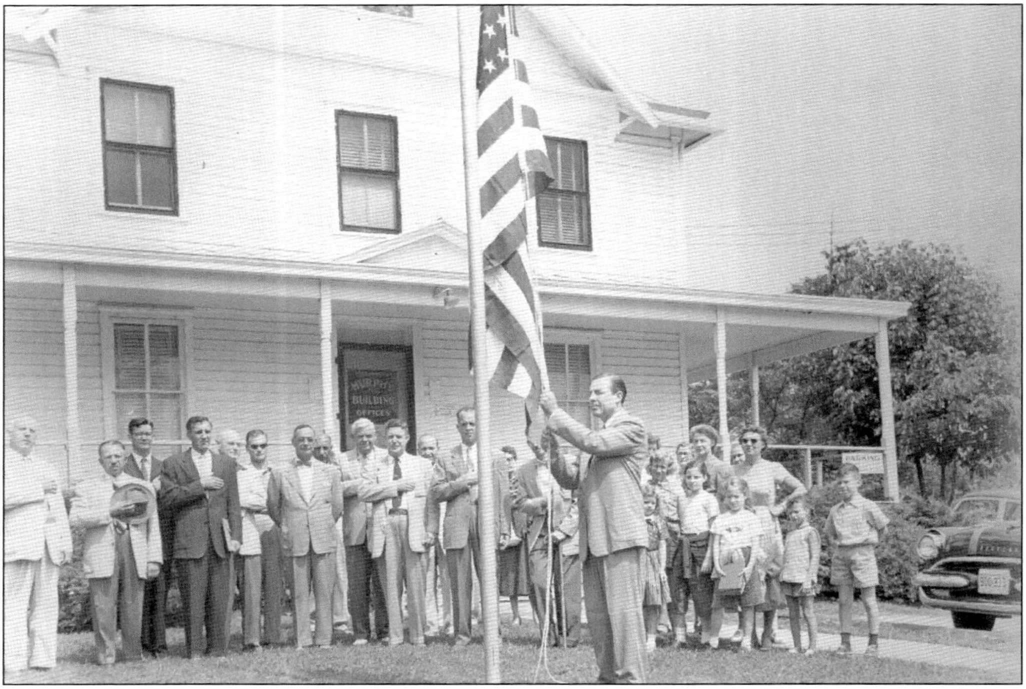

Much like the converted farmhouse housing the library prior to the land donation by the Riley-Styles family, the previous municipal offices were held in makeshift converted spaces such as the tiny police station on South Washington Street, the First Congregational Church building, and the Luttrell Murphy House on North Washington Street.

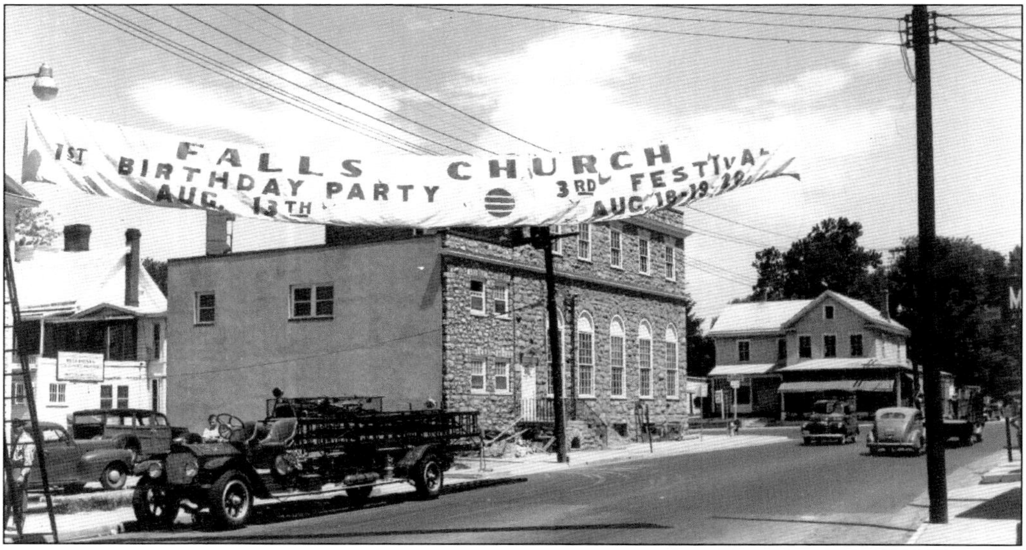

When the city celebrated its first birthday party as an independent jurisdiction, farm fields still ringed the town. A year later, the population was 7,535, almost triple the 2,576 population of a decade earlier. Despite continual growth at the residential and municipal levels, the base and character of the town had been solidified through the efforts of early residents who believed and worked for the future.

Six

EDUCATION

The first Falls Church school was reportedly an "Old Field" school, a simple one-room log cabin constructed on a tobacco field no longer capable of producing. Early residents also provided education to schoolchildren of the village inside their homes. Education of children, able and disabled, has always been a top priority for the leaders of Falls Church.

From the inception of the imposing Jefferson Institute in 1882, after the town incorporated, to the founding of Mattie Gundry's pioneering Virginia Training School for the mentally disabled, the foundation was laid to provide top-notch public and private schools to citizens. The St. James Catholic parish followed by founding its own wildly successful school for parishioners. Mary Ellen Henderson, for whom the current middle school is named, worked tirelessly to ensure the black community a stellar education prior to desegregation.

As the town grew, so did its award-winning schools. When Falls Church became an independent city following the 1948 charter, it extricated itself from sharing schools with Fairfax County. The school system created, based on the vision of those early founders, has become one of the most sought-after districts, making Falls Church an even more desirable location to live.

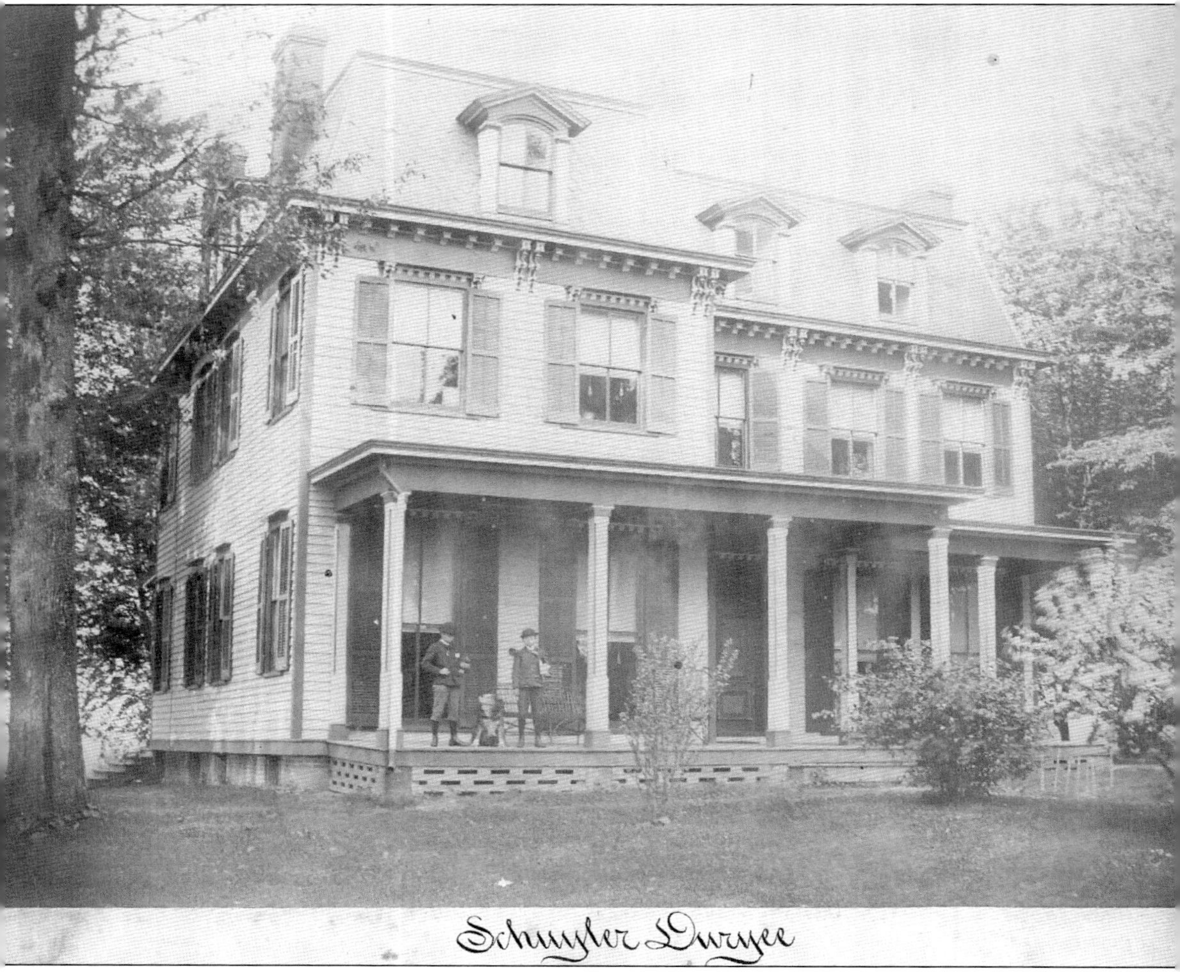

Mattie Gundry first started the Gun-Well School in 1893 at the rented Home Hill house on Lawton Street with her partner, Miss Weller. In 1899, Gundry purchased the Shuyler Duryee house in the 300 block of West Broad Street, enlarged the building, and developed a campus for the Virginia Training School, previously known as the Gundry Home & Training School for Feeble Minded, which she operated successfully for almost 50 years. She taught her mentally disadvantaged students useful knowledge and skills in order to live enriched lives and became well known for her leadership and research in national matters concerning mental handicaps. Gundry was elected to the town council along with Mrs. P.H. Smyth in 1921, before it was common for women to serve in the public sphere.

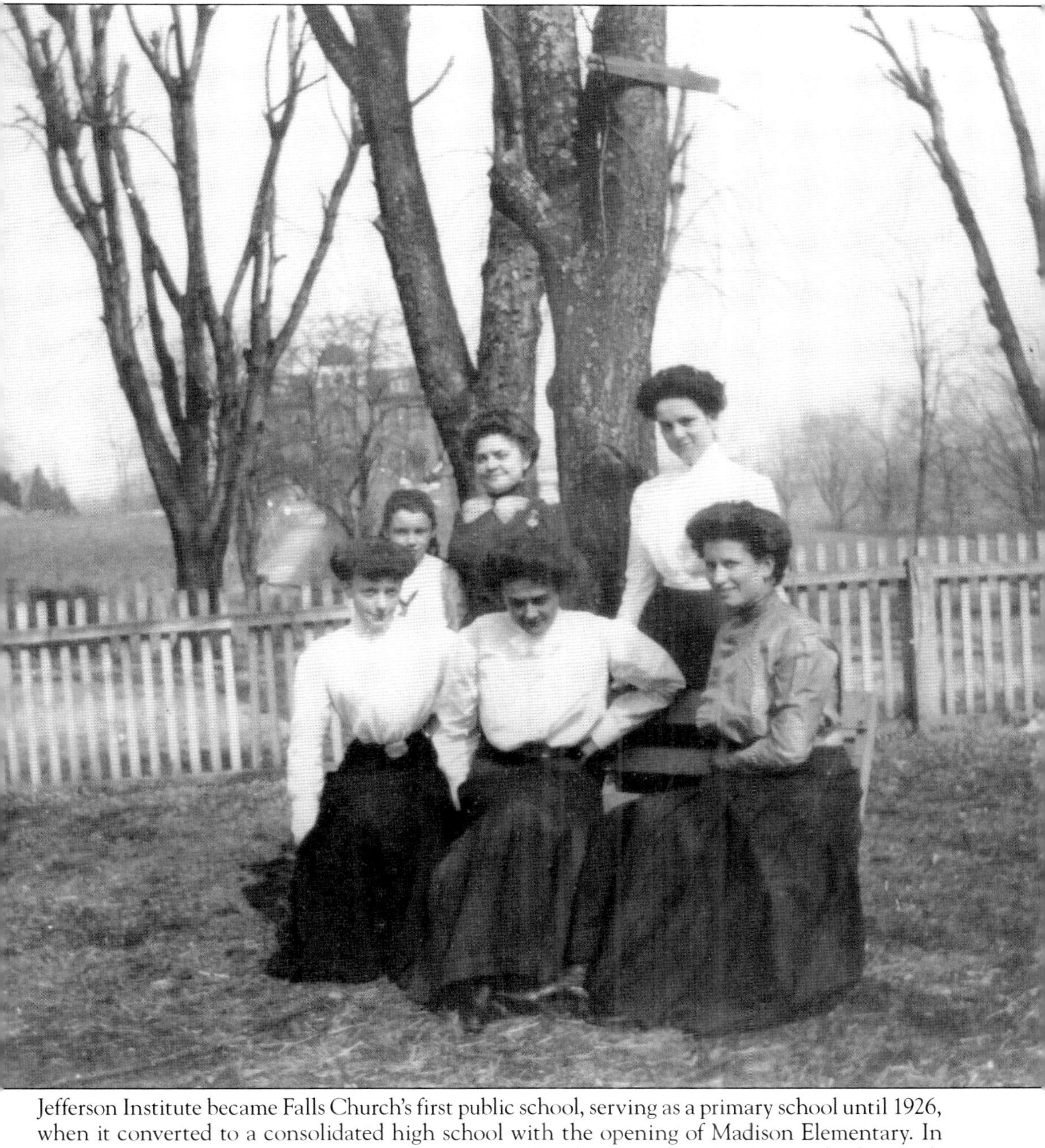

Jefferson Institute became Falls Church's first public school, serving as a primary school until 1926, when it converted to a consolidated high school with the opening of Madison Elementary. In 1945, it again became an elementary school when Falls Church High School opened. This Birch family photograph was taken with the Jefferson Institute in the background around 1910.

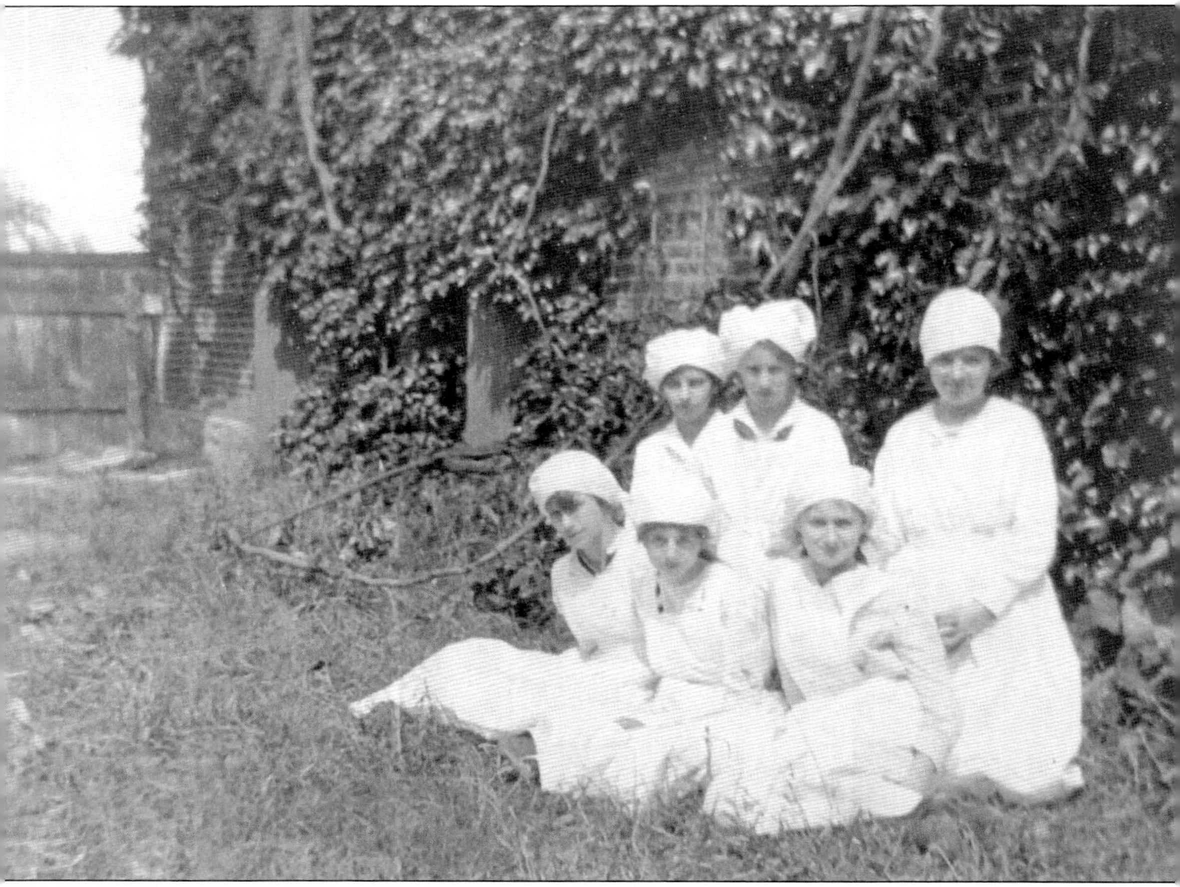

A Jefferson Institute cooking class poses outside the west wall of the school around 1917. The board fence divided the girls' play yard from the boys'. Marian Birch, seated in the front right, was the granddaughter of Joseph Birch, who donated the land for the school with the stipulation that it always be used for educational purposes.

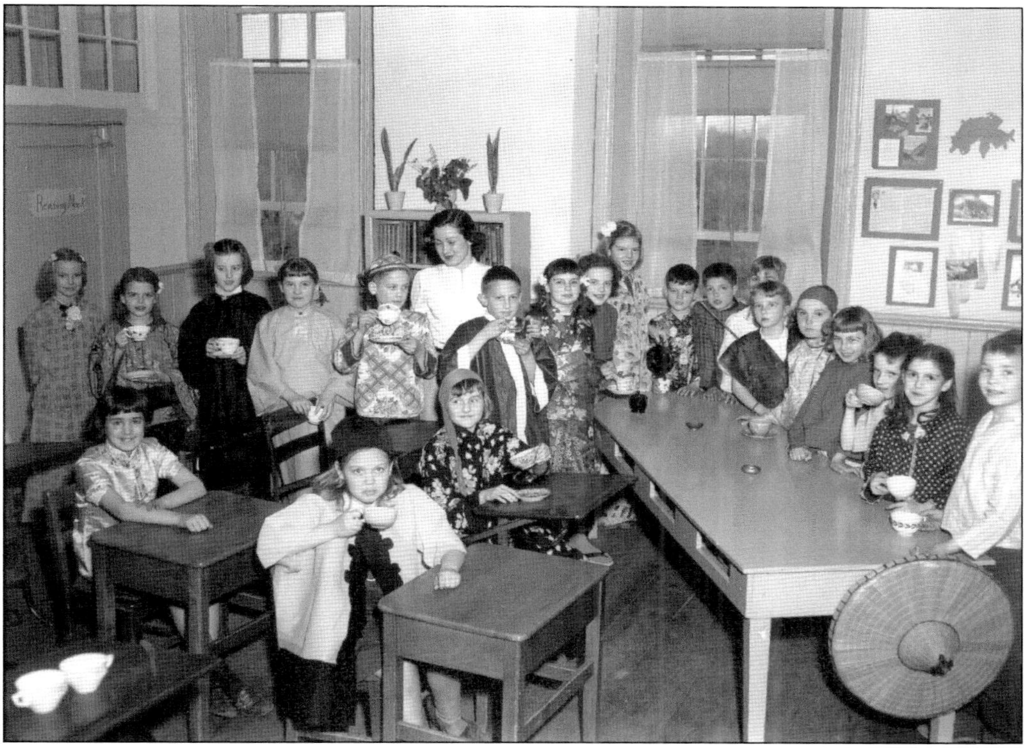

By 1949, Jefferson Institute became one of two city-owned public schools. Here, children enjoy a tea party in 1951, five years before the school was closed permanently. In 1958, the imposing two-story brick structure was torn down, cited as a fire hazard.

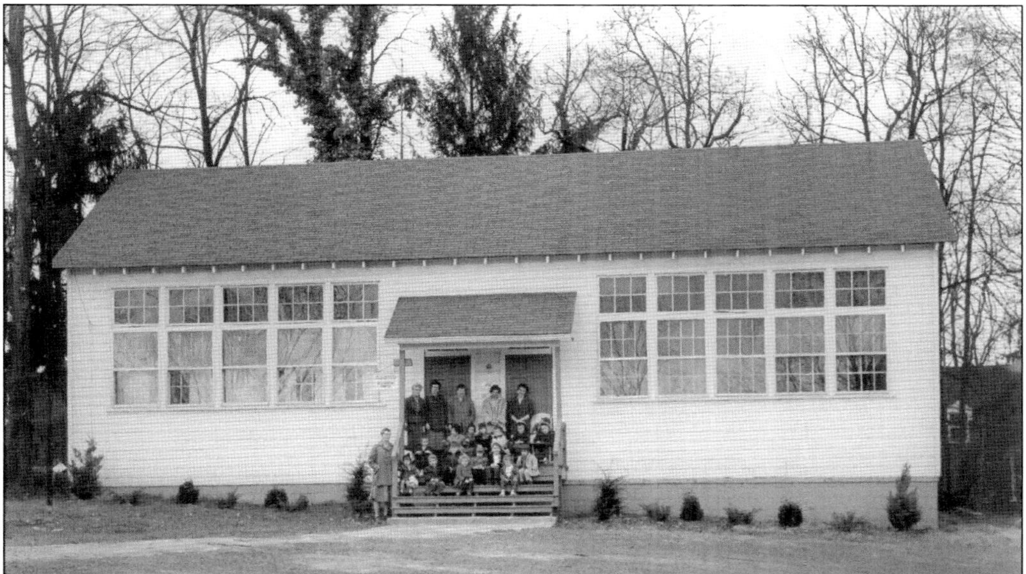

In the spirit of Mattie Gundry, the United Cerebral Palsy center continued on the grounds of the Jefferson Institute after its demolition. (MRSPL 1956, Porter.)

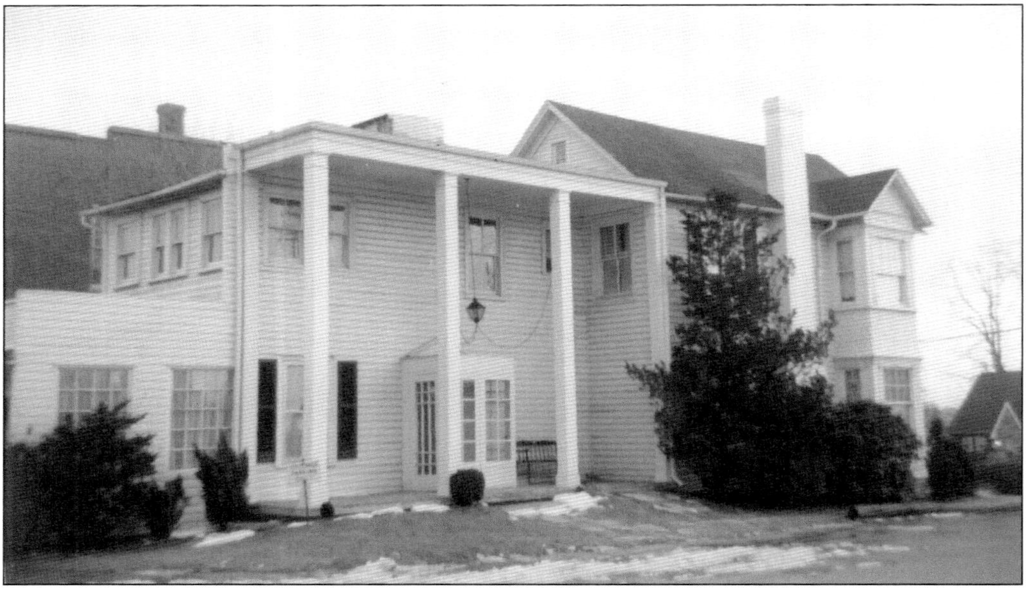

The Falls Church Beauty School filled the former home of Dr. George B. Fadeley on West Broad Street, next to the Independent Order of Odd Fellows (IOOF) Hall. Dr. Fadeley saw patients in his home, as was the practice back then, before the house became a salon school.

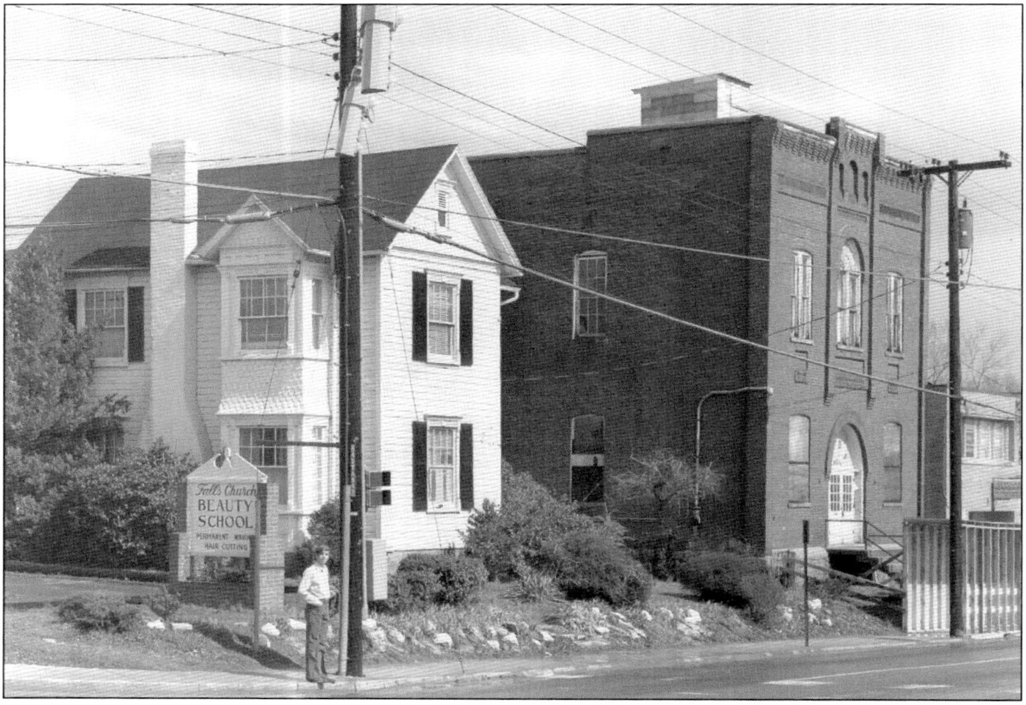

While a beauty school is not necessarily part of the primary education otherwise focused on in this chapter, it was a prominent landmark on Broad Street in the 1950s next to the IOOF. The former doctor's residence was originally entered from Broad Street and eventually became an antique shop.

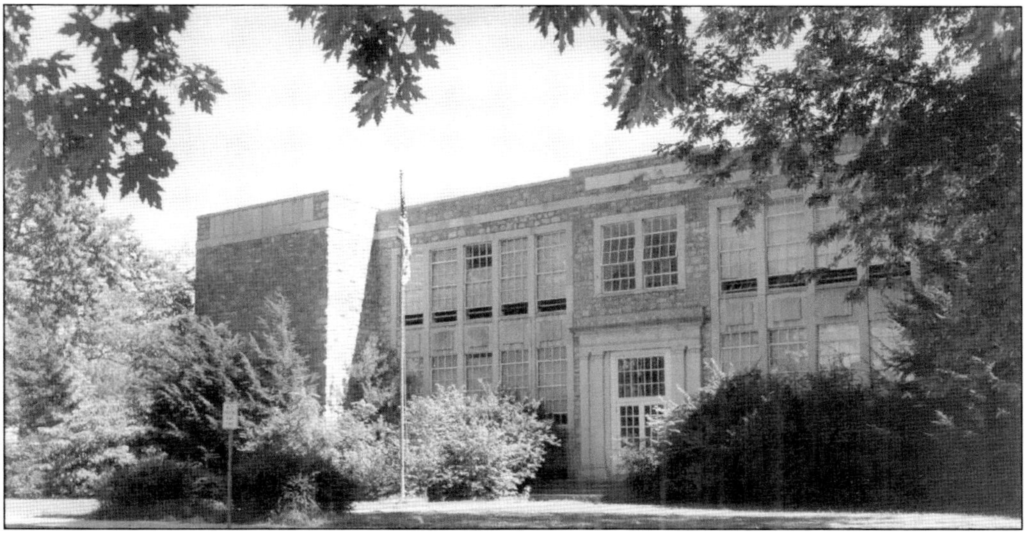

Even before becoming an independent city, education was a top priority for citizens of Falls Church and those elected to represent it. Joseph S. Riley stated "this matter of public schools is of vast importance and something should be done by the Council in order that an effort may be made to have a public school in the Corporation." The Jefferson Institute, the first public school in Falls Church, was born out of that statement. The Commonwealth granted Falls Church its own school district in 1924, and two years later, the Madison School opened at 334 North Washington Street to serve students in grades 1–7 and Jefferson Institute became a four-year high school. North Washington Street consisted mostly of homes and farmland at that time. The Madison School was demolished in 1979 after consolidation from the city's purchase of the Oak Street School from Fairfax County. (Both, MRSPL, Historical Commission, 1946.)

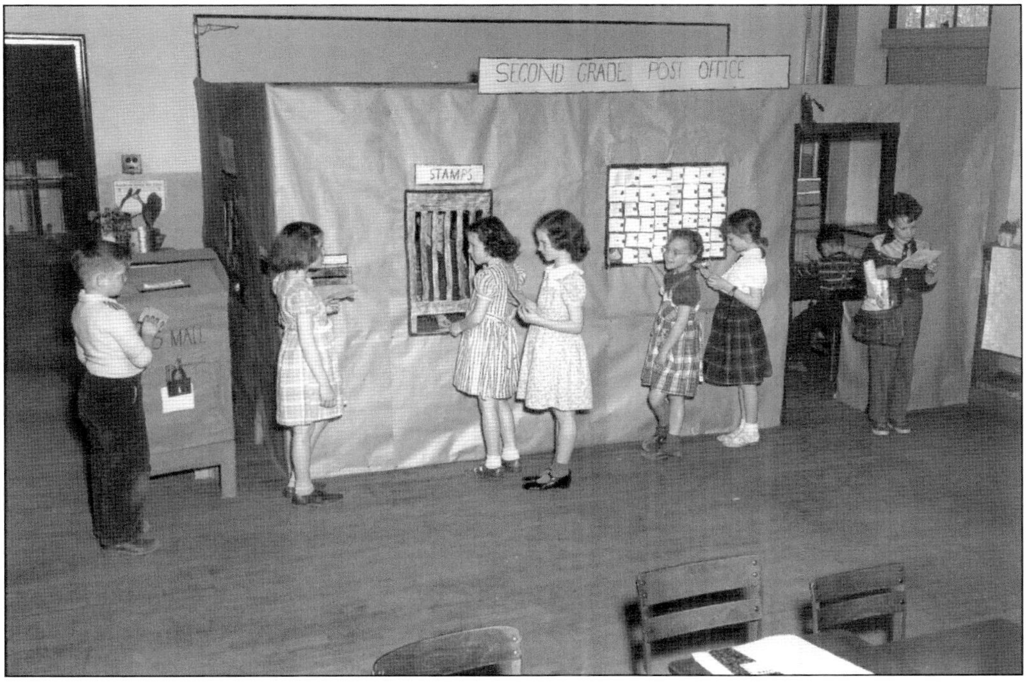

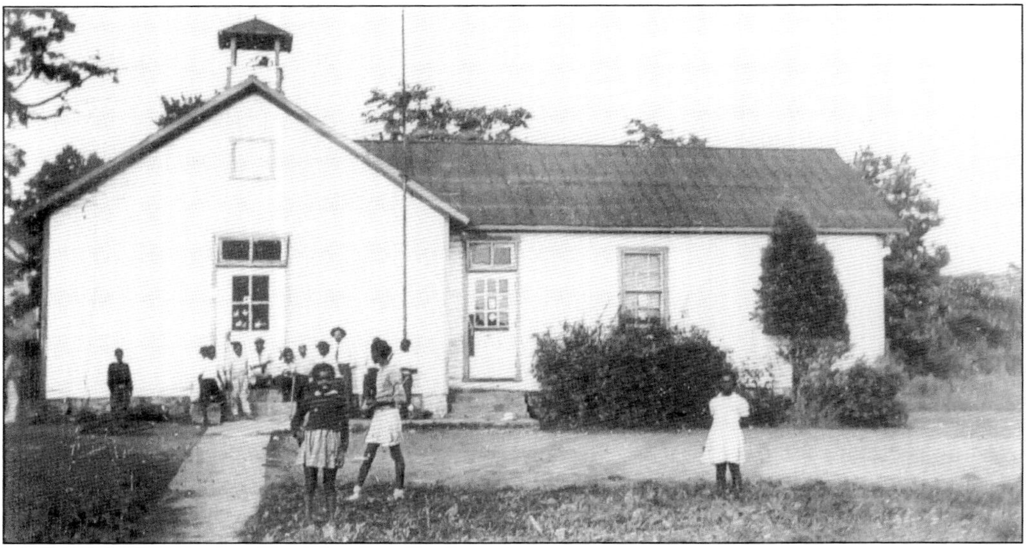

Prior to instituting desegregation in 1961, segregation played a role in Falls Church's education history. The city paid tuition to send African American elementary students to Fairfax County's James Lee Elementary School on Annandale Road and black high school students to Manassas. The school chose the ideal woman for its principal, Mary Ellen Henderson. (Courtesy of the Tinner Hill Heritage Foundation, Barbara Williams Collection.)

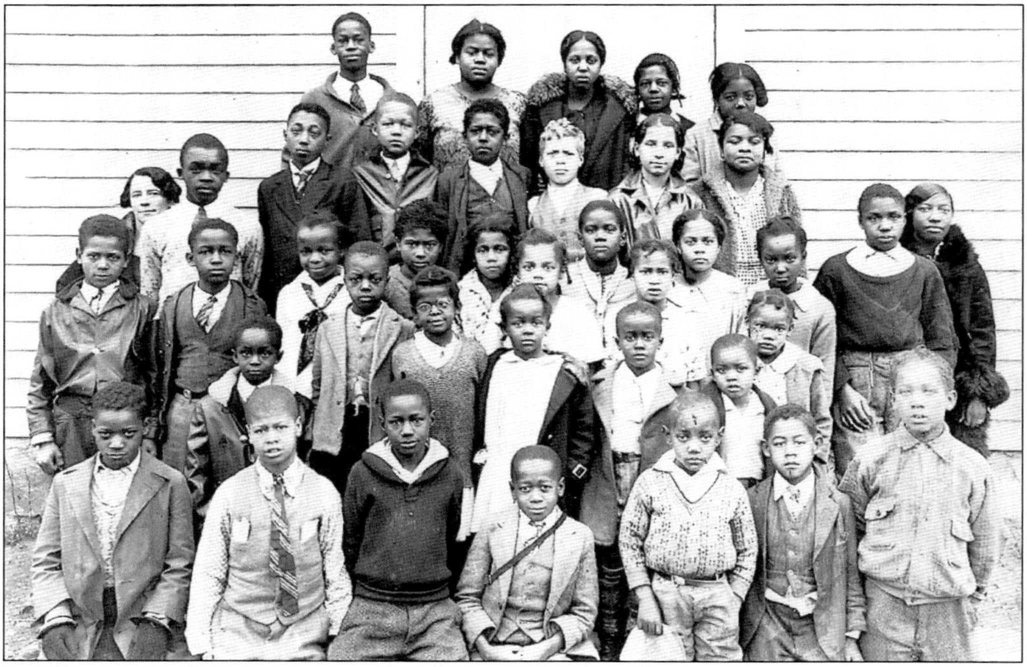

In 1919, the black community implored Mary Ellen Henderson to reopen the school, which closed because it had no teacher. She then served as principal and also taught grades 4–7 in one room of the two-room schoolhouse, recruiting another teacher to teach in the other. The overcrowded building lacked common conveniences such as running water, heat, or indoor toilets. (Courtesy of the Henderson Family Collection.)

OUR DISGRACE AND SHAME

SCHOOL FACILITIES FOR NEGRO CHILDREN IN FAIRFAX COUNTY

WHITE SCHOOLS	NEGRO SCHOOLS
1 All brick or stone, except 4 wooden buildings	1 One to three room wooden buildings
2 Have running water, janitorial service, inside toilets, central heating	2 All have outside "pit" toilets for teachers and children, no running water; all stoves in the rooms
3 Children ride in heated busses.	3 No janitorial service—teachers do all cleaning, haul water, make fires
	4 Three schools have no water on premises
	5 Some children walk from 4 to 6 miles to school
	6 Buses are old and rickety and are not heated.

HOW SCHOOL FUNDS ARE SHARED

In 1935 the School Board sought a grant of $153,022.50 from PWA and a bond issue (which was defeated) to raise $187,027.50. Of this total of $340,050.00 it was proposed to spend for:

WHITE SCHOOLS....................$330,750—97.4 per cent
COLORED SCHOOLS .... 9,000— 2.6 per cent

In 1935 this county owed the State Literary Fund $188,739.32 (all of which had been spent on white schools). In that year the colored population of the county was 19 per cent.

The 1945-46 PROPOSED budget provided among other items:

FOR WHITE SCHOOLS		FOR COLORED SCHOOLS
Administration	$18,380	0
Operation of School Plant .... (Salary of janitor, light, telephone and fuel)	80,350	?
Capital Outlay	$745,000	$45,000

The following proposed expenditures of a proposed loan from the State Literary fund were approved:

WHITE SCHOOLS	COLORED SCHOOLS
$50,000 for Herndon High School	0
$40,000 for 2 classrooms, wash room and cafeteria at Vienna	0
$20,000 for 2 classrooms at Lincolnia	0
$10,000 to complete 2 classrooms at Groveton	0
$40,000 additional was secured to add elementary rooms to Madison School	

Mary Ellen Henderson, known to her students as Miss Nellie, spent the next 30 years appealing to the community and appearing in front of the Fairfax County School Board, imploring for equality in education for her colored students, who mainly got by with castoff textbooks and supplies from their white counterparts. She also championed the push for a new school with modern facilities. After spending decades speaking and appealing, she decided to try a new approach that was ultimately much more successful. Using the 1936 school budget, Mary Ellen launched a study in the disparities in the learning environment and resources between the white and black school facilities, publishing a disparity study showing that 97.3 percent of the budget went to educating the white students. Her work led to the formation of an interracial committee in Fairfax County. Finally, Mary Ellen Henderson saw her decades of tireless work come to fruition. (Both, courtesy of the Henderson Family Collection.)

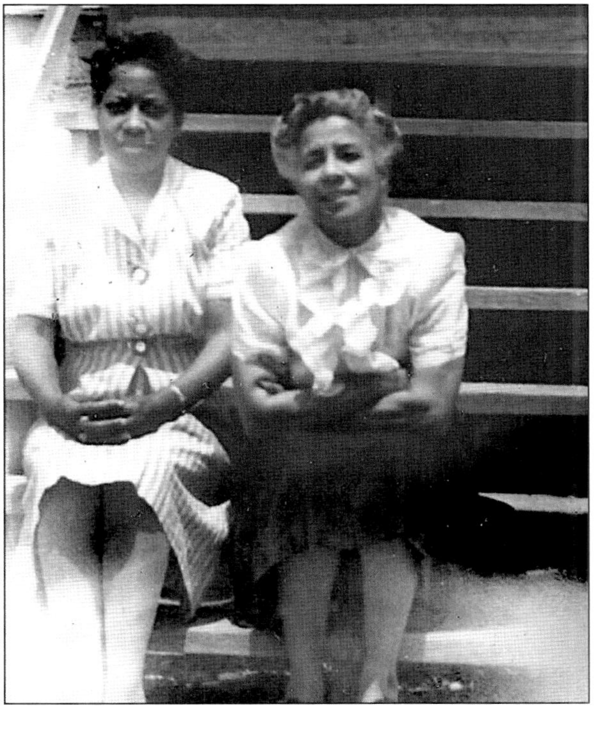

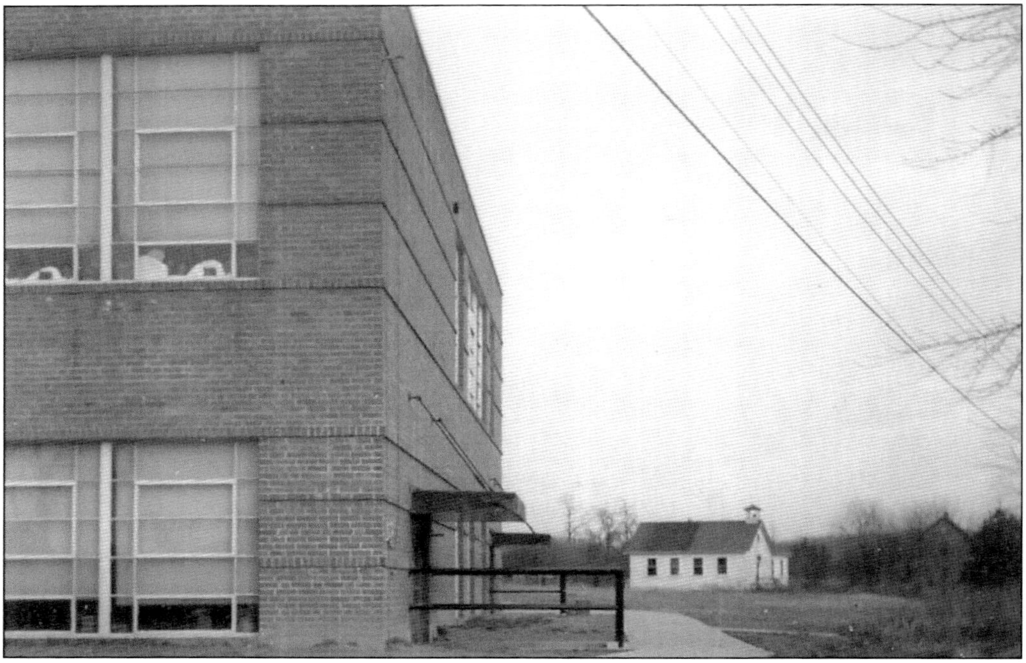

Mary Ellen Henderson's work led the school board to build the first new school for African American children. The new James Lee School was constructed on the same land where the two-room school stood, donated by James Lee. The school dedication took place in 1948. Henderson's successful efforts for educational redress became the model used nationwide. Along with her husband, E.B. Henderson, the couple's endless efforts spent promoting equality positively impacted their local community and helped shape the nation as well. (Both, courtesy of the Henderson Family Collection.)

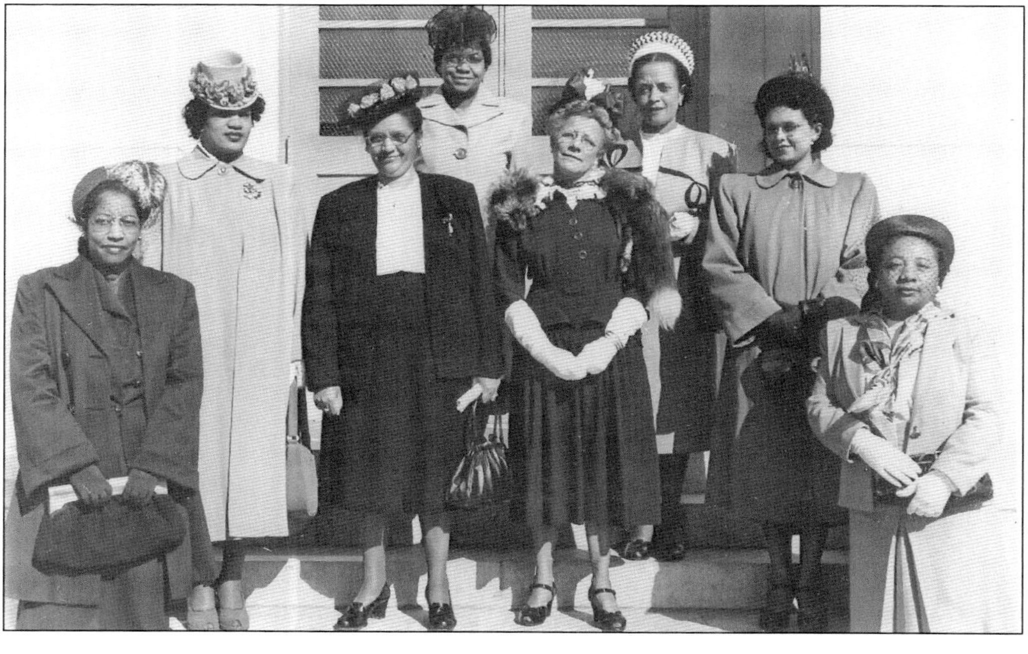

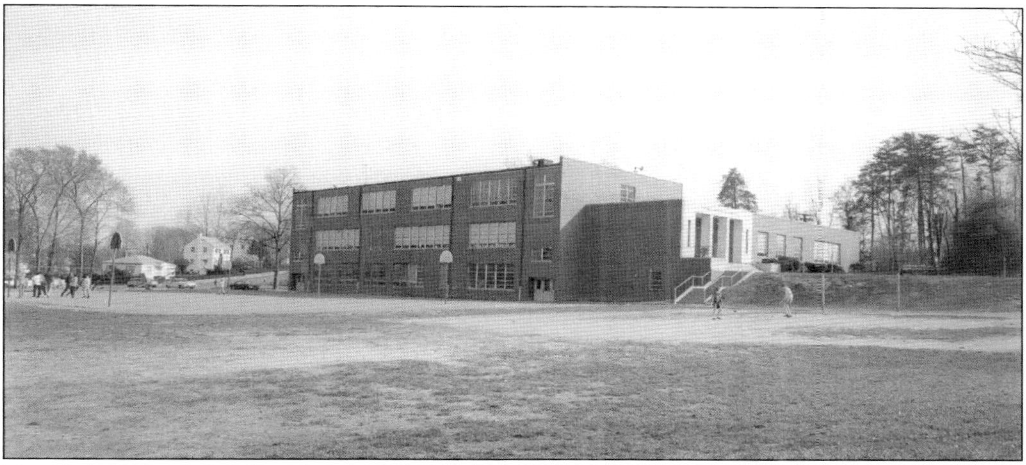

The Oak Street School on South Oak Street was opened by Fairfax County in 1948. With the city becoming independent from Fairfax County and assuming control of its own school district, the need for more elementary school space arose. Falls Church purchased the school from Fairfax County and assumed control in 1955, renaming it Thomas Jefferson Elementary. Mount Daniel Elementary was built on land just outside the city limits on the opposite north end of Oak Street and opened in 1952. The young city filed an annexation suit but lost, so the school remains outside city limits to this day. Thomas Jefferson Elementary remains the only school in the Falls Church district within the city. Along with an outstanding indoor curriculum, an outdoor classroom program began in the early days, allowing students to reforest and maintain plants along the banks of Tripps Run and tend to an adjacent butterfly garden.

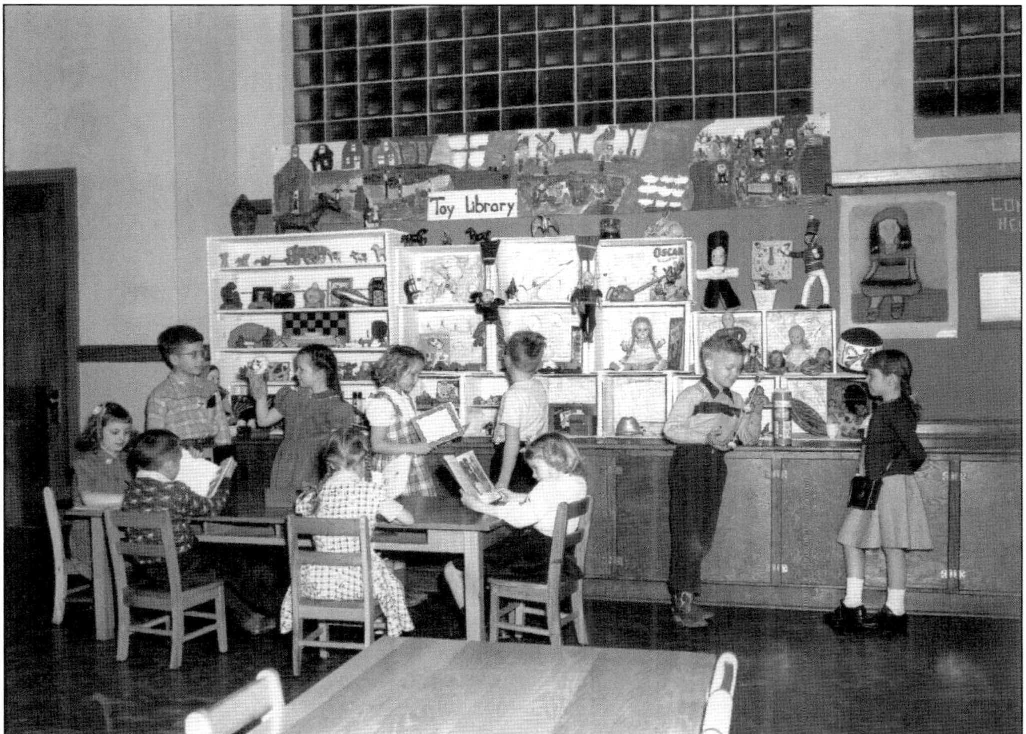

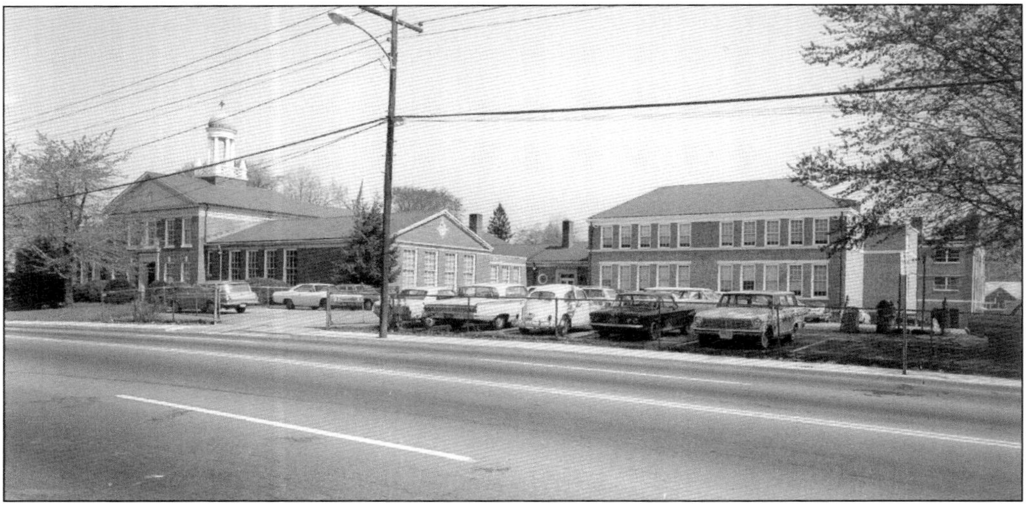

In addition to the award-winning public education system developed in Falls Church, the city has also been home to St. James Catholic Elementary School for more than a century. After receiving formal recognition as a Catholic parish in 1892, the St. James parish grew rapidly, and a school for the parish children was established. In 1905, a two-story, eight-room building was constructed to serve the school, and shortly after, the brick convent followed. The school continued to grow, and by 1934, student boarders from kindergarten through eighth grade had to be housed in three separate locations. One sister was assigned to teach a sixth-and-seventh-grade class on the stage of the auditorium in front of a small kitchenette. A common question during that cramped time was, "Is that textbook stored in the oven or the refrigerator?" Additional land was purchased and a new school was dedicated in 1948, but due to growth, it also continued expanding. In 1949, a kindergarten was added as a permanent part of the school.

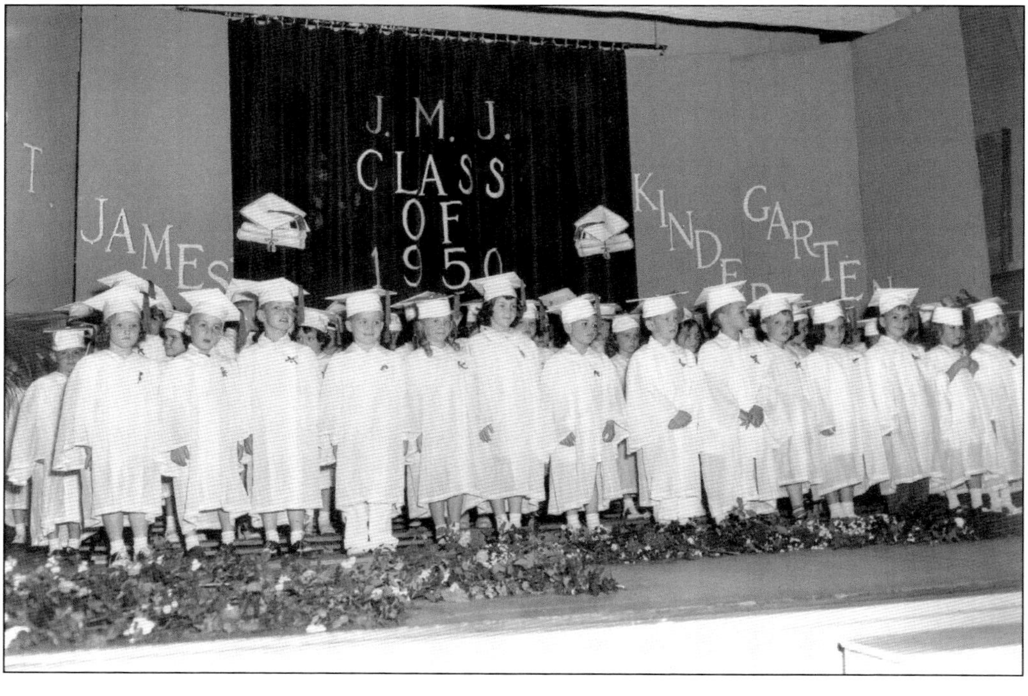

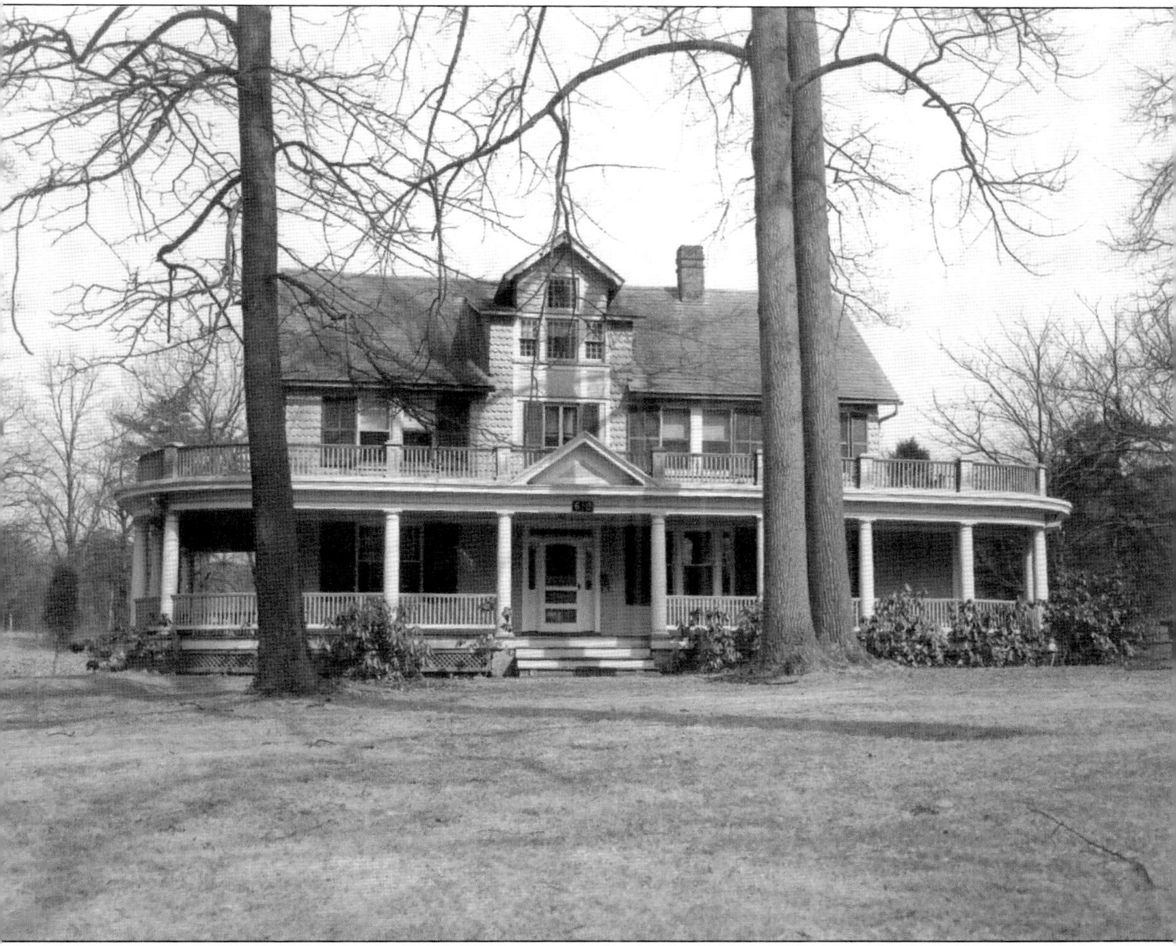

Over the years, a few small schools were established in homes throughout the city, such as Mattie Gundry's start in Home Hill. In 1943, new owners purchased Rice Home from the Eisenhowers, renaming it Tallwood and leasing it to the Tallwood School for two years. E. Edward and Eileen Schefer began a school at 119 South Oak Street before moving it to 610 Fulton Avenue known as Woodland House, just south of the Rothsay train station on the south side of the tracks. The Schefer School offered special tutoring and individual curriculum. In 1981, the school purchased the Albertson/The Triangle/Cook House at 407 Little Falls Street to restore and use as an adjunct to its school for gifted children. The school ended up under the direction of the Schefers' son, Anton. Prior to becoming a school, Woodland was a grand estate with tennis courts and riding horses.

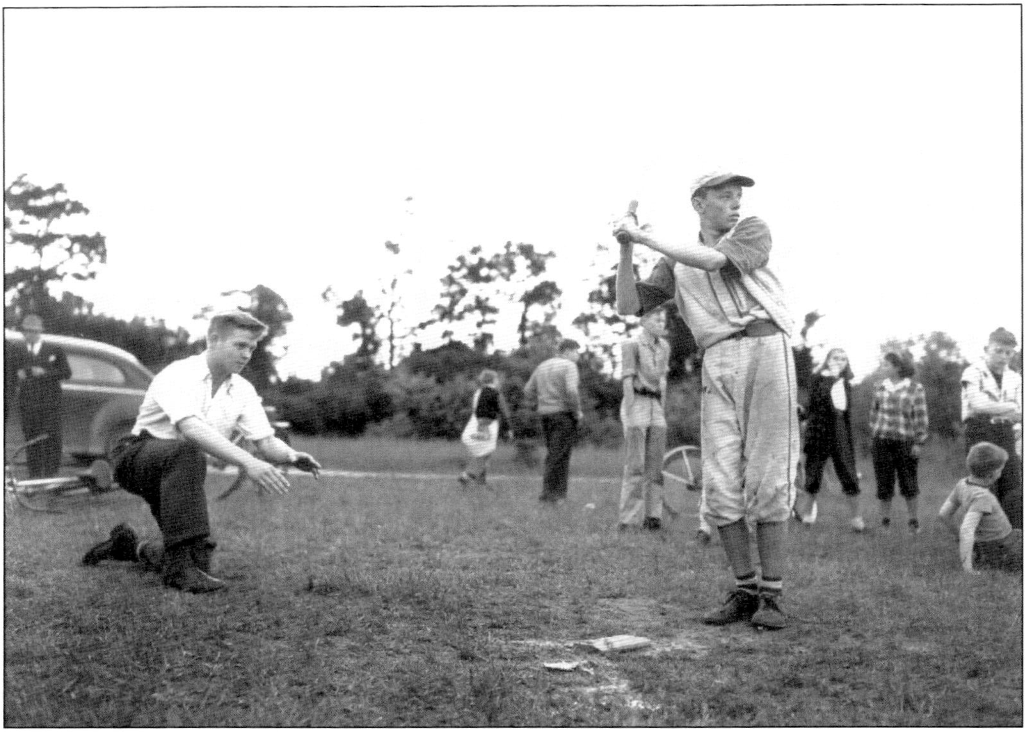

Sports have always been an integral part of the youth community. Many of the children who grew up in Falls Church spent their entire childhood in the city, playing and learning with the same peers.

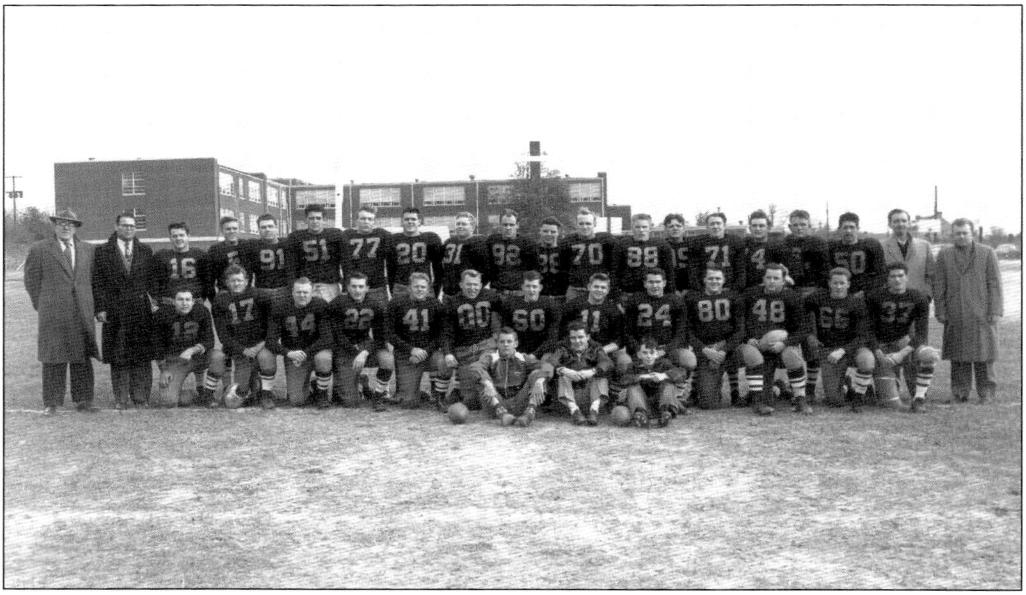

Despite a booming population over the years, as well as the exploding development of the rest of Northern Virginia around Washington, Falls Church managed to maintain a small-town atmosphere and community—a key goal.

Seven

Merchants and Community

In addition to churches, the community centered around the local shops and providers such as blacksmiths. Even the earliest settlers knew their business had a better chance of prospering by positioning it in a high-traffic area. Thus, the log Big Chimneys tavern sat at a rare crossroads in the area, and Wren's Tavern and the Falls Church soon followed.

As the area grew up, forward-thinking founders continued to try to manipulate development to draw the most traffic to the town. With a major turnpike cutting through the center of town and three train stations, Falls Church at one point fancied itself a tourist destination and overnight stop for travelers heading in and out of Washington, but the tourist idea was never fully realized.

Once a major center of merchants and services, the little city thrived, but it has recently been overshadowed by neighbors. With the explosive growth of Tysons Corner and Seven Corners on either end of Falls Church, the community has struggled to create a solid and lasting business model to draw in consumers from outside its borders. Still, just as it was in the beginning of the settlement, businesses feel like family in the town, where everybody knows each other's names.

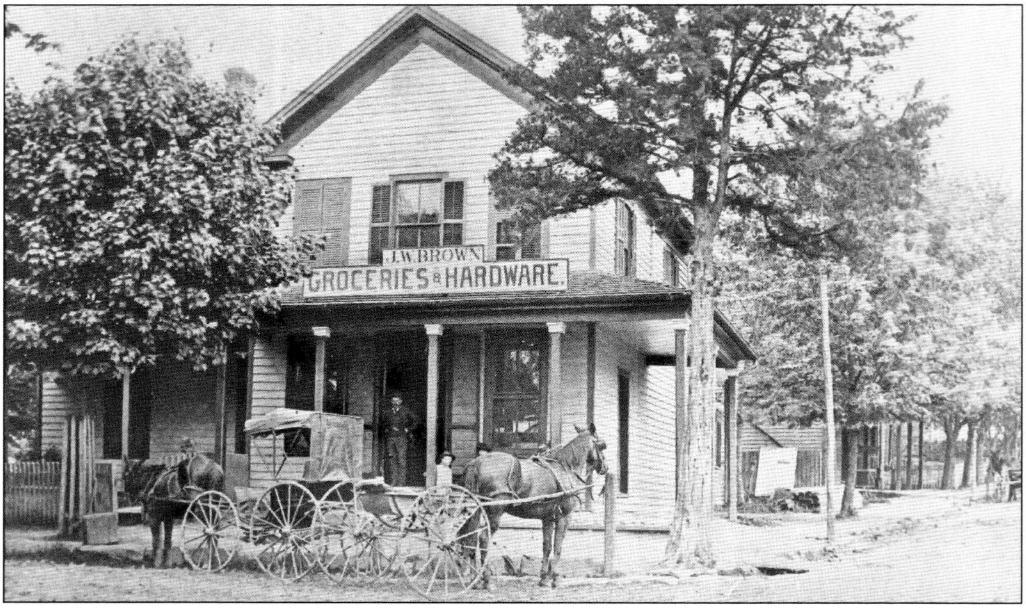

Edward Birch, no apparent relation to the long-standing Birch family of Falls Church, built a home at the corner of Washington and Broad Streets in 1866. Birch succeeded George B. Ives as postmaster of Falls Church, serving from April 1872 through June 1881, spanning the first incorporation of Falls Church as a town. The home served as a post office during his tenure.

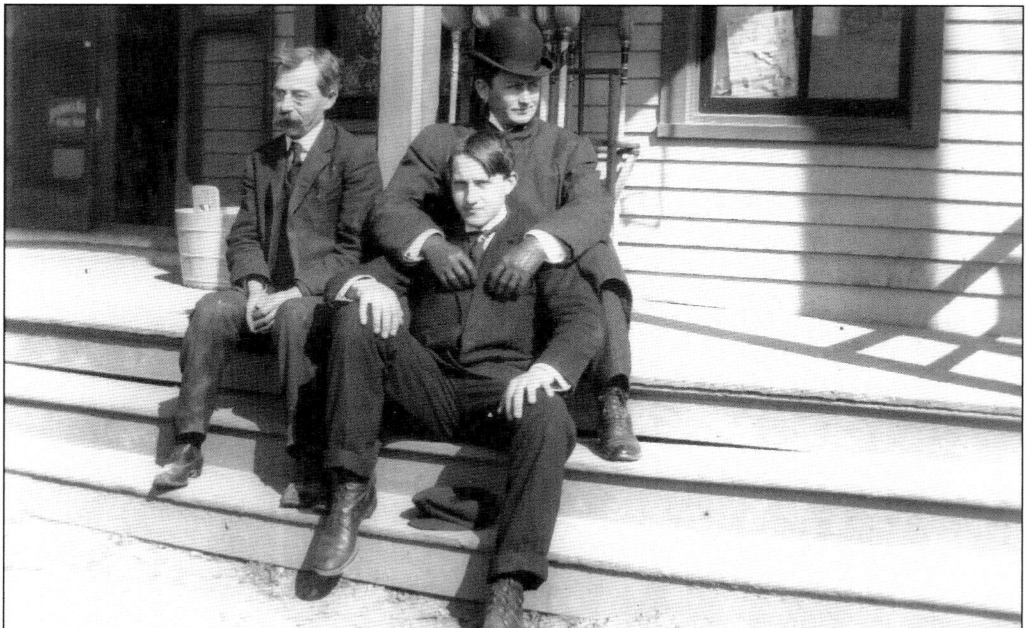

James W. Brown arrived in Falls Church from Loudoun County, where he had been a schoolteacher. He purchased the Birch home in 1883, and Brown's Hardware operated in this building across from the Star Tavern for more than 60 years. James W. Brown, seen here on the steps of his store in gloves, died in 1904 and his son, Horace (in front), took over the store at 18.

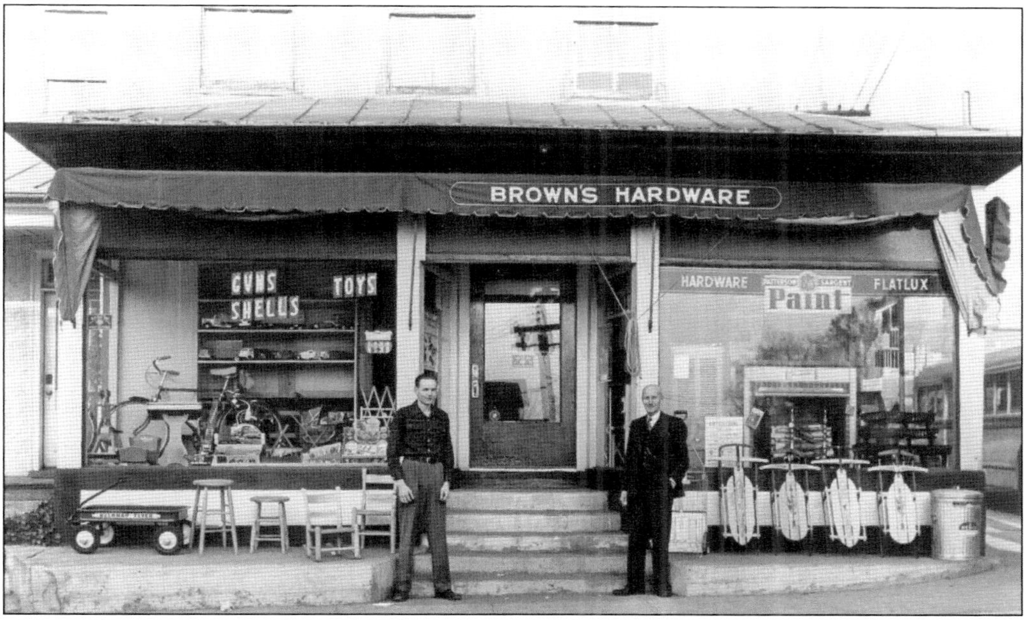

In 1942, the Browns moved out of the living quarters of the store. One of Brown's sons, also named James W., moved into a house on the cul-de-sac at the end of East Jefferson Street in 1936, renting the space to Tom Eastham, a later mayor of Falls Church. The Horace Brown family purchased a home on the corner of Little Falls and Great Falls Streets. Brown's Hardware sat across the street from Merton E. Church's Spofford & Church drugstore. In 1959, a new hardware store was built, and the old home was torn down later that year. The store was then run by Hugh R. Brown, grandson of James W. Brown. Brown's Hardware is still in business today and has the honor of being the longest continually operated business in the city. The photograph below shows the interior shelves and counter around 1940.

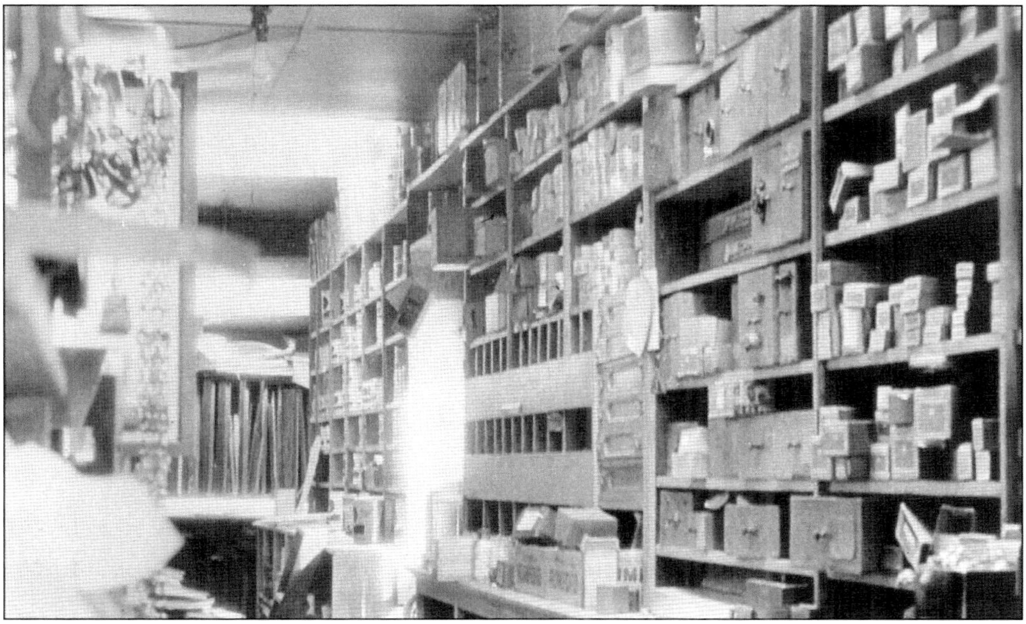

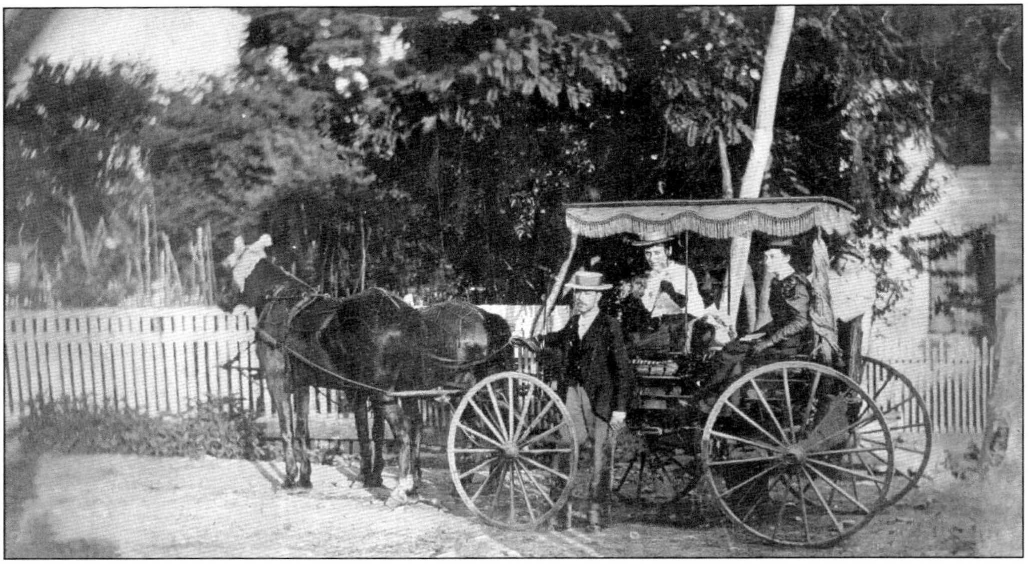

George W. Mankin arrived in Falls Church following the Civil War and purchased Cloverdale, the old Clover farmhouse on Park Avenue. His son, George T. Mankin, served in many capacities for the city, including as the fire warden and as Falls Church Registrar during World War I, when he registered more than 100 men in a two-month period, second only to Vienna in recruits.

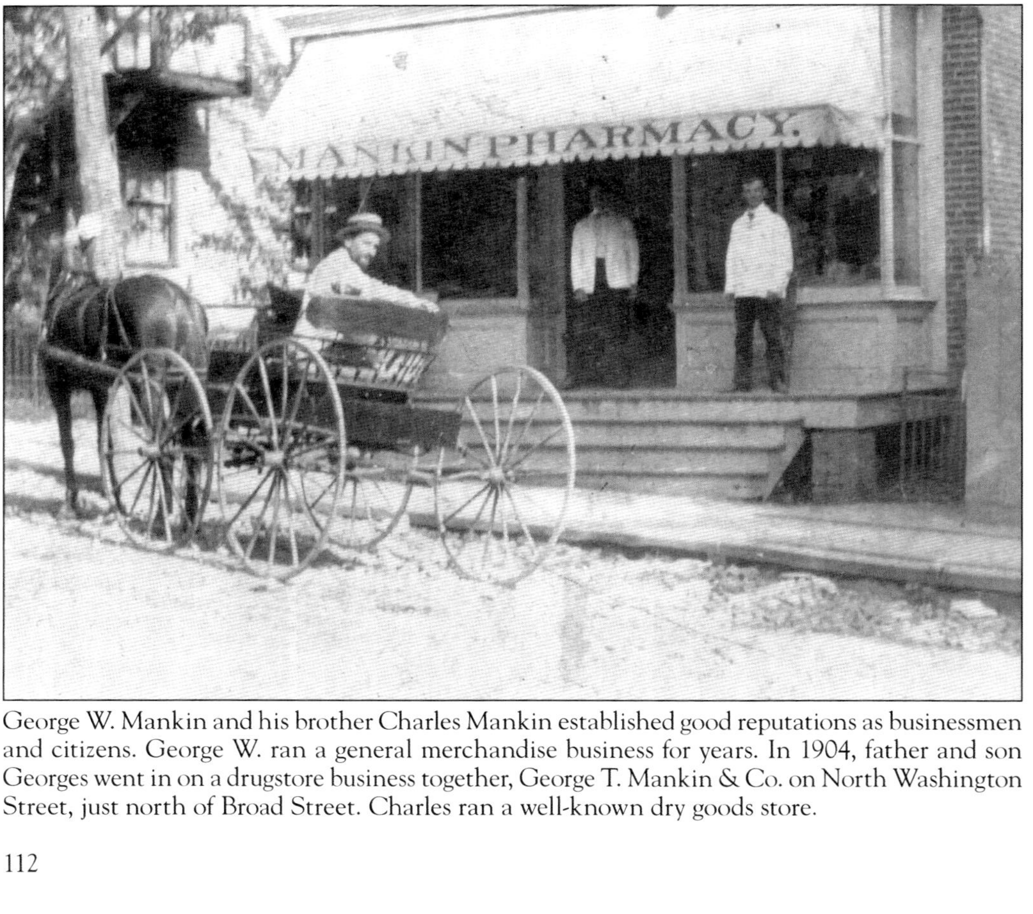

George W. Mankin and his brother Charles Mankin established good reputations as businessmen and citizens. George W. ran a general merchandise business for years. In 1904, father and son Georges went in on a drugstore business together, George T. Mankin & Co. on North Washington Street, just north of Broad Street. Charles ran a well-known dry goods store.

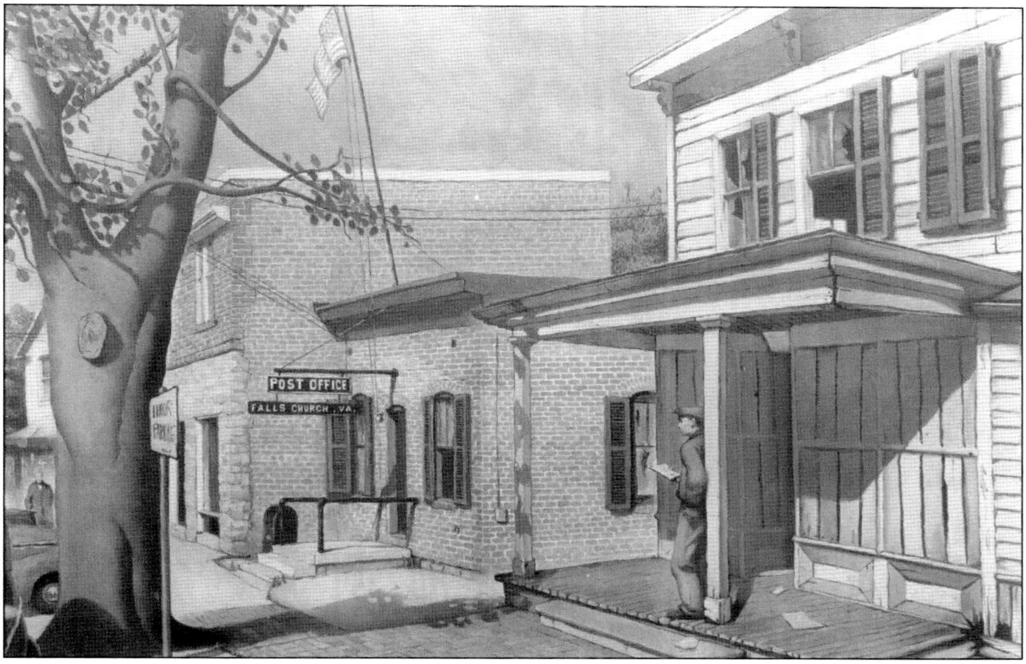

Pharmacies, general goods and grocers, taverns, feed stores, a post office, and florists clustered around the commercial center of Washington and Broad Streets. Over time, the undisturbed land and residences on Washington Street north of Broad Street rolled over into commercial properties.

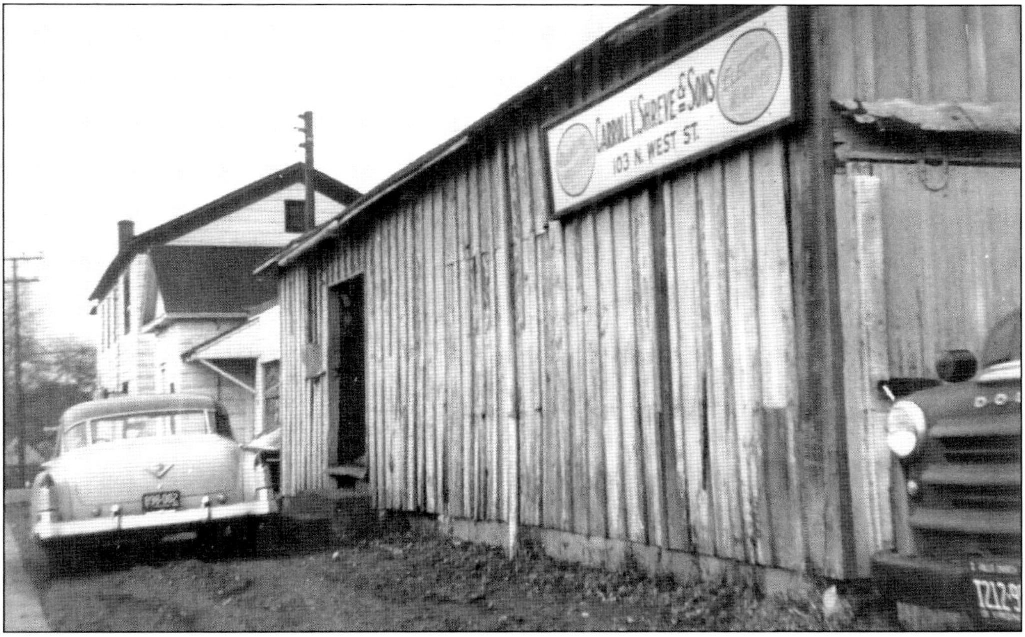

On the West End, a field of brooder houses once stood on South West Street south of Broad Street. Many still-familiar names once occupied residences or ran businesses in Falls Church. The Merrifield family lived in a house and owned a cottage on North Washington Street. Carroll V. Shreve & Sons once occupied 123 North West Street.

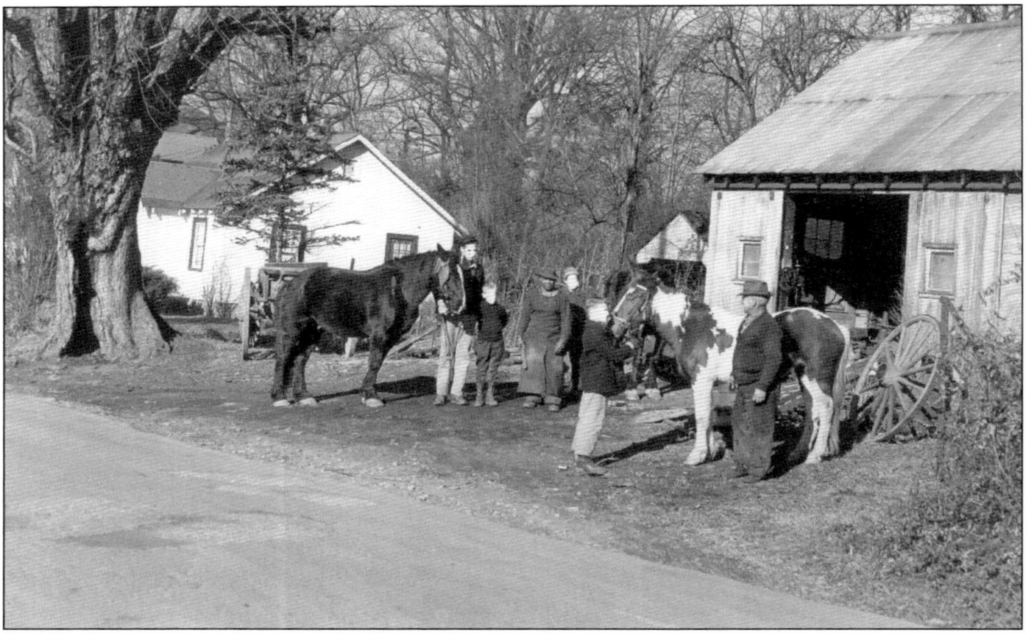

William Nathan Lynch arrived in Falls Church in 1854, operating a feed store and a blacksmith shop near The Falls Church on East Fairfax Drive and holding positions of prominence in the community. Many years later, in 1938, Robert Harmon started and ran the blacksmith shop at the rear of Meese Flower Shop.

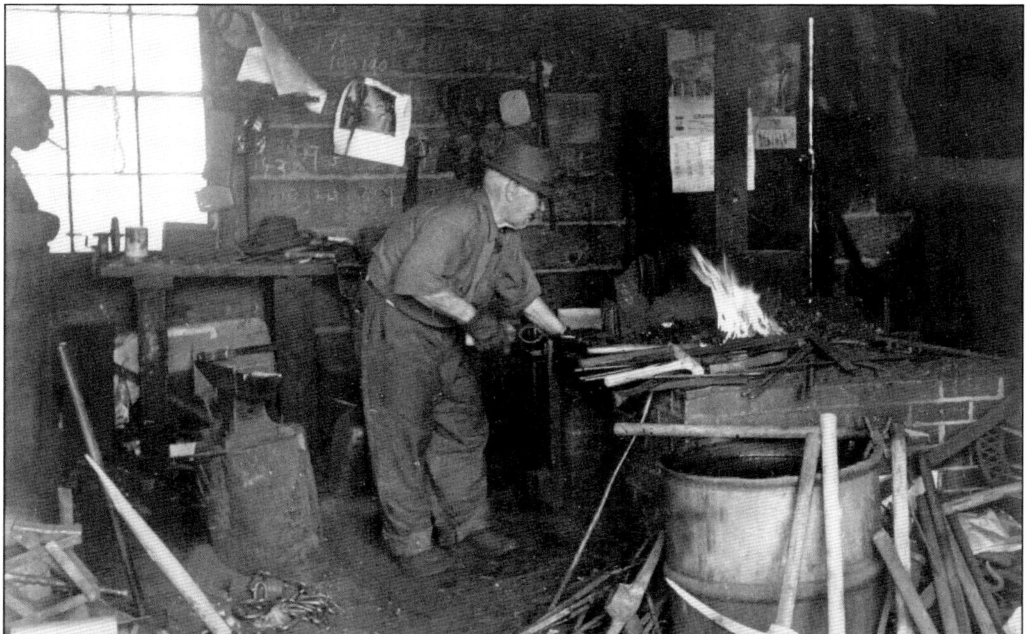

Blacksmiths were vital in farming towns, particularly in the days of horses and buggies. Shoeing horses was a regular task, as was repairing the metal parts of buggies and carts. Blacksmiths also produced skillets and pots for kitchens as well as farm implements.

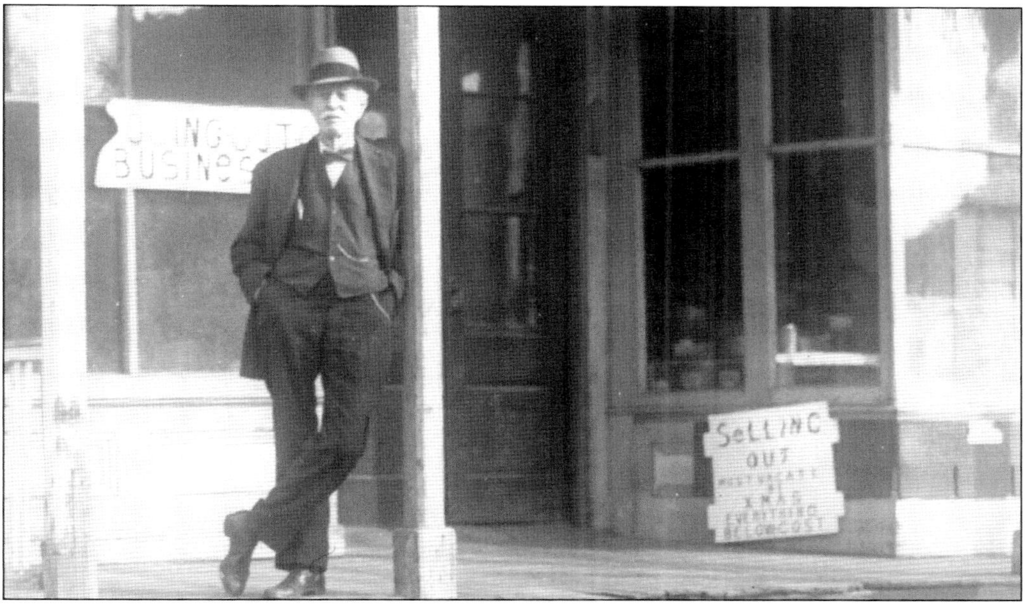

William Nathan Lynch built his home in 1898 at 304 East Broad Street, complete with a two-story cow barn. He sold milk from the cows at his home. Lynch's feed store was two blocks west, next to the old brick post office building on East Broad Street. In 1939, handwritten signs in the feed store windows advertised a Going out of Business Sale.

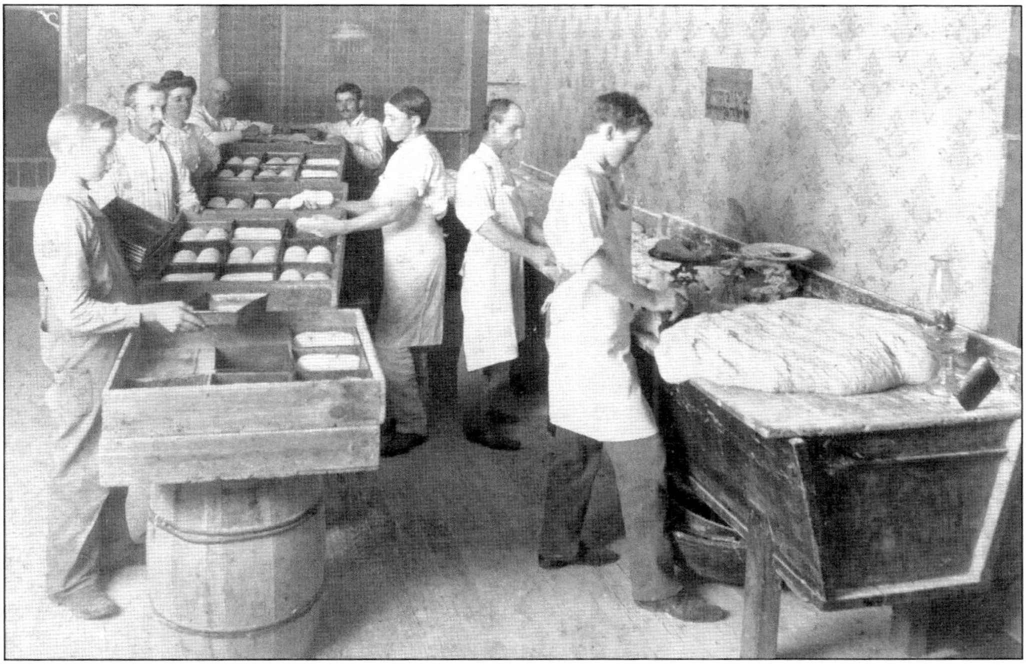

Erwin's Bakery doughboys prepare for the day's baking. A small barn at the rear of the Erwin house, at 300 West Great Falls Street, contained delivery horses for the bakery at one time. Some of the doughboys from Erwin's spent several months during World War I in training at Camp Lee, Virginia, and fought in some of Europe's bloodiest battles.

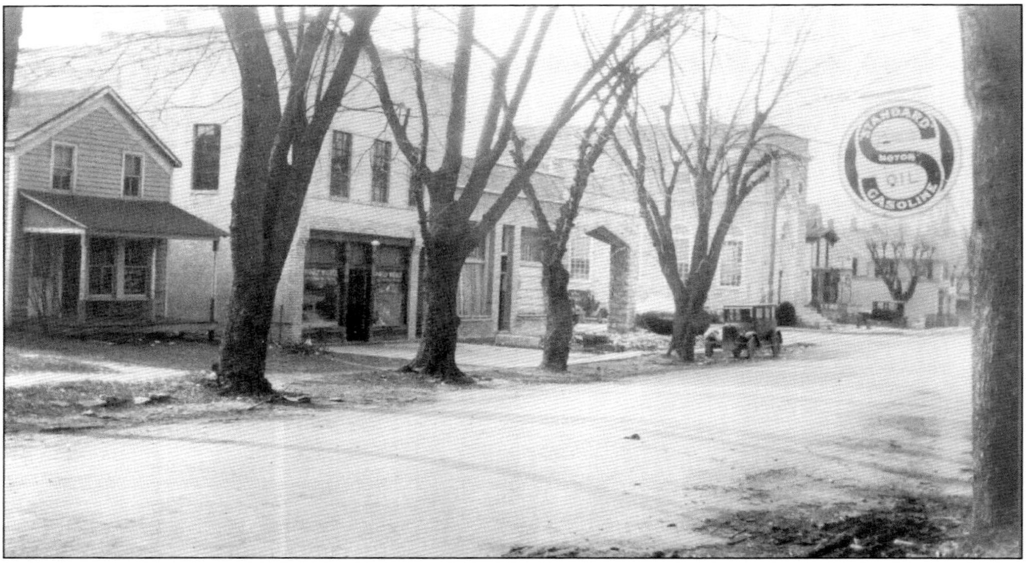

Residences near the intersection of Broad and Washington Streets gave way to burgeoning business during the booming 1920s. The Falls Church Bank with the stone gas station across Washington Street is in the distance of this photograph, which looks west down Broad Street from the northeast side of Washington Street around 1925.

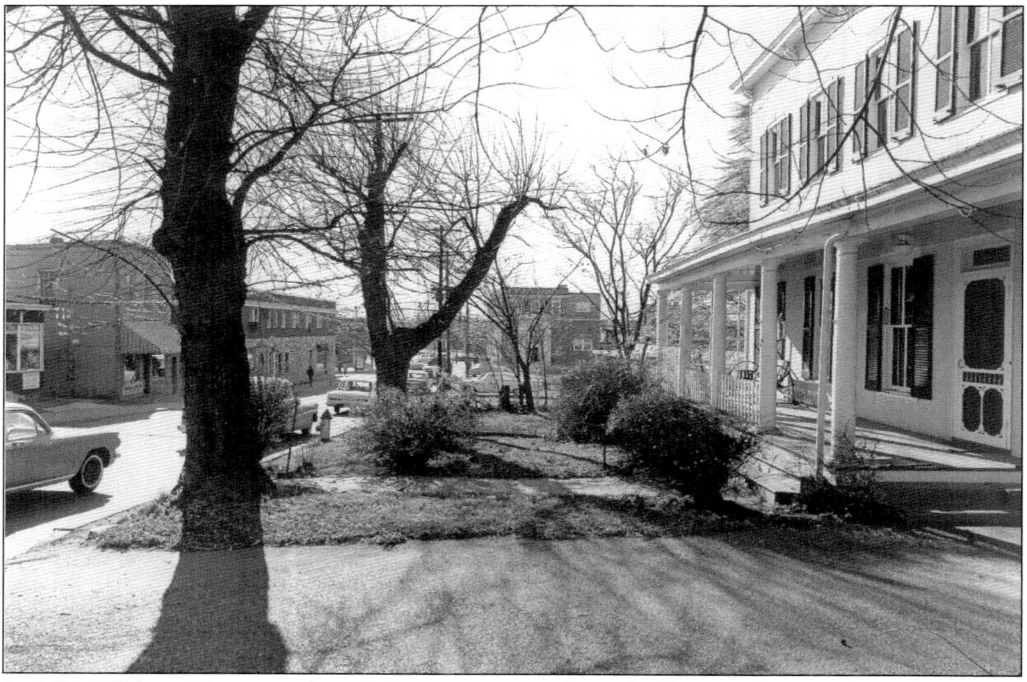

In 1874, William Tyson purchased the property on the right from Williston Clover, building a combined house and general store. It continued to serve as a commercial location until June 1927, when it was sold. North Washington Street continued transitioning from residential to commercial all the way up to Fairfax Drive, on the former Crossman farm property, extending the commercial center tradition started in the days of Wren's Tavern.

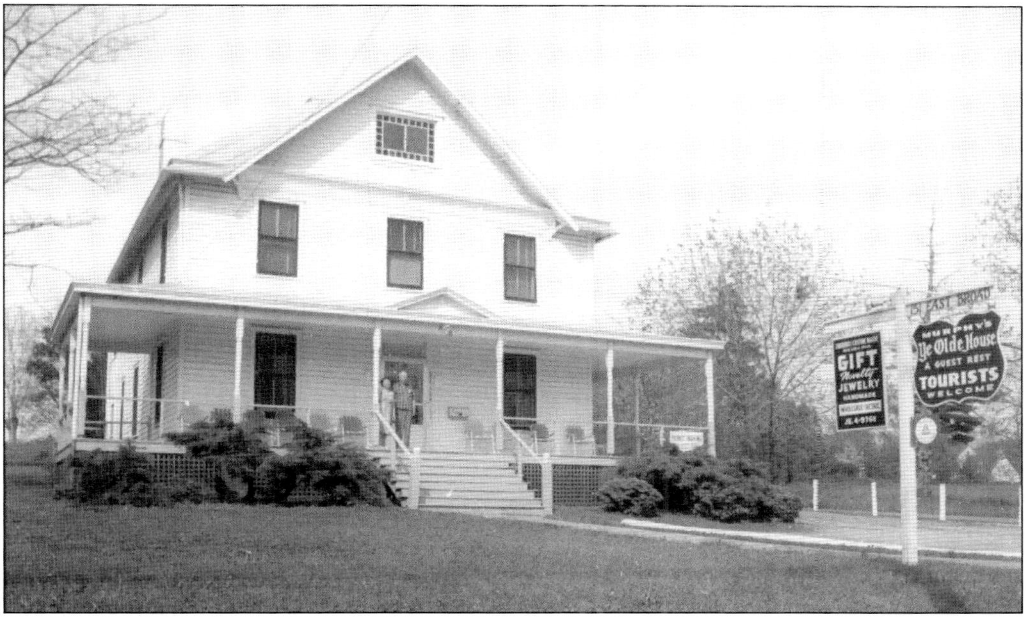

Falls Church spent some time trying to fashion itself as a tourist destination. "Ye Olde House, Tourists Welcome," enticed a sign outside the Luttrell/Murphy House on Broad Street in the first block east of Washington Street. A handful of houses near the commercial center of town spent some time as tourist homes and motels, including the Maple Shade Guest House, built in 1899 on North Washington Street.

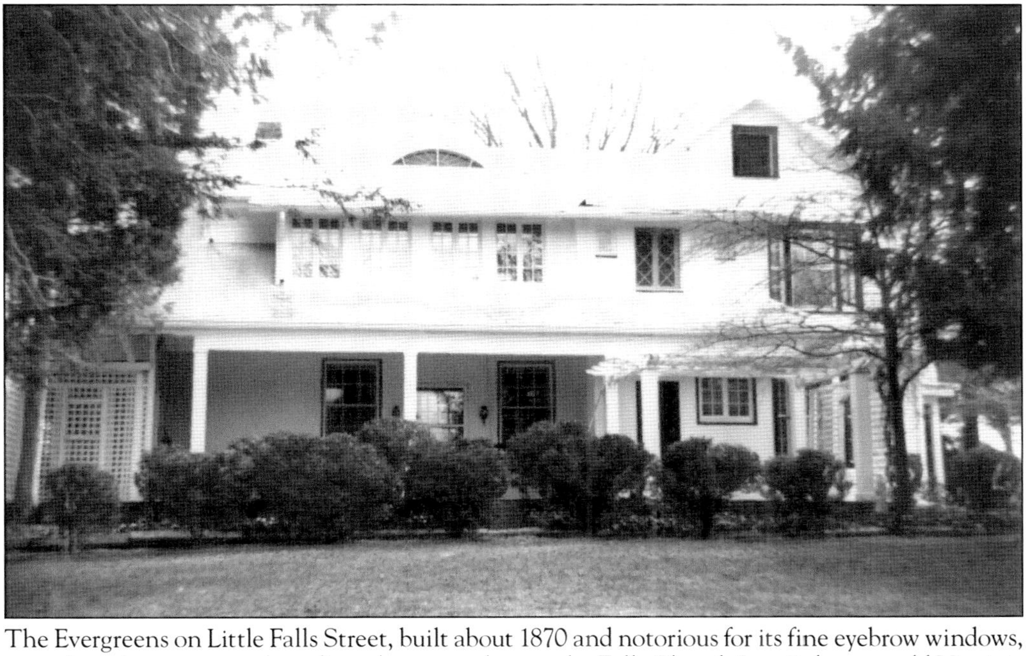

The Evergreens on Little Falls Street, built about 1870 and notorious for its fine eyebrow windows, served as a large summer boarding place next door to the Falls Church Inn, "where an old Virginia welcome awaits the way-farer, accommodated transient and regular boarders," according to the original *Virginia Village*, written in 1904.

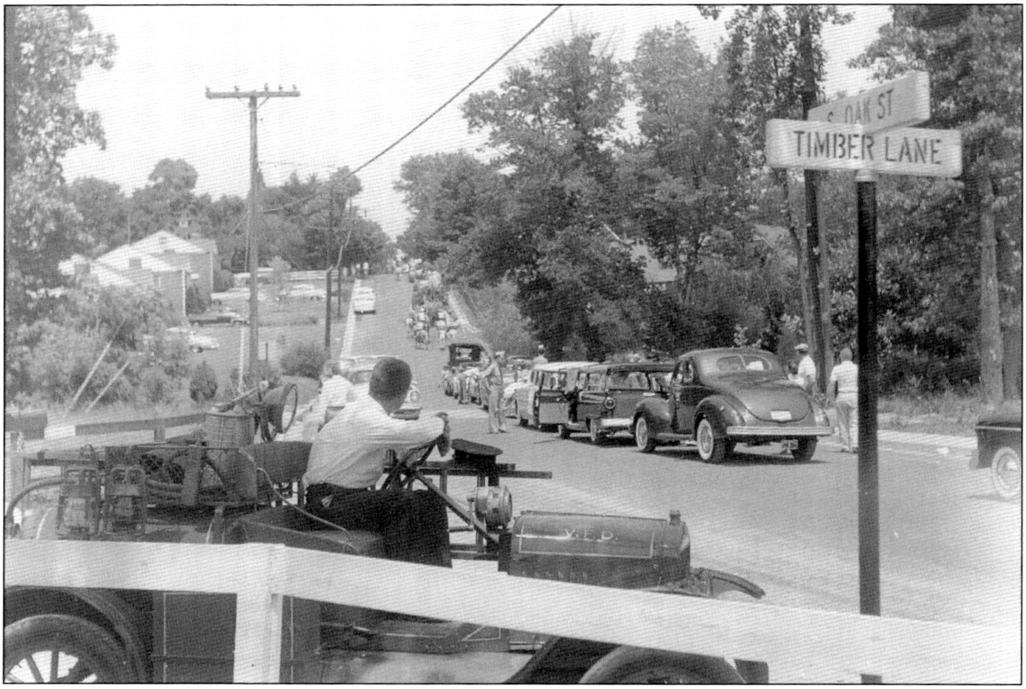

Parades have been a long-standing and much anticipated community event for decades, bringing families from the small city together. If not lining up to participate as members of a local civic organization or political affiliation, townspeople meet with neighbors at preplanned locations along the parade route. Here, cars are lined up in preparation for the 1957 parade at Tripps Run on South Oak Street.

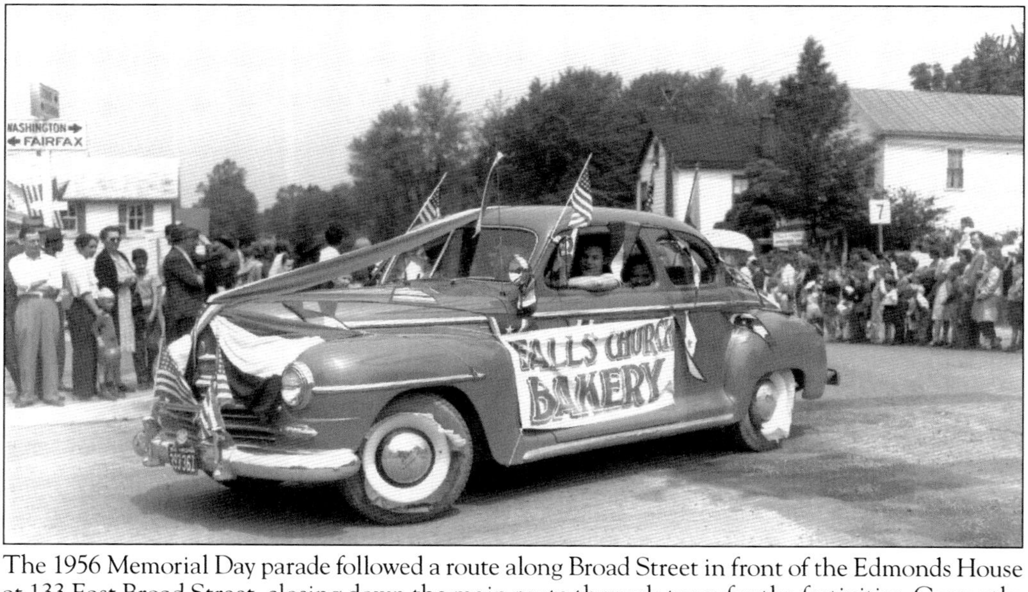

The 1956 Memorial Day parade followed a route along Broad Street in front of the Edmonds House at 133 East Broad Street, closing down the main route through town for the festivities. Currently, the parade route travels down Park Avenue—a block north and parallel to Broad Street—past the Cherry Hill farmhouse, library, and city hall.

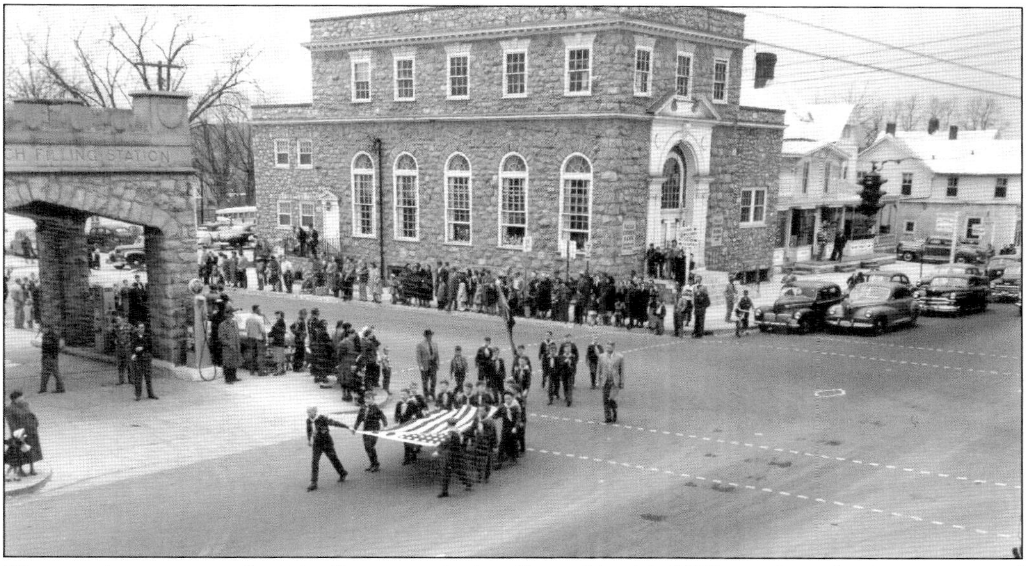

The merchant core and spirit of community is reflected in this 1952 parade at the intersection of Broad and Washington Streets showing Merton Church's Falls Church Bank building and opposite gas station, both made of granite. By that point, Broad Street had been widened to four lanes.

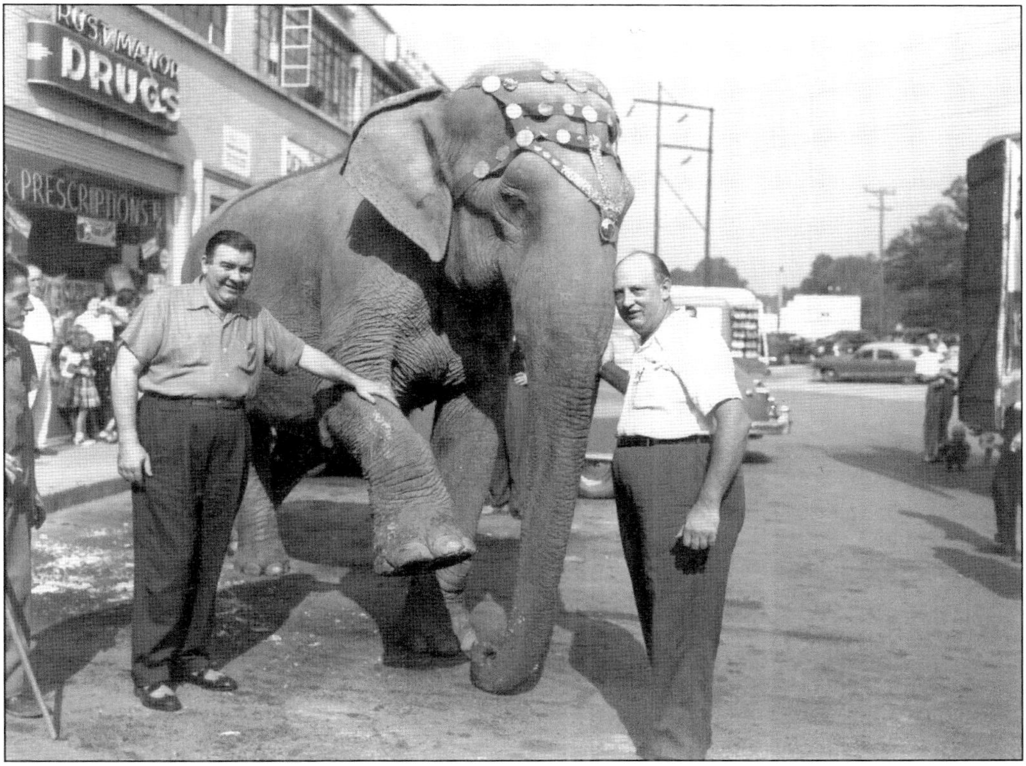

The Bailey family of Barnum & Bailey Circus lived nearby in Arlington and trained animals in a circular riding ring. Occasionally, the animals practiced routines through Falls Church. This elephant was celebrating his birthday in Falls Church years after the Bailey family first came to town.

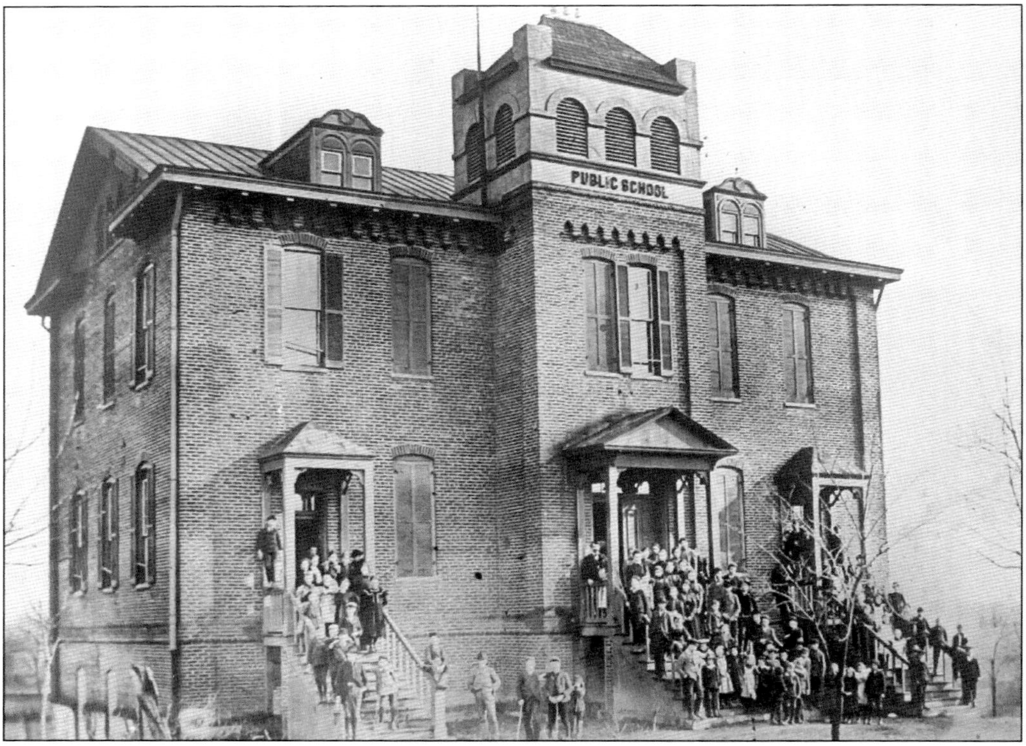

In addition to providing a top-tier education to the children of the town, the founders also focused on civic-mindedness and lay the foundation for years to come. The Village Improvement Society inaugurated the first Arbor Day observance in the commonwealth of Virginia at the Jefferson Institute in 1892.

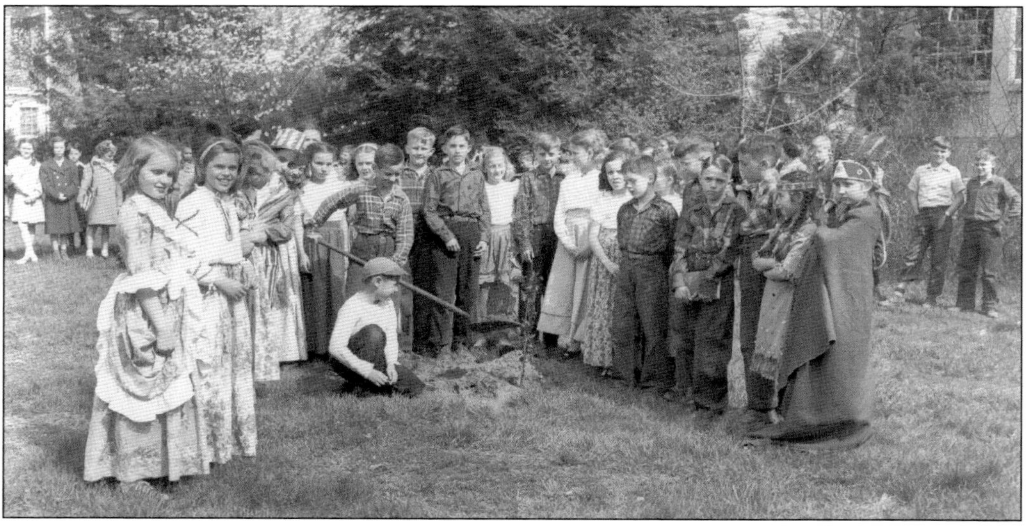

Madison students celebrate the same annual Arbor Day celebration in 1948. The successor to the Village Improvement Society, the Village Preservation and Improvement Society (VPIS) created an inventory of protected historic and notable trees throughout the city. Falls Church has been named a Tree City, USA, annually since 1978.

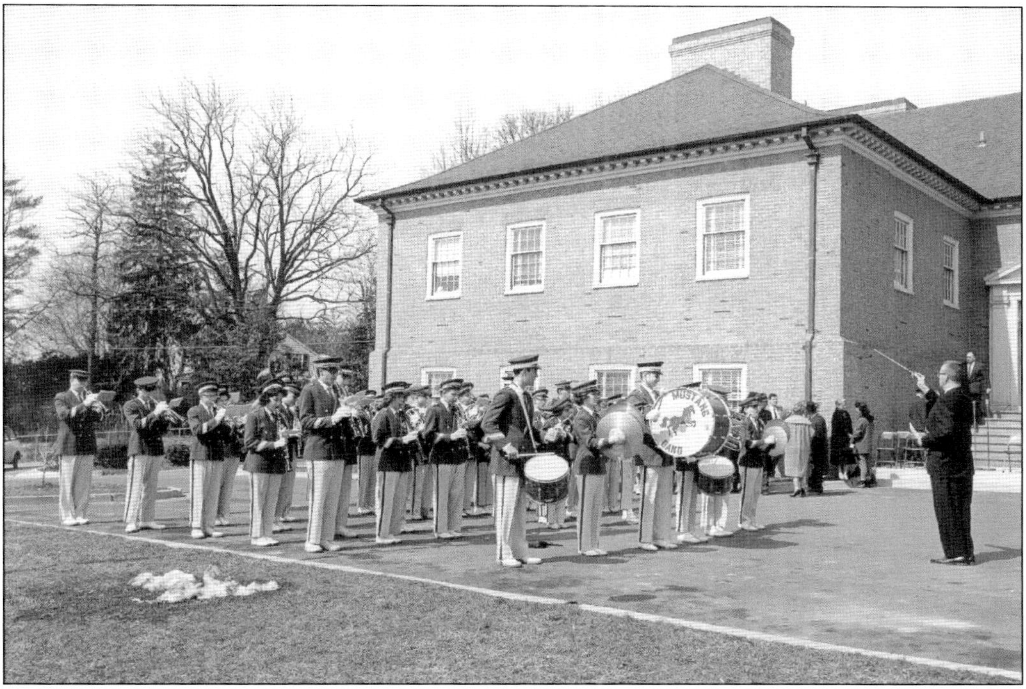

The city's progressive civic program secured it the All-America City award from the National Municipal League and *Look* magazine in 1962. Pres. John F. Kennedy cabled, "Warmest congratulations to Falls Church, Virginia." According to contest judges, who praised the city's nonpartisan atmosphere, the city showed "noteworthy accomplishments through alert, continuing citizen participation. Such is the only way to make self-government effective."

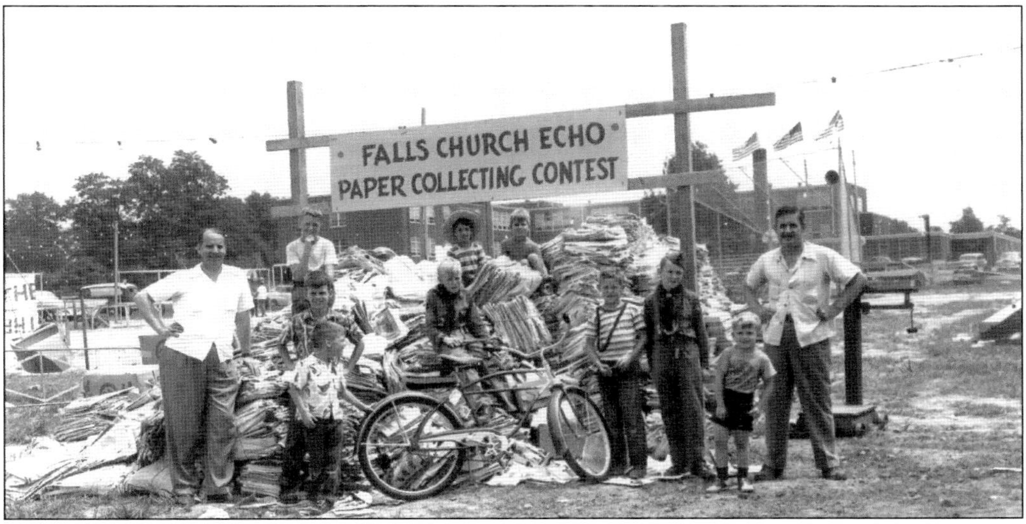

Environmentally friendly programs have always been important, taught in the schools through fun projects and friendly contests and competitions. Community businesses also participate in creating awareness and ecologically friendly attitudes among those growing up in the city. The green bin program and recycling center opened in 1990, and Falls Church was early to adopt a recycling program not requiring separate recyclables.

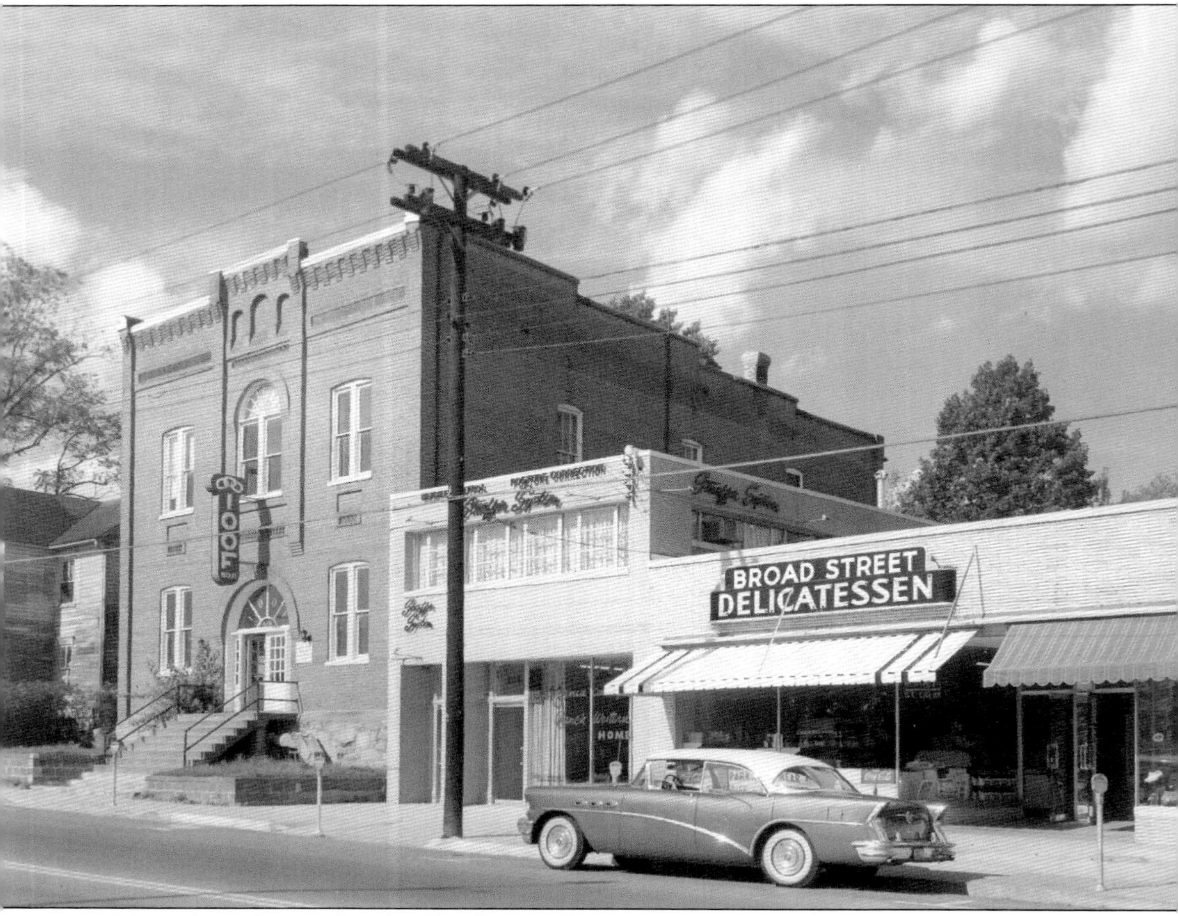

The Independent Order of Odd Fellows, Falls Church Lodge No. 11, was organized on October 24, 1890. The two-story brick building near the corner of West Broad and Little Falls Streets served as the town's only meeting place and community center for many years. Early member Charles Mankin gave money and land for the project. The main floor housed an auditorium, theater, or meeting room—adapted as needed. The order made a specialty of giving attention to its members during sickness and paid funeral expenses upon death. The lodge numbered among its members some of the most influential citizens of the town, among them Dr. George B. Fadeley, whose home and office was next door and eventually became the Falls Church Beauty School, and Thomas Hillier. The city ultimately built a new community center on the same parcel of land city hall was on, with a full slate of programs. The IOOF Hall was torn down in 1970.

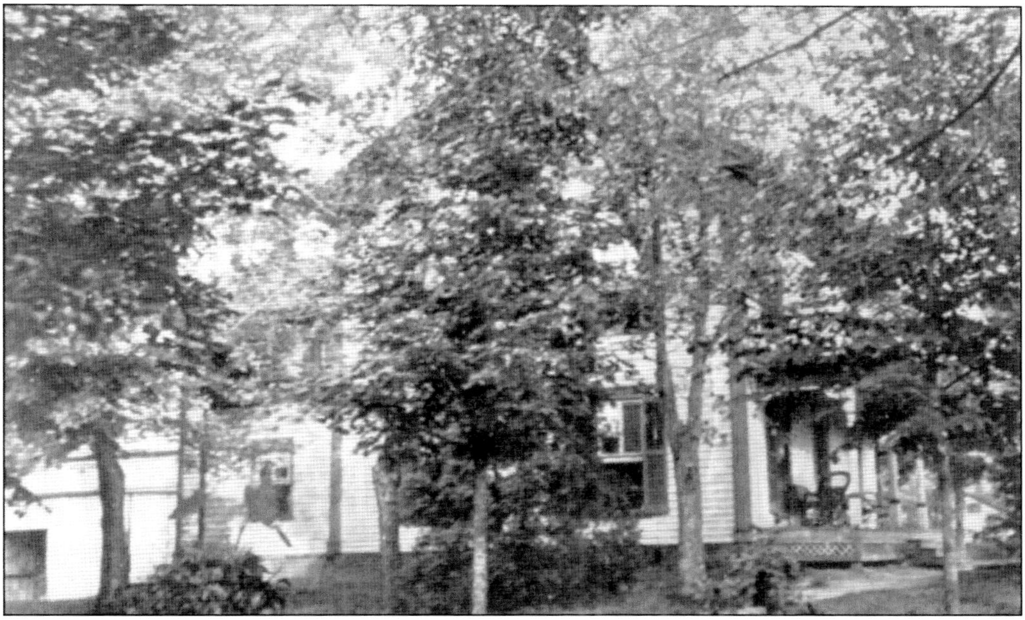

The Eagle House on North Washington Street, next door to the First Congregational Church, was the town's only hotel for many years. As the town grew, so did its appetite for social engagement opportunities. The Eagle House burned in 1920, and the State Theatre opened in 1936 on the same site. Billed as the finest theater in Fairfax and Arlington Counties, the State Theatre provided air-conditioning, a luxury not typical at the time. Flyers advertised the innovation as "manufacturing its own weather throughout the year," and the community flocked to marvel at the wondrous new theater. A white clapboard-style house at 105 Park Avenue across Washington Street was used as storage and parking for the State Theatre in the 1970s. The First Congregational Church next door went through several iterations as a school and recreation center. In 1961, it was sold to the Woman's Club of Falls Church and served as a meeting place. The bell tower was removed and the entrance was moved, and it eventually became home to the League of Women Voters.

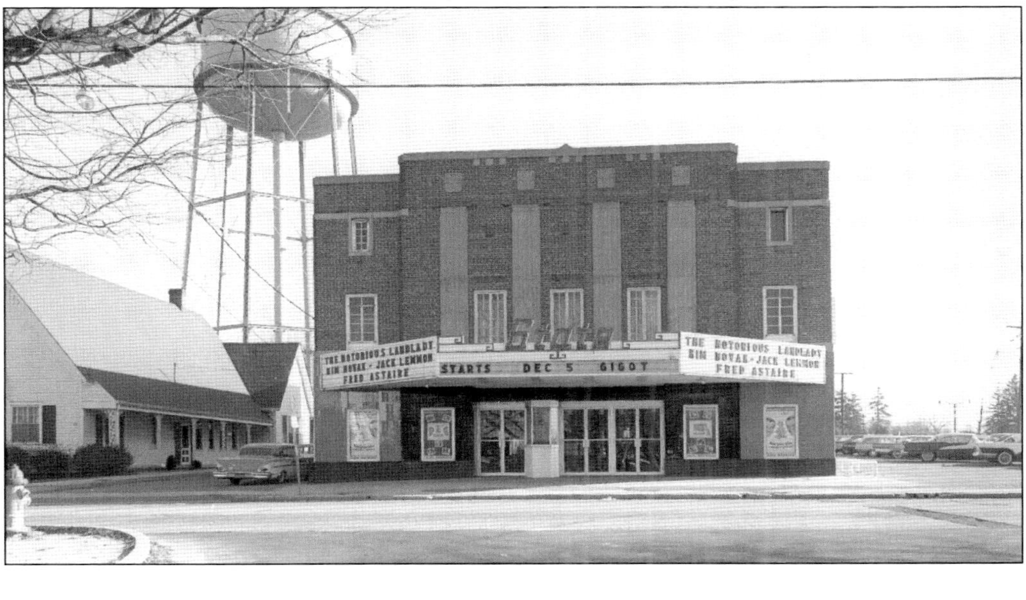

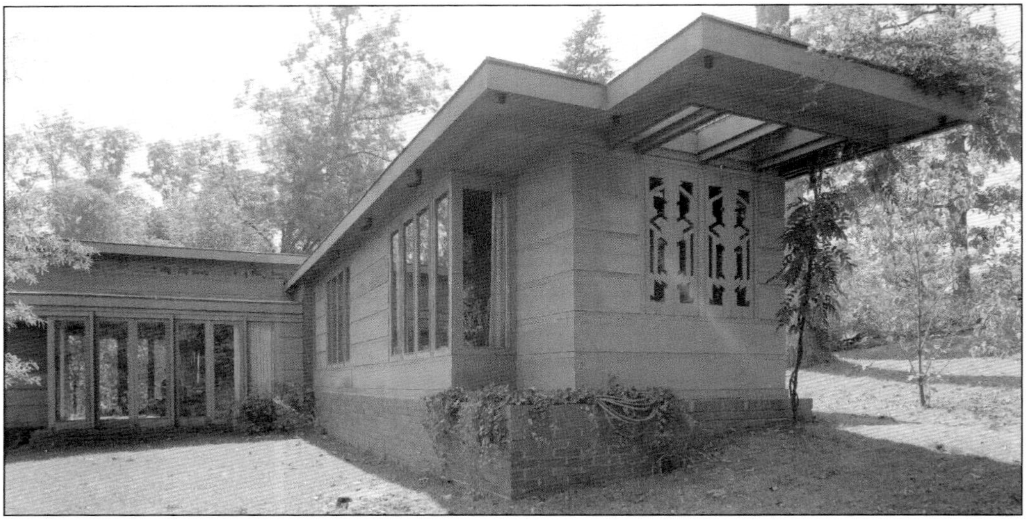

In addition to brushes with famous Founding Fathers of the country, Falls Church also hosted a few other famous characters. "Of course I am ready to give you a house," replied architect Frank Lloyd Wright in 1939 to an entreaty by Loren Pope. Wright spent time in Falls Church while building the Usonian Pope-Leighey House on Locust Drive. The doors rotated on piano hinges, and the house used radiant heat to warm the interior space over a concrete floor coated with red wax. Threatened with demolition during the planning of Interstate 66, a livid Loren Pope fumed in 1962, a federal cabinet official intervened, and a gift of the house by the owner at the time, Marjorie Leighey, saved the house. It was dismantled and reconstructed on Woodlawn Plantation on Richmond Highway near Mount Vernon, completed in 1965. The Pope house was the first Wright house in the area and only the second on the eastern seaboard. (Both, LOC, HABS VA, 30-FALCH, 2-.)

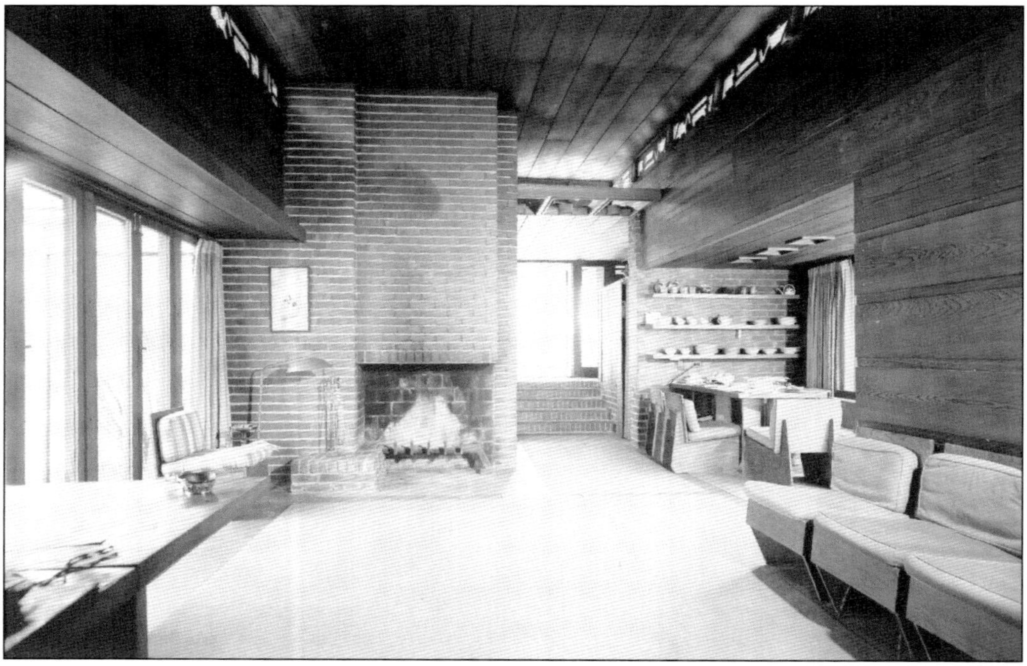

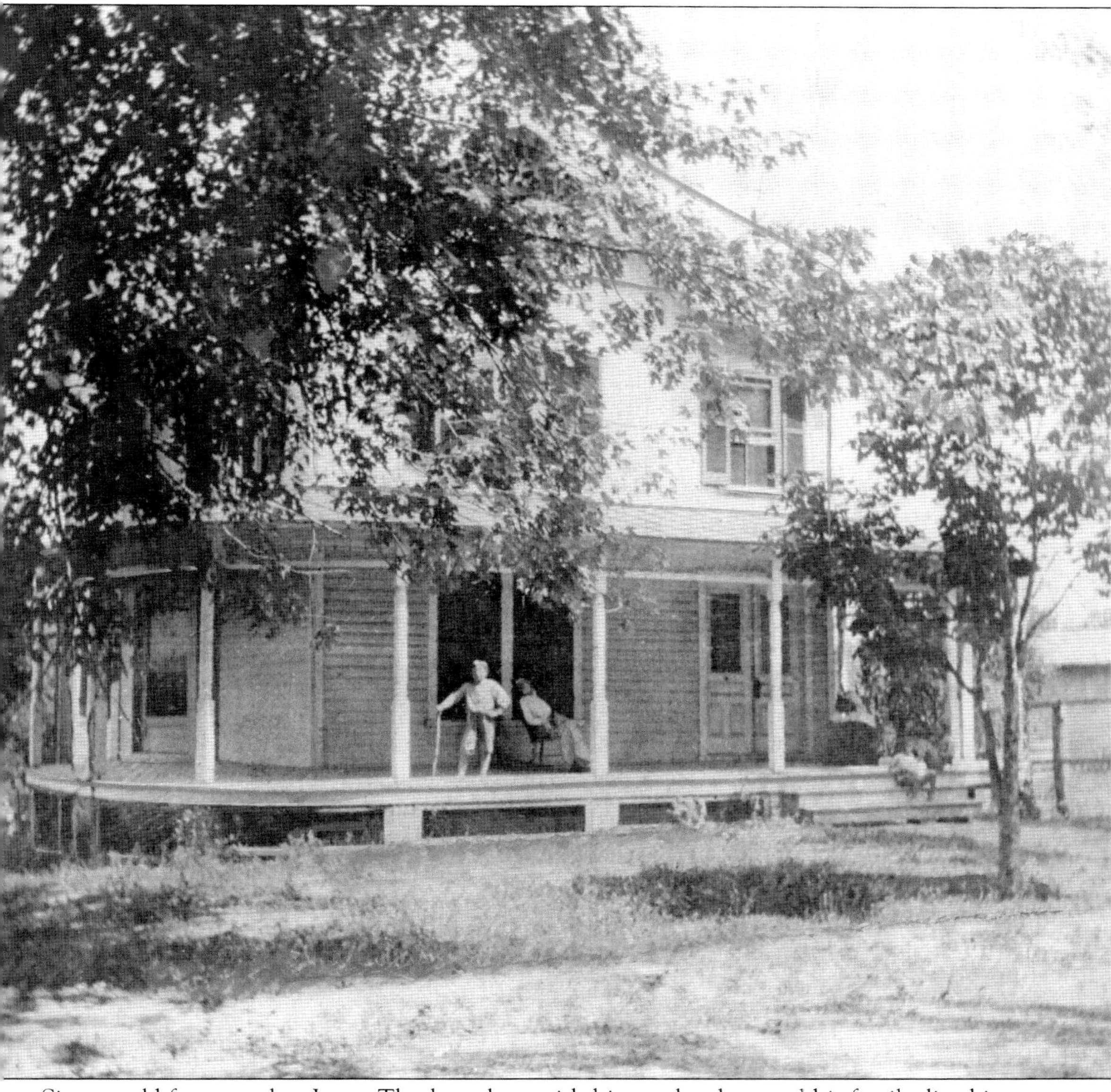

Six-year-old future author James Thurber, along with his two brothers and his family, lived in Falls Church in the summers of 1901 and 1902, renting the Crocker House at 319 North Maple Avenue. Thurber later recalled of his time spent there that garbage was collected by an ancient white-haired black man, Pete Gillam, whom Thurber described as "Not more than five feet tall, whose two-wheeled oxcart was pulled by a brace of oxen. His appearance never failed to enchant us boys, for he was not only out of the South, but out of the past, even out of fiction, as remarkable as old Uncle Tom himself." Thurber lost one of his eyes as the result of a childhood accident in Falls Church. Henry Crocker was an early Falls Church mapmaker and town leader who built this two-story house around 1890. A similar house at 321 North Maple Avenue, the home of E.P. Crocker, was demolished when the James Thurber townhouses were built.

Bibliography

Douglas, H.H. *Falls Church Places and People*. Falls Church: Falls Church Historical Commission, 1981.

Gernand, Bradley E. *A Virginia Village Goes to War: Falls Church during the Civil War*. Virginia Beach: The Donning Company Publishers, 2002.

Gernand, Bradley E., and Nan Netherton. *Falls Church: A Virginia Village Revisited*. Virginia Beach: The Donning Company Publishers, 2000.

Harwood, Herbert H. Jr. *Rails to the Blue Ridge: The Washington and Old Dominion Railroad, 1847–1968*. Falls Church: Northern Virginia Regional Park Authority, 2000.

Pendleton Stuntz, Connie. *A View of Falls Church, Virginia Including Its Western Neighbors Thru the 1881–1889 Diaries of Edmund Flagg, Esq*. Falls Church: Higher Education Publications, Inc., 2005.

Rust, Jeanne. *All-American Crossroads*. Fairfax: The Virginia Press, 1970.

Steadman, Melvin Lee Jr. *Falls Church, Virginia—By Fence and Fireside*. Westminster, MD: Heritage Books, Inc., 1964.

Stewart, Charles A. *A Virginia Village*. Falls Church: 1904 text reprinted by Village Preservation and Improvement Society, 1985.

Volpe, Margie Miller, Betty Hughes Cline Melton, and Susie Bachtal. *The Brigham-Cline Family Cookbook*. Falls Church: self-published, 1988.

Wrenn, Tony P. *Falls Church: History of a Virginia Village*. Falls Church: Historical Commission of the City of Falls Church, 1972.

INDEX

Consistent with our mission to preserve history on a local level, this book was printed in South Carolina on American-made paper and manufactured entirely in the United States. Products carrying the accredited Forest Stewardship Council (FSC) label are printed on 100 percent FSC-certified paper.

MADE IN THE USA